PRAISE FOR *TRANSFORMING TRAUMA IN CHILDREN AND ADOLESCENTS*

T0351552

"SMART is a ground-breaking new approach to treating traumatized children, based on the combination of keen clinical observation, sensory integration, and a deep understanding of the latest advances in the neuroscience of trauma. A focused, embodied, and engaged sense of self depends on learning to integrate sensory, muscular, emotional, and cognitive input, which is profoundly damaged by early trauma and disrupted attachment. With simple and affordable equipment, SMART creates a sensory space that helps children activate their sensory and physical needs and expressions, which in turn helps them to befriend their internal sensations and manage their actions and interactions. SMART fosters this core foundation for becoming a functioning human being, and thus it can help children to access and activate their rational brains and become full partners in connection, play, learning, and language."

—BESSEL A. van der KOLK, MD, founder and medical director, emeritus at the Trauma Center, president of the Trauma Research Foundation, professor of psychiatry at Boston University School of Medicine, and author of *The Body Keeps the Score: Brain, Mind and Body in the Healing of Trauma*

"Incredible! SMART is a revolutionary approach that exquisitely weaves together the authors' profound clinical wisdom and observations with the science and theory of the leading thinkers and scientists in our field. A must-read for mental health professionals, this book will help move us forward, updating the common, but narrow lens focused only on behavioral and top-down approaches. Keeping regulation and relationships at the heart of the approach, combining what we now know about the embodied brain and the far-too-often neglected sensorimotor system, this book will expand the perspective on and efficacy of the practice of many professionals, and it will support integration for so many families impacted by trauma."

—TINA PAYNE BRYSON, LCSW, PhD, best-selling coauthor of *The Whole-Brain Child* and *The Power of Showing Up* and founder of TheCenterforConnection.org

"Housed within the framework of the tenets of Sensory Integration, the authors have developed a triune intervention model that threads together the aspects of somatic regulation, trauma processing, and attachment-building in order to widen the window of tolerance for the dysregulated behavioral, emotional, and relational challenges faced by children and adolescents with a history of developmental trauma. The Sensory Motor Arousal Regulation Treatment (SMART) intervention model addresses the most fundamental mechanisms of traumatized children in a bottom-up, nonverbal language treatment option that not only prompts kids to ask—Do I get to play in there!—while peeking into his or her therapist's office, but more fundamentally, helps them make meaning of their traumatic experiences through the combined therapeutic actions of movement and sensory processes. Thus, while SMART focuses on the body it nonetheless changes a child's state of consciousness. This book is a clinical must-read for therapists who treat traumatized children or adolescents."

> —MARILYN R. DAVILLIER LCSW, MSSA and Ed Tronick, PhD, founders of the Infant-Parent Mental Health Fellowship, University of Massachusetts Boston

"I am so grateful for the commitment of the authors to provide clinicians with an additional, accessible treatment model to help the children in their care heal from the devastating impact of childhood trauma. People—especially children—experience overwhelming sensations and feelings that they are unable to put into words. SMART's emphasis on helping children take effective action using their whole body to better understand and regulate these sensations and feelings is central to healing."

> —STEVE GROSS, MSW, chief playmaker and founder of The Life is Good Playmakers

TRANSFORMING TRAUMA IN CHILDREN AND ADOLESCENTS

An Embodied Approach to Somatic Regulation,
Trauma Processing, and Attachment-Building

ELIZABETH WARNER · ANNE WESTCOTT

ALEXANDRA COOK · HEATHER FINN

FOREWORDS BY MARGARET E. BLAUSTEIN, PHD *AND*

RUTH A. LANIUS, MD, PHD, AND SHERAIN HARRICHARAN, PHD

North Atlantic Books
Berkeley, California

Published by
North Atlantic Books
Berkeley, California

Cover art © arka38/Shutterstock.com
Cover design by Howie Severson
Book design by Happenstance Type-O-Rama

Printed in Canada

Transforming Trauma in Children and Adolescents: An Embodied Approach to Somatic Regulation, Trauma Processing, and Attachment-Building is sponsored and published by the Society for the Study of Native Arts and Sciences (dba North Atlantic Books), an educational nonprofit based in Berkeley, California, that collaborates with partners to develop cross-cultural perspectives, nurture holistic views of art, science, the humanities, and healing, and seed personal and global transformation by publishing work on the relationship of body, spirit, and nature.

North Atlantic Books' publications are available through most bookstores. For further information, visit our website at www.northatlanticbooks.com or call 800-733-3000.

MEDICAL DISCLAIMER: The following information is intended for general information purposes only. Individuals should always see their health care provider before administering any suggestions made in this book. Any application of the material set forth in the following pages is at the reader's discretion and is his or her sole responsibility.

Library of Congress Cataloging-in-Publication Data

Names: Warner, Elizabeth, 1951– author. | Westcott, Anne, 1962– author. |
  Cook, Alexandra, 1967– author. | Finn, Heather, 1978– author.
Title: Transforming trauma in children and adolescents : an embodied
  approach to somatic regulation, trauma processing, and attachment
  building / Elizabeth Warner, Anne Westcott, Alexandra Cook, Heather
  Finn.
Description: Berkeley, California : North Atlantic Books, [2020] | Includes
  bibliographical references and index. | Summary: "A new somatics and
  attachment theory treatment protocol for therapists working with
  children and adolescents who suffer from complex trauma and neglect,
  using movement and sensation to target the neurological structures that
  support emotional and behavioral regulation"—Provided by publisher.
Identifiers: LCCN 2020003913 (print) | LCCN 2020003914 (ebook) | ISBN
  9781623172589 (trade paperback) | ISBN 9781623172596 (ebook)
Subjects: LCSH: Psychic trauma in children—Treatment. | Psychic trauma in
  adolescence—Treatment. | Child psychotherapy.
Classification: LCC RJ506.P66 W37 2020 (print) | LCC RJ506.P66 (ebook) |
  DDC 618.92/8521—dc23
LC record available at https://lccn.loc.gov/2020003913
LC ebook record available at https://lccn.loc.gov/2020003914

1 2 3 4 5 6 7 8 9 MARQUIS 25 24 23 22 21 20

This book includes recycled material and material from well-managed forests. North Atlantic Books is committed to the protection of our environment. We print on recycled paper whenever possible and partner with printers who strive to use environmentally responsible practices.

We dedicate this book to the clinicians who invited us into their work. Their curiosity and eagerness to learn a new approach to treatment and their spirit infuse the model today. Most of all, we dedicate this book to the children and families who have journeyed with us in the development of SMART. They have shared their pain and their strength with us, and through their openness, we have all learned and grown.

CONTENTS

ACKNOWLEDGMENTS

To the National Child Traumatic Stress Network and the members of the Trauma Center who contributed to its inception and ongoing work to establish a network of people across the United States devoted to the treatment and study of children and adolescents and interpersonal complex trauma. Without the NCTSN, and the knowledge gained, we would not be where we are as a field.

To all the people, including Bessel van der Kolk and Alexandra Cook, a member of our team, who contributed to the study that led to identifying Developmental Trauma Disorder (DTD) as a clinical entity, separate from PTSD. The ongoing work to validate DTD continues to deepen our understanding of child trauma. It describes our clients and better represents their diverse needs in a way that assists all those who work with them.

To the Trauma Center's clinical team during SMART's first decade, because it afforded space and time for SMART to bloom. The special climate of curiosity and innovation, and the drive to find better treatments, emanated from Bessel van der Kolk's philosophy of housing clinical work alongside research, education, and training so that each informed the others. Able teams, led by Joe Spinazzola, Margaret Blaustein, Alexandra Cook, Marla Zucker, and later, Hilary Hodgdon and Heather Finn, pursued these endeavors, to the benefit of SMART's development throughout its first years. There have been numerous clinicians and trainees at the Trauma Center and at JRI who have contributed their clinical experience and their enthusiasm. We especially thank Erika Lally, Dan Williams, Wendy D'Andrea, Amy Fingland, and Robbie Aikin. In addition, we thank Tiffany Naste for her contribution to the application of SMART by In Home Therapy teams, Michelle Vaughan, to the application with Residential Treatment teams, and Jennifer Moore, to the informed consent process with child clients. No other kind of environment could have fostered the development of SMART so well.

To the Trauma Center's research team, who challenged us to articulate and operationalize the SMART method and mechanisms of change. Joe Spinazzola was particularly instrumental in pushing us to be researchers and publish our work. Mara Renz Smith helped us refine our Child Descriptors, which contributed to our SMART Regulation Map. Nancy Muse has been invaluable as both a researcher and an editor. Marla Zucker provided significant feedback and encouragement about the manuscript. Mia Greenwald captured our young clients in action in her drawings, and Adam Moorman conveyed complex SMART concepts in simple, yet elegant, visual images.

We express gratitude to our external funders, the Cummings Foundation, the Bainum Foundation, and especially to Susan Miller, for the seed money for SMART that supported us in the beginning, and for her ongoing moral support. We also thank North Atlantic Books for supporting this book through to the end.

Finally, we must acknowledge the vital contribution that Jane Koomar, PhD, OTR/L, FAOTA, made to the early development of SMART through teaching us about the core body senses, the role of sensory seeking and sensory avoiding in auto-regulation, and the role of sensory satiation in self-regulation and a core sense of being. Her collaborative spirit allowed for a true multidisciplinary process for our first edition SMART manual, before she passed away in 2013.

Thank you to my husband, John Conforti, for his endless hours of encouragement, boundless support, and tender love—I am eternally grateful; and to my children, David, Christina, and Dylan, for their modeling in the SMART photographs and, more importantly, for being my source of joy and inspiration. A special thank you to my mother for being my original rock and model of how to overcome trauma.

—ALEXANDRA COOK

Thank you to my wife, Sinead McLaughlin. You are my biggest support and co-regulator, and I could not imagine doing this work without you. And to my family and friends for their endless patience and encouragement throughout this journey.

—HEATHER FINN

To my husband, John Stein, for his ongoing support and wide window of tolerance for my time away from our daily life together; to my daughters, Hannah and Sarenna, for their love and curiosity about what I was doing; and to my grandchildren, Kai, Elyas, and Lidianna, for being enthusiastic models for SMART videos and photos, and for just being themselves so I could understand better how kids develop into wonderful human beings with vitality and spirit.

—ELIZABETH WARNER

To my husband, Phil, for his kind patience with my many hours with my nose in a computer, and to my two daughters, Molly and Sarah, who tolerated modeling and testing and transporting SMART equipment. Most of all, I love them for reminding me of the power of presence and joy of play.

—ANNE WESTCOTT

FOREWORD

BY MARGARET E. BLAUSTEIN, PHD

In every field, movement forward is marked by watershed moments—shifts, both large and small, that influence our understanding of how, what, and why. The field of traumatic stress has been no different, carried forward on the shoulders of the many pioneers who have influenced our understanding, first, of the tremendous impact that traumatic stress has on the development and functioning of individuals and communities; followed by our growing understanding of the myriad, intertwining impacts of this stress on behavior, relationships, neurology, cognition, emotion, and physiology; and of the range of factors—individual, contextual, and systemic—that rightfully must influence our approach to intervention.

Perhaps one of the most significant shifts in the field of traumatic stress in the past decade has been a growing understanding that trauma impacts not just mind, but—at its deepest core—body; that traumatic experiences are carried forward in the physiological responses, the nonverbal imprints, the action urges and frozen actions, the surges of arousal and numbing that drive the day-to-day experience of children and adults whose lives have been marked in part by their experiences of overwhelm. The empirical literature has established clearly that—along with the more visible impacts on behavior, emotion, and relationship—trauma impacts those critical determinants of self and functioning that are hidden under our skin, influencing the development of neurological structures (e.g., Bremner 2002; De Bellis et al. 2002; Morey et al. 2016), shifting neurological pathways (e.g., Ito et al. 1998; Stark et al. 2015), and affecting patterns of physiological arousal and dampening (e.g., De Bellis and Thomas 2003; De Bellis and Zisk 2014; Schore 2001; Teicher et al. 2003).

This impact is stark in the youngest cohort of trauma-exposed individuals. As we more clearly define and study developmental trauma—those adversities that are experienced early in life, and that overlay and shape the child's course of development—it is increasingly clear that dysregulation at all levels is the defining outcome of these experiences (e.g., Dvir et al. 2014; Ford et al. 2013;

Jennissen et al. 2016; van der Kolk 2005), and it is not surprising that perhaps the most apparent service needs among symptomatic, trauma-impacted youth are those that address behaviors and emotional and relational challenges that appear driven in part by dysregulated neurological systems (e.g., D'Andrea et al. 2012; Greeson et al. 2011; Kisiel et al. 2009).

Despite this growing understanding of body in the impact of trauma, the role of language continues to be elevated in our clinical world as the most critical, if not the sole, vehicle for addressing and supporting the needs of our clients. Clinicians are taught language-based methods for building relationship, for gathering information, and for invoking and resolving traumatic experiences. In therapeutic work, all too often our attention is drawn only to what is said—by the client, and by ourselves as providers.

And yet, anyone who has ever sat with a child knows that children make meaning of the world with their whole beings. From birth, children process their experiences through all of their senses—through taste and smell and touch, through sound and sight, and through action. Young children learn about their world in part through the ways that they act upon it, and through the ways the world responds to and/or acts upon them. For all of us, meaning is made first—and perhaps most deeply—on the level of the physical, the sensory, and the viscerally experienced.

We learn about our earliest caregivers by scent and by feel, by the physical and affective imprints that are laid down according to the nature of their interactions with us. We learn our capacities and our limits by the successes or failures of our actions—by the ways we stand, and move, and throw, or by the ways we stumble and fall. We learn the rhythms of our body by the ways that we experience the ebb and flow of our arousal, our emotions, and our most basic physiological needs. And we learn comfort and control over these rhythms—or distress and unease—based on our growing understanding of the ways we are able, or not, to have mastery over our own physical experiences.

Like many of us, my earliest experiences as a clinician were marked by training and supervision that emphasized language. I was taught to interview, to reflect, to identify and map cognitions, and to challenge beliefs. I was taught how to support the building of narrative, and how to use language to develop a beginning, middle, and end to my clients' stories. I brought audiocassettes of clinical sessions to my supervision meetings, and sat and listened to the playback of the words that were said, in the absence of any real awareness of the meaningful spaces that filled the silences, or the physical context in which the words were uttered.

But as my training, and then my professional experience, progressed, I sat with more children. With the thirteen-year-old girl who refused to speak, whose silence was a dare at every meeting. With the seven-year-old whirlwind who rejected any attempt at structured activity, but who moved and bounced and ultimately calmed when running his hands through sand. With the ten-year-old girl who wrapped herself in a blanket in the corner of the room, and who would only engage from behind a fort constructed of chairs and pillows. With the sixteen-year-old who could talk nonstop if there were a ball in his hand, but who shut down the moment he sat in a chair.

And as my work with children and adolescents progressed, I learned that the audiotapes I had been taught to study left out perhaps the most important source of information about the young people we worked with, and I found myself increasingly aware of, and curious about, the rhythms and energy, the movements and stilling, the silences and speech patterns of the children and adolescents I was seeing, and the ways these shifted according to relationship, context, and internal and external experiences.

I credit a great deal of that curiosity to the authors of this book. In the early 2000s, I found myself reflecting, along with other colleagues, about the nature of intervention for childhood trauma, and began working to co-develop a framework for supporting youth and families who have experienced overwhelming stress. During that same time period, one of the authors of this text, Elizabeth Warner, came to work at our center, bringing her knowledge and expertise in the field of child therapy, along with her previous experience working with youth on the autism spectrum and with other sensory challenges. She expressed a deep interest in better understanding the sensory imprints of trauma in childhood, along with identifying the ways to integrate that understanding into our clinical work. She quickly connected with like-minded colleagues, including co-authors Anne Westcott and Alexandra Cook, experts in sensory motor approaches and in childhood development, and they began to work together to develop the foundations of the Sensory Motor Arousal Regulation Treatment (SMART) approach described in this text. They collaborated with and drew in the expertise of a widely respected occupational therapist, Jane Koomar, and over time their work was enhanced by other contributors, including co-author Heather Finn, an experienced child clinician.

The SMART team pushed the providers at our center to dive deeply into the sensory and physical worlds of the young people we worked with. And in parallel to our understanding that meaning is made on the physical level, they pushed us to learn through experiencing. Perhaps one of the most influential early moments for my own growth in understanding of the nature of the sensory was a "field trip" that the SMART team arranged to the occupational therapy center founded by Dr. Koomar. Our entire clinical team spent a day exploring the equipment at the center, and reflecting on our physiological responses, the shifts in our arousal, and the ways that the physical and the sensory influenced our mood and our energy. I recognized that I became quickly anxious with fast movements—like swinging or spinning—and that my body settled and calmed with deep pressure. These observations meshed with my knowledge of my sensory preferences—I deeply prefer the quiet and the calm to the highly stimulating—but I had never before taken time to truly pause, explore, and really reflect on my physiological preferences. Well over a decade later, the concept of *curious reflection* and the ways we cultivate it has become a cornerstone of my own work with youth and adults who have experienced traumatic stress.

Curiosity about the physical and the sensory led the SMART team to install video equipment in several therapy rooms at our center. Recording sessions and reviewing them—not just for the words spoken, as so many of us had learned to do, but for the observed, and critically for the shifts and transitions in energy and arousal, in connection and relationship, in mood and affect, and in the use and cessation of language—became one of the most important tools our clinicians had for understanding the process of intervention. We learned to *microtrack*—to notice not just what occurred session to session, but moment to moment.

Critical to this process were the facilitating space and equipment. The authors designed and created a sensory space, such as is described in this text, and thoughtfully filled it with the equipment that would allow a child to enact in a manner dictated by their own bodies and their sensory and physiological needs. Such a space draws a child in; like many other working parents at our center, I brought my own children to work on occasion, and even with therapy room after therapy room filled with toys, there was no part of the center my children were more drawn to than the SMART room. The opportunity to bounce, to build, to swing—or to cocoon and contain—is naturally regulating, and innately appealing to the physical nature of children.

This physical appeal is, of course, only a piece of the critical import of attuning to the body in the treatment of children. It is not just the physical alone—although there is certainly an argument to be made for the importance of naturally regulating physical activity as a key part of intervention with young people; there is a growing literature, for instance, highlighting the healing nature of activities such as sports, yoga, theater, and dance (e.g., Beltran et al.

2016; D'Andrea et al. 2013; Ehud, An, and Avshalom 2010; Kisiel et al. 2006; Palidofsky and Stolbach 2012). As relates to intervention with youth who have experienced trauma, however, perhaps most critical is the way that this physical and sensory exploration facilitates the child's mastery over their surrounding space, their experiential opportunity to regulate their internal sensations, their actions, and their interactions; and the way these shifts in physiological organization in turn enable the child's ability to make use of connection, attachment, and—ultimately—language. It is truly only when we are in a regulated state, in rhythm with those around us and in our world, that we are able to effectively make use of our higher cortical processes—to be curious, to express, to process, and to engage—and it is because of this that the fluid attention to both mind and body is an essential component of effective clinical practice with youth.

We owe the youth with whom we work the obligation of our curiosity—of truly observing, and then working to understand and intervene in rhythm with their expression. I challenge the readers of this text to observe any young person in your world, and to engage your curiosity about the ways that they connect, communicate, regulate, and reflect; to notice the ways that language intertwines with the physical, the sensory, the relational, and the rhythmic; and to reflect on your own interactions and responses, and the ways your connection shifts when you engage on all of these levels.

Our ability to learn, to grow, to expand our understanding, and to become increasingly effective in our practices is one of the defining features of any scientific field, and is in fact one of the defining features of human development. I personally owe a debt of gratitude to the authors of this text for facilitating a watershed moment in my own professional development. In this field, our understanding of traumatic stress and its imprints has continued to evolve, and so too must our methods for addressing it. This text, and the work of its authors, is representative of a critical movement forward in that process.

FOREWORD

BY RUTH A. LANIUS, MD, PHD, AND SHERAIN HARRICHARAN, PHD

The infant–caregiver attachment relationship lays the foundations for how an individual first experiences their internal and external worlds. When an infant first enters the world, close interaction with the caregiver provides key sensory input, including the sound of the caregiver's voice, the sight of the caregiver's face, the feel of the caregiver's gentle touch, and the taste of the nourishment provided by the caregiver. This plethora of sensory experience forms the core of the child's internal world of sensations and feelings. Through ongoing interactions and play with the caregiver, the child then begins to discover their external world and to develop a center of gravity, balance, coordination, as well as an ability to locate their body in space. In addition, a new sense of agency in motion later emerges, helping the child to navigate through the challenges of the external world. As the child transitions into adolescence and adulthood, the cerebral cortex, where sensory and motor experience is integrated, completes its development thus providing the cornerstone of cognition, emotion regulation, agency, and an integrated engagement of the embodied self with the world.

Psychological trauma and attachment disruptions, however, affect significantly sensory experience, having a profound effect on how an individual experiences both their internal and their external worlds (Engel-Yeger, Palgy-Levin and Lev-Weisel 2013; Schore 2002; Stewart and White 2008). Traumatized individuals often feel cut off from their internal sensations and feelings, perhaps unsurprising given how intolerable and futile they felt when the trauma was experienced (Feeny et al. 2000; Frewen and Lanius 2006). For example, during traumatic experiences, it is often impossible for the traumatized person to flee from intense emotions associated with the event such as terror or rage. Coupled with a compromised ability to fight back against an aggressor, the mind, brain, and body learn quickly that feelings are not only pointless but also unendurable, thus leading to a disconnection from the inner world of sensations and feelings. Afterward, intense emotional numbing often becomes a facet of everyday life, to the point that traumatized individuals frequently lack the capacity to experience fully love and compassion for self or others.

Not only do traumatized individuals become disconnected from their internal experiences and their body, but their experience of the external world may also be altered (Koomar 2009). Here, the feeling that the world is unreal is a common reality of many persons who suffer from trauma. Moreover, the world is often experienced as being intensely unsafe. Profound disconnection from one's sensations and feelings can also affect one's ability to move fluidly in space thus altering the body's interaction with the external world (Schimmenti and Caretti 2016; van der Kolk 1994). Traumatized individuals may also feel frequently unbalanced, clumsy, and uncoordinated and have difficulty knowing where their bodies are located in space. This experience is particularly common in persons with significant signs of disembodiment, which can involve feelings such as the sensation that one's hands or feet are disconnected from one's body and the absence of a boundary around one's body (Blanke and Arzy 2005; De Ridder et al. 2007; Lopez, Halje, and Blanke 2008). Unsurprisingly, these experiences can have a powerful effect on how one interacts with the environment.

The combined, synchronous experience of the internal and external environment lays the foundation for an embodied self coordinated in space and time. As described eloquently in the chapters that follow, an embodied self requires: 1) a sense of stability and a center of gravity; 2) being able to locate one's body in space; 3) ego motion or the experience of agency in motion (i.e., why do I move?, guided by interoceptive experience, and where do I move?, directed by exteroceptive signals); 4) first-person perspective; and 5) self-location in time. However, many of these components may be sorely lacking in the aftermath of trauma, where individuals frequently experience an unstable center of gravity and an inability to locate their bodies in space. Indeed, the experience of being cut off from internal/interoceptive signals and the inability to locate one's body in space renders agency in motion an arduous task. Finally, first-person perspective and self-location in time are often compromised, thus leading to the sensation of a timeless and often fragmented sense of self.

How can we understand the brain mechanisms underlying the processing of internal and external sensory information and their relationship to crucial processes, including physiological regulation and homeostasis, the ability to perform motor actions, cognition, and emotion regulation, key elements associated with an integrated and successful engagement of the self with the world? Here, it is critical to note that the brain stem and midbrain play a central role in receiving sensory input from the body as well as from the external world (Bechara and Naqvi 2004; Geva et al. 2017). A midbrain structure, the periaqueductal gray, receives direct input from internal bodily signals and can, through its connections, influence brain stem, limbic, and cortical areas (Craig 2003; Faull et al. 2019; Pollatos et al. 2007; Seth, 2013; Terpou et al. 2019). By contrast, the superior colliculus, another midbrain structure, receives visual, auditory, and sensory input from the external environment and represents a critical first entry point of sensory information into the central nervous system (King 2004; Stein 1998). The superior colliculus is, in turn, connected to midbrain structures that are connected to brain stem, limbic, motor, and cortical brain regions, thus allowing a bidirectional dynamical interplay among all three levels of the brain (i.e., brain stem/midbrain, limbic system, cortex) and helping to explain not only why brain stem/midbrain structures can influence limbic and cortical regions (bottom-up processing) but also why brain stem/midbrain brain regions can be impacted by limbic and cortical brain areas (top-down processing) (Bell and Munoz 2008; Doubell et al. 2003; Meredith and Stein 1985; Nicholson et al. 2017; Olivé et al. 2018).

The balance or vestibular system is another important system necessary for processing multisensory input, including auditory, visual, and somatosensory information, thus setting the stage for synchronous processing of both internal and external experience (Day and Fitzpatrick 2005; Lopez, Halje, and Blanke 2008). The vestibular nuclei in the brain stem have connections with brain regions key to processing viscerosensory information from the internal environment (posterior insula), as well as sensory information from the external environment (temporoparietal junction) (Harricharan et al. 2017; Hitier, Besnard, and Smith 2014; Lopez and Blanke 2011). Information relayed to these regions is subsequently transmitted to the dorsolateral prefrontal cortex, where multisensory integration occurs (De Waele et al. 2001). Here, it is critical to note that the dorsolateral prefrontal cortex not only plays a crucial role in cognition and emotion regulation, but also underlies the experience of agency in motion, i.e., why do I move where? (Farrer et al. 2003; Kohn et al. 2014; MacDonald et al. 2000). It is only once sensory, motor, emotional, and cognitive information are integrated fully at this level that an embodied self that is integrated in space and time comes online (see Hierarchy of Development, Insert 2). Taken together, recent efforts to identify the neural pathways underlying sensory processing have revealed the central role of sensory information derived from the internal and external world in motivating motor and higher cortical functioning including agency, cognition, and emotion regulation (Dixon et al. 2018; Harricharan et al. 2019; Simmons et al. 2013). These findings have significant implications for therapeutic interventions involving bottom-up versus top-down processing (Cohen and Mannarino 2008; Ogden and Minton 2000; Shapiro, 2001; Solomon and Heide 2005; Taylor et al. 2010).

SMART is a therapeutic modality that focuses on bottom-up processing of sensory, vestibular, and proprioceptive (the sense through which we perceive the position and movement of our body, including our sense of balance) input that is known to be significantly affected by trauma (Champagne 2011). In other words, SMART postulates that by intervening at the basic sensory, vestibular, and proprioceptive levels mediated by the brain stem/midbrain, we can influence motor functioning, cognition, emotion regulation as well as agency facilitated by the limbic and cortical regions via the brain connections described above. Therapists utilizing SMART have shown elegantly how working with sensory input, including deep or light pressure, rotation, and proprioception, can have a profound impact on the integration of sensory, motor, emotional, and cognitive information and thus lead to an embodied self that is capable of successful engagement with the world. It is often moving to see videotapes of this work and observe how children seek exactly the sensory input they require for more optimal emotion regulation when they are exposed to an environment that provides them with a choice of sensory inputs. Once this occurs, it is also fascinating to observe the emergence of the traumatic narrative, previously unavailable when traumatic memories were relived in the form of sensory flashbacks only. When this comes about, one can often witness the transformation from *reliving* to *remembering* traumatic memory—memory that is now integrated in time and space and can be communicated in the form of a narrative. Recent research has revealed that this transformation involves a shift from right, posterior brain regions involved in sensory memory recall to left prefrontal brain regions involved in verbal memory recall and multisensory integration (Lanius et al. 2004). Once the traumatic narrative has emerged and cortical brain regions have come online, top-down emotion regulation therapies, including cognitive behavioral treatments, are frequently facilitated (Deblinger et al. 2011; Ehlers et al. 2005; Foa, Steketee, and Rothbaum 1989).

This work not only has critical implications for working with traumatized children, but also points to the necessity of future research examining this approach in adults. Even though we have made significant progress in the treatment of trauma-related disorders, a remarkable number of individuals suffering from chronic, repeated trauma do not benefit fully from the treatments available to date (Bisson et al. 2007; Ford et al. 2013). SMART offers a treatment with a sound clinical and neuroscientific theory that has the potential to be of benefit in both adult and child trauma populations. It will also be crucial to examine SMART as a potential treatment for populations who exhibit language barriers. A focus on sensory processing may alleviate significantly language barriers that are often present when more standard treatments are employed. This may be particularly relevant to refugee populations, where language barriers are often inevitable. Finally, SMART may represent an important preventative strategy to enhance resilience and optimum functioning in both children and adults. Here, providing children and at-risk adult populations, including military members and first responders, with regular multisensory integration training such as SMART may prove useful in ameliorating the long-term effects of trauma exposure by facilitating cortical top-down emotion regulation through bottom-up sensory processing. Future research focusing on this topic is urgently needed.

In summary, SMART has the potential to be a ground-breaking new approach for the treatment of traumatized children and adults. It begins by targeting sensory experience and eventually leads, through bottom-up processing, to the integration of sensory, motor, emotional, and cognitive information that is critical to an embodied self capable of integrated and successful engagement with itself and with the world. Increased incorporation and bidirectional interaction of all brain levels, including the brain stem/midbrain, limbic system, and cortex, are a much-needed paradigm shift in research and in the neuroscientifically informed treatment of trauma-related disorders. Here, SMART is at the forefront and has the ability to enhance our understanding of the origin, brain underpinnings, and treatment of the often devastating effects of psychological trauma.

1

INTRODUCTION
TO THE BOOK

Early Steps in the Development of SMART

*Chronic childhood trauma interferes with the capacity to
integrate sensory, emotional and cognitive information
into a cohesive whole and sets the stage for unfocused and
irrelevant responses to subsequent stress.*

    —STREECK-FISCHER AND VAN DER KOLK 2000, 903

*Many children have problems with coordination, balance,
body tone and they are easily disoriented in time and space.
Having problems interpreting incoming information
makes them react inappropriately.*

    —STREECK-FISCHER AND VAN DER KOLK 2000, 911

Clinicians treating children and adolescents with complex trauma regularly witness major problems in their clients' ability to organize responses to everyday tasks and demands. Almost two decades ago, observant trauma therapists were noticing the way fundamental neuropsychological processes, such as sensory perception and integration, orientation to time and space, body awareness, and behavioral organization, were deeply impacted by traumatic experience. Yet, trauma treatments have lagged behind in addressing such fundamental mechanisms. New embodied ways to manage dysregulation in traumatized children and their families were needed; thus, SMART, Sensory Motor Arousal Regulation Treatment was born.

In the beginning of the SMART project, a group of therapists from the Trauma Center, in Brookline, Massachusetts, interested in solutions to these problems visited a Sensory Integration clinic for a staff retreat. Dr. Jane Koomar, an occupational therapist and developmental psychologist, and founder of the clinic, extended the invitation because she was curious about the problems of trauma and attachment affecting the clients she was treating for sensory processing problems. Dr. Koomar had been trained by the founder of Sensory Integration, Dr. A. Jean Ayres, and understood the intertwined nature of sensory and psychic experience.

In 1972, Dr. Ayres, with prescience, said:

> As the natural developmental association between sensory input and psychic experience becomes better understood, the two forms of therapy may profit from joining forces. What is rocking and being cuddled other than tactile and vestibular stimulation plus an interpersonal relationship? Are not the neural traces for the sensory and the social aspects of the experience laid down as one in the brain? Are not many of the child's important emotional experiences in the first five years of life closely associated on an experiential and therefore neurological basis with their sensorimotor equivalents? (Ayres 1972, 266)

During our visit to the Sensory Integration clinic, we played on giant pillows stuffed with foam blocks, large inflatable Dolphin pillows, cocoon swings, rolling barrels, spinning boards, and weighted blankets. We paid attention to the effects on our internal states of arousal, and as we experimented, we noticed the immediate upregulating and downregulating effects. In this playful context, we imagined their potential value in the treatment of our clients whose inability to sit still, to sustain focus or goal-directed behavior, or to coherently express themselves were the acute impediments to their treatment, as well as their growth and development.

Most child and adolescent clinicians have used outdoor playgrounds or basketball hoops in therapy sessions, but Sensory Integration Occupational Therapy offered some elementary tools for helping arousal regulation that could expand mental health therapists' conceptual understanding and repertoire. The staff's exploration of the effects of using this equipment on their own arousal—an experiential approach to learning that has influenced the training method—convinced us that a more physically active approach, employing the sensory inputs and motor outputs in therapy with our clients, would be worth investigating.

The Creation of the SMART Room

Bessel van der Kolk, the founder of the Trauma Center, intuitively understood the significance of the geography of space, and offered us a large fourteen-by-seventeen-foot room. With Dr. Koomar's help, we designed a therapy space that could be replicated by other mental health settings. We installed gym matting on the floor and purchased equipment that did not require special training such as large physioballs, weighted blankets, a balance beam, a balance board, a tunnel, a sensory shaker, body socks, and big Cloud Nine pillows. With a video camera mounted on the wall, experienced and interested child therapists began providing therapy and videotaping their sessions for study.

The SMART room at the Trauma Center at the Justice Resource Institute (JRI), Brookline, Massachusetts

"Can I go in there?" children ask from the waiting room door as they peek into the SMART room. The "affordance" of the environment, to use psychologist James J. Gibson's (1977) concept, is an invitation to play. Even the most traumatized children and youth gravitate toward equipment and find ways to explore without mediation or guidance by therapists. Over time, the room has remained intact, with minimal signs of wear. The opportunity for sensory motor play has minimized destructive behavior displayed in other settings. Furthermore, as therapists learned to tend to physical safety in ways that affirm the client's natural inclinations for engagement (a "yes, and let's together make it safe" approach), the merits of such a therapeutic space became evident. We attribute this to the way the physical environment offers opportunities to address the anxiety, fear, and inner distress in ways that "speak" to the whole child, body, mind, and brain.

Meeting the Challenge of Arousal Regulation

In addressing this challenge, we found a set of tools that effectively addressed a bottom-up, or somatic, form of regulation in therapy sessions and could be generalized to home and community; this was our initial primary mission. In order to Track how our child clients were responding to the Somatic Regulation Tools, we needed a way to assess their arousal level. Thus, we refined an assessment tool, using widely accepted concepts and our observations of our child and teen therapy video recordings, that we now call the SMART Regulation Map. This map assists child therapists using a SMART room to Track observable behavior of psychological states in real time, and to identify the moments when a child is most accessible for intervention. In addition, our observations of children were organized into clinician-useful descriptors (see Child State Descriptors, Inserts 4 and 5), and eventually codified for video recording study.

As experienced child therapists and physically active people ourselves, we had used playgrounds with overly active clients and intuitively understood the effects of movement and physical play on arousal regulation. However, in order to be more intentional and effective, we needed the framework that Sensory Integration provided. Sensory Integration theory elucidated the way good sensory processing and integration is central to a child's functioning in daily life. Dr. Ayres had broken ground when she illuminated the foundational significance of the so-called proximal senses—the vestibular, tactile, and proprioceptive senses—in early development. Dr. Koomar's basic training in these sensory motor systems allowed us to identify what we saw as we watched session video recordings, to more effectively scaffold the child's efforts to use these sensory inputs, and to add Rhythmicity and Safe Space when the child needed ways to build relationships. Arousal regulation vastly improved as clients used these tools, and we built our Therapist Skills. We had found an effective and more efficient avenue to Somatic Regulation.

Had we written about our model after the first six months, our manual would have only included Somatic Regulation Tools, but we discovered how Somatic Regulation resulted in the spontaneous emergence of a fully embodied form of Trauma Processing. Thus was born the dance between Somatic

Regulation and Trauma Processing as our primary treatment model (Warner et al. 2011). However, the issue of how to integrate and work with the caregivers kept persisting. As we gained confidence in the work with Somatic Regulation and with Trauma Processing, we focused on the work we had been doing in building co-regulation and developing attachment relationships (Warner, Cook et al. 2014). Through watching video, we identified the many opportunities for Attachment-Building embedded in SMART room engagement of therapist and child or caregiver and child through active or subtle use of tools to support connection and communication between them. These three threads—Somatic Regulation, Trauma Processing, and Attachment-Building—became our Spiral that now tracks the full therapeutic process of SMART in sessions and over the course of treatment as will be illustrated in case studies.

The **SMART** Spiral

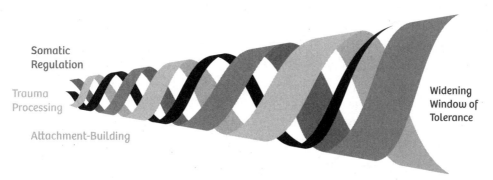

SMART Spiral capturing the dynamic therapeutic process expanding capacity

As our model evolved, we began training providers in the application of SMART. Some of these were open-enrollment trainings and some were through contracts with specific agencies. Through our collaboration with specific agencies, we were able to see how our model translated to areas like the Midwest (Kansas), the South (Tennessee), urban cities, rural environments, and other countries (Japan, Hong Kong). In addition, treatment facilities for different populations, such as those with hearing impairment and those with eating disorders, have also approached us to adapt SMART for their clientele. Through these collaborations we have learned how nonverbal language methods of engagement cut across many cultural divides, as well as how different cultures vary in their comfort with child-centered physical expression.

The Book

This book represents the culmination of our efforts to date. We are absolutely certain that the SMART model will continue to evolve and grow organically, as that is what our process has been. As described above, the SMART model began with a focus on Somatic Regulation, it grew to incorporate the dance between Trauma Processing and Somatic Regulation, and then it evolved again to address the process of Attachment-Building. These three threads form the basic structure and road map of this book.

We begin with chapter 2, "Foundations," which elucidates the key areas of research and influence that affected the development of the SMART model. The model was developed to help traumatized children, so we start with exploring the major contributions from the field of complex trauma. Then we address the relevant literature in each of the three threads: Somatic Regulation, Trauma Processing, and Attachment-Building.

Part 2 of the book is devoted to the tools and skills necessary for a SMART therapist, namely Tools of Regulation, Therapist Skills, and Video Reflection. The introduction to this part describes two concepts that are fundamental to SMART treatment and apply to all of the tools and skills: the SMART Spiral (described above) and the SMART Regulation Map that was developed through our video recording review and coding for research. The Regulation Map builds upon and expands the Modulation Model (Ogden and Minton 2000) and the familiar concept of the Window of Tolerance (Siegel 1999, 2012). This SMART Regulation Map provides the guidance for many of the decisions made about which tools and skills to use. Chapter 3 lays out the Tools of Regulation that we use in treatment. These tools were initially focused on three main sensory inputs—Tactile, Proprioceptive, and Vestibular—but grew to include other important facets of using these basic tools effectively, including Sensory Satiation, Rhythmicity, and Safe Space.

In chapter 4, we outline the Therapist Skills used in implementing SMART. These skills grew out of our efforts to understand what a SMART therapist actually does in session that is specific to SMART. First and foremost is Tending to Safety—physical safety, relational safety, and emotional safety. Next are Skills Internal to the Therapist—namely, Tracking Out and Tracking In, and Choice Points—meaning that there are no outward actions associated with these skills; they are simply taking place within the mind and body of the therapist. Lastly, there are several Skills External to the Therapist that typically result in some type of action: Embodied Attuning, Following, Full Participation, Leading, and Verbal Scaffolding.

In chapter 5, we discuss the importance of Video Reflection as an essential part of SMART treatment. Because this is a primarily nonverbal form of treatment, it is very difficult to describe in words what is happening in session. Thus, only through watching video recording can a therapist, supervisor, or consultant see what actually happened in session. Furthermore, building in this level of reflection has been part of our process from the beginning and when people have tried to do SMART without video recording, much of the process is lost.

Part 3 of the book addresses assessment and treatment in chapter 6. As we discovered through watching video recordings, these issues are intertwined and ongoing. Therefore, we combine them in the book and then explore them through the three threads of the SMART Spiral.

In Part 4, Embodied Treatment in Action illustrates SMART therapy through three case studies that represent different ages and show the evolution of treatment over time. These chapters illustrate how unique the weaving of the threads of the Spiral is to each child and family. The last chapter of this part—chapter 10—describes SMART collaboration with a variety of people and cultures, as well as implementation in several different treatment settings, including adolescent residential programs, preschool programs, In-Home Therapy programs, and private practice.

At the center of the book in the form of color inserts are informative full-page graphics of the following: SMART Spiral, Hierarchy of Development, SMART Regulation Map, Child State Descriptors, Brain Mappings, and the Tools of Regulation and Therapist Skills. At the end of the book, there is a helpful appendix detailing how to create a SMART Program, lists of SMART basic and additional equipment, description of video recording equipment, and considerations for informed consent with children. These inserts and the appendix are referenced throughout the text.

In order to protect the privacy of our clients, no identifying information or pictures are used in the book. The photographs utilize child models; the case studies alter important demographic information; and the drawings do not accurately depict the actual child or family member. However, the heart of the narrative and the process is preserved.

We end with our thoughts at this juncture knowing full well that our process will continue, so that the Conclusion is not a final conclusion, but rather a conclusion to this book.

PART 1

Theoretical and Therapeutic Principles

2

FOUNDATIONS

Aidan (age nine) begins treatment with a well-trained trauma therapist. He screams at the top of his lungs in session. He plays out scenes in the dollhouse that incorporate the swearing and violence he has been exposed to, but his play has no resolution. He bounces around the room with such ferocity that the therapist is often frightened for her safety. This is a weekly session that she has come to dread.

Aidan is a child who is trying to cope with his history of complex trauma and the resultant extreme dysregulation. In traditional trauma treatment, Aidan is the type of child that SMART was designed to help. In this chapter, we will present the foundations that have informed the development of the SMART model. We begin with the trauma framework, because the children and families wrestling with trauma and its aftermath are at the heart of our mission. Next we will describe the theoretical and clinical groundwork for the three threads of the SMART Spiral: Somatic Regulation, Trauma Processing, and Attachment-Building.

Trauma Framework

Children who have been exposed to complex trauma, which is a combination of chronic child maltreatment, neglect, witnessing violence at home or in the community, and importantly, attachment adversity, experience significant dysregulation across multiple domains. The Complex Trauma Task Force of the National Child Traumatic Stress Network (NCTSN) (Cook et al. 2003; Cook et al. 2005) described seven primary areas of dysfunction in traumatized children and adolescents: attachment, biology, affect regulation, dissociation, behavioral control, cognition, and self-concept. These provided the basis for the eventual framework of Developmental Trauma Disorder (DTD), proposed for possible inclusion in the *Diagnostic and Statistical Manual* (*DSM-5*) utilized in the United States (Ford et al. 2018; van der Kolk et al. 2009). This proposed diagnosis truly considers the traumatic antecedents, functional impairments, and symptom array of the children we serve. Furthermore, this proposed diagnosis overcomes the previously limiting requirement of the PTSD diagnosis that there be a client-identified experience of a perceived sense of threat to the physical integrity of self or others. DTD expands the definition of exposure to include multiple exposures, the chronicity of experiences, and the fact that many occurred in the context of caregiving relationships, combined with a subjective experience of rage, betrayal, fear, resignation, defeat, or shame (Cook et al. 2003). The authors recognized the need to consider the impact of trauma exposure on the unfolding development of the child, taking into account important factors, such as the timing of exposures, the age of the child, and especially sensitive periods in neurodevelopment (Teicher et al. 2018), as well as the need to have a framework that does not contribute to fragmentation with multiple diagnoses but embraces the whole child who needs good enough caregiving.

The World Health Organization will include Complex Post-Traumatic Stress Disorder (Complex PTSD) in the *International Classification of Diseases,* 11th revision (*ICD*-11) (World Health Organization 2018), effective January 2022 (Reed et al. 2019). Complex PTSD is strikingly similar in its description of symptoms to DTD; however, it was not formulated from a developmental perspective in the same way. Both the DTD framework and the Complex PTSD diagnostic category list dysregulation across three symptom clusters: affective and somatic, attentional and behavioral, and self and relational. SMART was designed for children struggling with just this profile.

Affective and somatic dysregulation is likely the most recognizable feature of complex trauma. The tantrums, the highs and lows, the "big" feelings that these children suffer from are taxing for them and for their caregivers. In addition to emotional dysregulation, the body and its ability to tolerate sensory input become extremely sensitive. Dissociation is one of the major coping efforts to manage these overwhelming feelings and thus is perhaps the hallmark of complex trauma. Essentially, dissociation occurs when an experience is so overpowering that it impedes the normative process of integrating information (Putnam 1997; Putnam 2016; Putnam and Trickett 1997; Wieland 2015):

> *For most children, it is a good thing to increase self-awareness and improve control over their behavior; for abused children, integrating different aspects of self means confronting emotionally disturbing material. It makes good psychological sense to evade anxiety and pain by avoiding mental leaps needed to unify fragments of identity into a more unified personality. (Putnam 2016, 227)*

Thus, the function of dissociation is to protect the person from being overwhelmed by experience by making it smaller and manageable through compartmentalizing, detaching, and/or forgetting.

Complex trauma is associated with a number of problems related to **behavioral and attentional dysregulation,** including substance abuse, running away, fighting, self-injury, and juvenile delinquency (Anda 2002; Felitti and Anda 2010; Greeson et al. 2014; Layne et al. 2014). The myriad of behavioral issues are manifestations of the internal arousal dysregulation and they are often the children's best effort to cope with or communicate their inner distress. Executive functioning is significantly impacted, including decision-making, impulse control, and planning. In addition, language is often compromised because of the overpowering nature of the affect and stress (Cook et al. 2005; Gabowitz, Zucker, and Cook 2008; Sylvestre, Bussières, and Bouchard 2015; Teicher et al. 2016; van der Kolk 2014). Moreover, the lack of development of basic capacities, such as arousal regulation and sensory motor development, makes the generation of more mature abilities, such as executive functioning, more challenging.

The third symptom cluster focuses on the **dysregulation of self and relationships.** One of the core features of complex trauma exposure is the decimation of a child's sense of value and worth through targeted verbal abuse, as well as pervasive neglect. In addition to the initial traumatic exposure, all of the dimensions of the resultant DTD mentioned above contribute to a negative self-concept that can perpetuate negative affect, a sense of hopelessness, and lack of motivation. Furthermore, many of the resources for developing a positive sense of self are missing for traumatized children; e.g., a warm attachment figure, a sense of competency and agency, and positive feedback from one's community. Without a strong sense of self and self-worth, it is difficult to form positive relationships. As a result, traumatized children have issues with trust, boundaries, defiance, aggression, and empathy.

DTD/CPTSD symptomatology is rooted in biological and attachment disruptions. **Attachment** is where development begins, and yet in traumatized families, it is also where the effects of complex trauma take hold and spread throughout a child's developmental trajectory. Typically, a child learns the basics of arousal regulation through the attachment relationship between caregivers and infant (Schore 2003; Siegel 2012; Sapolsky 2017). When this relationship is inconsistent, absent, or threatening, the child is not able to lay down the appropriate neural wiring for future social-emotional development (Schore 2003). Of particular note is the intersection of the autonomic nervous system with the social engagement system as described by Porges's polyvagal theory (Porges 2011, 2017). Specifically, when a child is safe, they are able to operate in a parasympathetic state that involves good connection with another. In a state of danger, the flight-or-fight sympathetic nervous system is activated. In a life-threatening situation, if flight and fight have failed, a shutdown state, or "freeze" state, emerges that reflects dorsal vagal activation; this state can become chronic. Thus, disruptions in attachment have far-reaching consequences for the traumatized child.

There is much research on the **biological** aftermath of child maltreatment and neglect that indicates the importance of the type of maltreatment and the age and gender of the child, whose stress-related biological systems are more sensitive during critical periods (Putnam and Trickett 1997; Teicher et al. 2018). In addition, the enduring effects of abuse and neglect have been shown to contribute to many of the leading physical health concerns, as well as psychiatric issues (Felitti et al. 1998; Lanius, Vermetten, and Pain 2010; Teicher and Samson 2016; Teicher et al. 2016). The most pertinent areas of impairment relative to SMART are autonomic nervous system dysregulation (Elbers et al. 2017; Sherin and Nemeroff 2011), disruption of left and right hemisphere communication (Teicher et al. 2003), executive functioning compromises (De Bellis, Hooper, and Sapia 2005; De Bellis et al. 2009; De Bellis, Woolley, and Hooper 2013), and disturbances in the default mode network that disrupt awareness of one's internal state, as well as the sense of the body in space (Bluhm et al. 2009; Daniels et al. 2011; Patriat et al. 2016; Qin and Northoff 2011; Tursich et al. 2015; Viard et al. 2019; Zeev-Wolf et al. 2019). Because traumatized children are exposed to threat and deprivation, their nervous systems are often in flight, fight, or freeze mode. Furthermore, there is research evidence that the corpus callosum is smaller relative to a nonabused counterpart, thus affecting the child's ability to integrate information from the left and right hemispheres (Teicher et al. 2003). Planning, organization, initiation, and behavioral inhibition are all significant issues for traumatized children, likely related to deficits in the connectivity of the brain stem and midbrain to and development of the prefrontal cortex. Lastly, the default mode network is a group of structures that keep the brain ready for action when there is no immediate cognitive demand (Buckner 2012). This network involves both interoception and exteroception—i.e., internal awareness and environmental awareness—both of which are often compromised in traumatized children.

SMART was designed for traumatized children and their families. Through our focus on Somatic Regulation, Trauma Processing, and Attachment-Building, we address the primary problems of attachment, biology, affect regulation, and dissociation. As a result of our interventions, we have noticed remarkable improvement in behavioral regulation, cognitive functioning—especially language, planning, and executive functioning—and sense of self.

Components of Trauma Treatment

In 1992, Judith Herman wrote a seminal book, *Trauma and Recovery*, in which she outlined a three-stage model that guided treatment for years. The stages were: Safety, Remembrance and Mourning, and Reconnection with Ordinary Life. Trauma treatment has evolved from a phase-based approach to a component-based approach in part because of individual differences, as well as the overlapping nature of the work. The Complex Trauma Task Force put forth the following components necessary to most trauma treatments: safety, skills building, growth of positive attachment relationships, meaning-making, trauma processing, and developing a positive sense of self (Cloitre et al. 2012; Cook et al. 2005). All of these components are essential in SMART treatment.

Foundations: Somatic Regulation

Our first thread—Somatic Regulation—provides the basis and foundation for all of SMART treatment. First of all, it was the primary presenting problem we were trying to tackle: dysregulation of affect, arousal, and behavior. Second, it matches our understanding of the importance of child development through bottom-up processing. Third, the other threads grew out of our initial focus on regulation of the body. Regulation is the anchor and the north star for our journey. In this section, we will explore the contributions of arousal regulation and its underlying neurobiology and the key sensory motor systems and their underlying neurobiology.

Sensory motor activity is fundamental to child development (Cuppini, Stein, and Rowland 2018; Piaget 1952; Winnicott 1964). During the months of gestation and continuing into a child's postnatal life, the senses are in operation, including hearing the mother's heartbeat and voice, sensing the rocking motion of her movement, and feeling the tactile input from outside pressure of the womb. Newborn babies begin to experience the touch of caregiving and the mother's voice, now coupled with the engagement of mutual gaze. The baby is also beginning to explore the world through looking about and reaching to touch. Within the first half-year, the baby seeks to move his body, often seeking to reach out beyond his arm's reach by rolling. Movement, which depends on the multisensory integration of tactile, proprioceptive, and vestibular information, organizes the brain for intentional, purposeful actions, rather than repetitive, nonfunctional movements. The integration of sensory motor experience starts with reflexive movements in utero but organizes quickly into actions—i.e., movement with intention—from birth on.

Abuse and neglect disrupt this normal developmental trajectory. Whereas neglect is the absence of developmental nutrients, abuse interrupts, disturbs, and distorts typical developmental experience. Our perspective is that these distortions are traumatic adaptations that allow a child to live in a threatening environment and that the ensuing brain changes reflect the adaptation of the organism to survive (Teicher and Samson 2016). As described by the DTD research, complex trauma leads to a variety of problematic outcomes. The children and adolescents who come to SMART therapy with problems of self-regulation are alternately overreactive and underreactive to the ordinary events, demands, and stressors of life. In order to understand the outward manifestation, it is important to appreciate the underlying mechanisms of arousal regulation and the fear system.

Arousal Regulation and the Autonomic Nervous System

Arousal refers to the psychophysiological states from wakefulness and alertness to sleep and coma, and is generally understood to impact consciousness, attention, information processing, and the ability to organize behavior. Three neurobiological systems are involved in arousal: the ascending reticular activating system, which regulates wake/sleep, alertness, and levels of consciousness; the neuroendocrine system, in particular, the stress-regulating hypothalamic–pituitary–adrenal (HPA) axis, which stimulates glucose production for the energy needed to respond to stimuli and stressors; and the autonomic nervous system (ANS). The ANS, because of its immediate response to stimuli and stressors, is the most important in relation to the SMART therapy session. The sudden shifts we see in our clients' psychological states in the therapy room result from the activation of the ANS.

The ANS is a key, front-end, physiological system to respond to external and internal stimuli and stressors. Its neurons extend from the periphery of the body and the viscera to the spinal cord up through the brain stem and thalamus to the somatosensory cortex, and back down via motor neurons to actively respond. The ANS causes heartbeat, breathing, the organs of ingestion, digestion, elimination, muscular tension and engagement, and sexual response—in fact, the entire internal milieu—to up- or downregulate so the organism responds effectively to events.

The ANS is a full sensory motor engine and braking system. The sympathetic nervous system (SNS) branch of the ANS activates the body's visceral organs and the motor systems to respond quickly, and if threat is perceived, to galvanize the whole body for flight-or-fight responses. The complementary parasympathetic nervous system (PNS) branch returns those visceral and motor systems to baseline, or homeostasis, for necessary rest and recovery. The overactivity and reactivity of the traumatized child reflects a sensitized SNS that is working overtime, with an underperforming PNS that does not give enough rest to the child's body. Thus, the complementarity of "get up and go" and "rest and relax" is out of balance. Over time—often by adolescence—the exhaustion of the child's physiology and desensitization to stress can be seen in depression, numbing, and associated behaviors. Underlying this dysregulation are many fears and triggers that children and caregivers often cannot explicitly identify. Neuroception, a term coined by Stephen Porges (2004), is "how neural circuits distinguish safe, dangerous, or life threatening people or situations" (19). This subconscious system for threat detection is in overdrive, and many situations and people trigger defensive and avoidant responses.

Under immediate physical or psychological threat, what does the human being do to survive? The ANS readies the organism to immediately engage in the so-called defense cascade. Typically, the steps in this fast-acting survival system are the following: (1) freeze and scan the environment, (2) flee the threat, (3) if not possible, fight off the threat, and (4) if that is not possible, submit in fright through tonic immobility, a kind of temporary paralysis (Cannon 1929 in Bracha et al. 2004, 448; Kozlowska et al. 2015; Levine 2010; Volchan et al. 2017). In each case, the SNS galvanizes the entire internal biological milieu and various sensory and motor systems to act to survive. Therapists are familiar with the hypervigilant flight-or-fight responses in clients because these are the behavioral patterns that lead to referrals for mental health services. However, there is another important option: the attach response, and it is central to the recovery of our clients. Developmentally, this response is critical to survival. Under threat, young humans as well as other immature mammals immediately search for the caregiver for protection. In the case of the young child, the auditory and visual sensory systems scan and orient the young to the location of the caregiver for safety. The motoric responses then activate to seek physical proximity.

This "approach response" (as opposed to the "avoidance" responses of the overall defense cascade) is necessary for survival of the young mammal and for attaining restoration of homeostasis through co-regulation. When proximity to the caregiver is attained, the young seek co-regulation via the sensory systems of tactile and auditory input. Fortunately, eye contact is not necessary in this situation because the caregiver must scan the environment for further threat and a way out. In this case, deep touch and voice suffice to physiologically slow the rapidly beating heart and deepen the breathing, thus creating the "felt sense of safety" (Gendlin 1982, 2012) in the body. This protective factor can make the difference for a child between an experience of terror or one of modulated anxiety. Adequate co-regulation by the adult restores homeostasis in the psychobiological systems of the child and, with that, a felt sense of safety.

Among the most debilitating effects of neglect and abuse on developing children is instilling avoidance or fear into their experience of caregiving adults. The chronic absence of an attachment figure to provide this calming function is what maintains the hyperarousal that afflicts neglected children. The lack of co-regulation trains the nervous system how to remain in a hyperalert state, but not how to rest and to attain calm alertness, a resting state, or restful sleep. In the case of psychological or physical maltreatment, the nervous system is completely overwhelmed by fright, and without the modulation of co-regulation, over time many adolescents develop blunted affect and physiological responses. When there is exposure to multiple trauma types, including abuse, blunted ANS reactivity to a stressor is reflected in a slowed heart rate and lower skin conductance (D'Andrea, Pole, et al. 2013). This reflects a kind of immobilization in the nervous system that may be the basis for dissociation. Avoidant or withdrawn adolescents, prone to hypoarousal and dissociation, show us the seeds of this pattern. This pattern extended into adulthood is evident in complex trauma adults with the dissociative subtype of PTSD in which the brain shows no evidence of the exteroception necessary for accurately navigating the environment (Harricharan et al. 2017).

Sensory Motor Systems: Tactile, Vestibular, and Proprioceptive Inputs

Sensory motor processing and physiological arousal regulation provide the foundation for all higher-level development of behavioral organization, social engagement, emotion, cognition, and language. (See Hierarchy of Development and Brain Mapping, Inserts 2, 6, and 7.) Analogously, the brain stem, where the heart of these functions resides, and the part of the brain that ensures our survival, undergirds the higher-level cortical networks of the midbrain and the neocortex (Damasio 2010, 258–62; Kandel et al. 2013, 340–41).

Hierarchy of Development

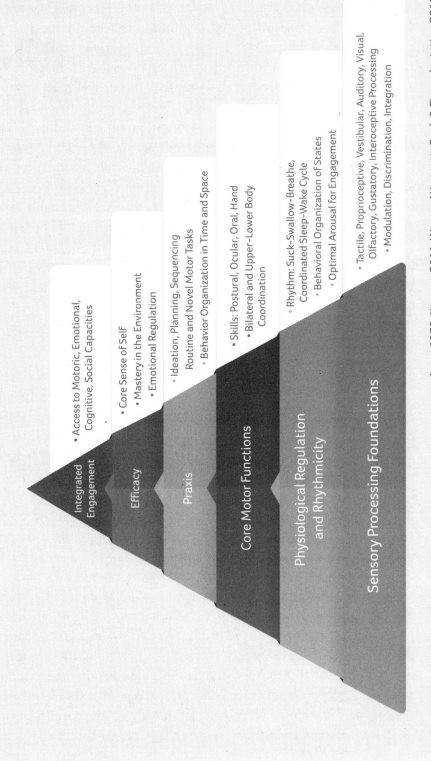

- Access to Motoric, Emotional, Cognitive, Social Capacities

Integrated Engagement

- Core Sense of Self
- Mastery in the Environment
- Emotional Regulation

Efficacy

- Ideation, Planning, Sequencing Routine and Novel Motor Tasks
- Behavior Organization in Time and Space

Praxis

- Skills: Postural, Ocular, Oral, Hand
- Bilateral and Upper-Lower Body Coordination

Core Motor Functions

- Rhythm: Suck-Swallow-Breathe, Coordinated Sleep-Wake Cycle
- Behavioral Organization of States
- Optimal Arousal for Engagement

Physiological Regulation and Rhythmicity

- Tactile, Proprioceptive, Vestibular, Auditory, Visual, Olfactory, Gustatory, Interoceptive Processing
- Modulation, Discrimination, Integration

Sensory Processing Foundations

Ayres 1979; Koomar 2011; Warner, Westcott, Cook & Finn adaptation 2019

Pyramid showing the "bottom-up" nature of development and the corresponding capacities in the child's organization of state and behavior

Information from the senses of smell, taste, hearing, and vision, along with input from the tactile, vestibular, and proprioceptive senses, travels to the brain and becomes integrated, beginning at the midbrain superior colliculus, to organize the person's responses to and actions on the environment. In SMART, we have prioritized the latter three senses—tactile, vestibular, and proprioceptive—because these sensory inputs and motor outputs form the core experience of the body, and thus, most effectively facilitate self-regulation, contributing to a more vibrant, grounded, and integrated sense of self in traumatized children and adolescents. As Blythe and colleagues (2017) note, "While the sensory systems provide information about the environment (feeling), integration of sensory experience takes place as a result of action or motor output in response to sensory signals (doing)" (22), an understanding that goes back to Sir Charles Bell in 1833 (Bradley 2014; Kandel et al. 2013, 456–57). Afferent sensory input to the brain and efferent motor output from the brain are looped together, one informing the other. When working well together, these support good physiological arousal regulation and rhythmicity.

The Tactile Sense

Tactile sensory input emanates primarily from receptors in the skin, the largest organ of the body. The many types of receptors variously respond to deep pressure, more dynamic pressure generated by a poke or pressure moving across the skin, light touch, pain, temperature, vibration, chemical sensitivity, itch, and skin stretch. SMART has found deep pressure and lighter or moderate touch to impact arousal regulation most effectively of all the various types of tactile experience. It is also important to consider pain processing, specifically whether the child notices and attends to it. Pain will generally upregulate arousal; however, traumatized people often have unusual responses to pain such as hyposensitivity or hypersensitivity.

Discrimination of types of touch is greater or lesser in different parts of the body, with more nerve endings in some parts of the body than others. This is of significance in particular when considering touch triggers in clients. As we have observed numerous times in the SMART room, clients appear to have developed sensitivities in places where there was an injury, or negative touch through physical or sexual abuse. In addition, the hands, the feet, and the face and mouth proportionally have many more receptors and take up a larger portion of the somatotopic mappings of the body on the somatosensory cortex, by the number and location of the neurons (Craig 2015, 133–34; Kandel et al.

2013, 363–65, 374–78). When asking children to take off their shoes, we take advantage of the fact that more deep pressure Tactile Input to the feet, a caregiver's foot massage, or a gentle tickle will increase body awareness.

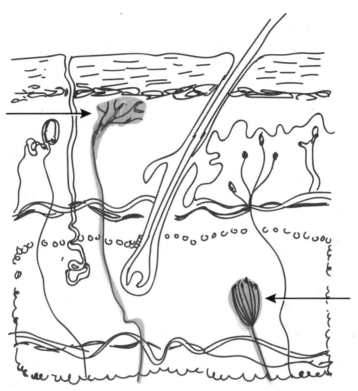

Skin receptors for tactile input: light touch (upper arrow); deep touch (lower arrow)

The Vestibular Sense

The vestibular sense has receptors in the inner ear adjacent to the auditory receptors of the cochlea. Vestibular information is generated whenever the head moves and tiny hairs within the receptor structures move in fluid, which stimulates the release of neurotransmitters (Balaban 2016). The vestibular receptors consist of the otoliths, which process linear information in the horizontal and vertical planes, and govern our relationship to gravity, and the semicircular canals, which process head rotations (Kandel et al. 2013, 917–19). When a child jumps on a trampoline, the otolith utricles are activated, and when moving straight ahead, as when running or moving back and forth in a glider rocker, the otolith saccules are activated. When the head is inverted, such as when a child does a headstand or hangs from the monkey bars by her legs, or a parent playfully hangs a young child upside down, the relationship to gravity is processed by the otoliths. As the very young child learns to stand upright, fall, and return to upright, the otoliths process the relationship to gravity while the proprioceptive receptors help organize the full body—all parts having to work together—to stand up.

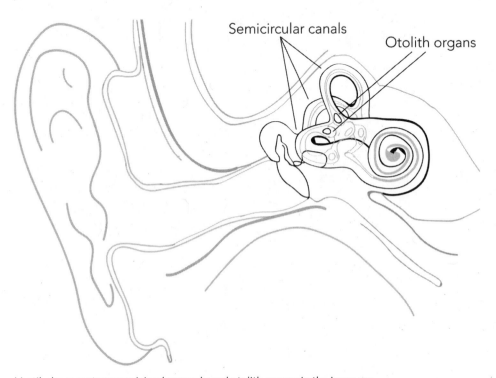

Vestibular receptors: semicircular canals and otolith organs in the inner ear

The semicircular canals process angular head movements that occur in three planes of space as when the head nods up or down or side to side or tilts left or right. When a child runs in a circle, rolls over a ball, does a cartwheel, spins in an office chair, rhythmically traces an arc in a swing, or twists and rapidly untwists in a swing, information is processed in three dimensions, contributing to a spatial mapping of his body in relation to himself and to the surrounding environment. The vestibular network is the GPS of the brain; it is crucial to experiencing a center of gravity and a sense of stability and groundedness in the world.

Head movement in three-dimensional space and the vestibular receptors

The Proprioceptive Sense

Proprioception lets us perceive movement, location, and action of the parts of our body in relation to each other, as well as the sense of effort, muscle tension, and weight (Ayres and Robbins 2005, 41, 94–95; Proske and Gandevia 2012). Proprioceptive receptors reside in the muscles and joints throughout the body and are called muscle spindles, Golgi tendon organs, and joint receptors. These provide input to the brain about the angles of the joints and muscle length, which in turn affects the force of muscle contraction and extension through the motor neurons. The proprioceptors are activated with all of the crawling, clinging, rolling, hopping, jumping and leaping, pushing and pulling, lifting and throwing, hanging, and weight-bearing that young children and teens do in and outside of the SMART room (Kranowitz 2005, 136–38). This information contributes to awareness of the location of the body parts in relation to each other and the location of the body in space in relation to the surrounding environment. A body schema, or a sense of the body as an organized whole, is built on this foundation, along with tactile and vestibular information (Kandel et al. 2013, 482–84).

Proprioceptors: Golgi tendon, muscle spindles, joint receptors

Movement-Based Senses and a Core Sense of Being

When the sensory motor systems are working well together, the child experiences a core sense of being as she moves about the world (Bundy and Koomar 2002; Koomar and Bundy 2002). The subjective experience of the full embodiment of the self depends on brain networks identified by neurobiologists that create a sense of embodiment, groundedness, and continuity through time. The brain pathways are activated when sensory inputs originating from the vestibular, proprioceptive, and tactile receptors travel via afferent neurons to the brain stem, midbrain, and thalamus through networks to the temporoparietal junction, the insula, the somatosensory cortex, parts of the prefrontal cortex, and the cerebellum (Blanke, Slater, and Serino 2015; Hara et al. 2015; Lenggenhager, Smith, and Blanke 2006; Namkung, Kim, and Sawa 2017; Pfeiffer et al. 2013).

The *embodiment* of a sense of self comprises the following elements: *self-location*—"I experience myself as located within my body borders and I know where I am in space, relative to others and my surrounding environment" (Blanke 2012; Ionta et al. 2011; Ionta et al. 2014; Pfeiffer, Serino, and Blanke 2014); *first-person perspective*—"I am looking out at the world from me" (Hoover and Harris 2015; Ionta et al. 2014; Pfeiffer et al. 2013); and *agency*—"I am the author of my own actions and thoughts" (Lenggenhager and Lopez 2015). The vestibular network contributes to the experience of being physically grounded and balanced, which in turn contributes to *mental groundedness and stability*—"I can feel my center of gravity grounding me" (Harricharan et al. 2017). Finally, a continuous sense of *self across time* is coded in the temporoparietal junction along with self-location—"I have a continuous sense of myself across time, with a past, present, and future" (Arzy, Molnar-Szakacs, and Blanke 2008; Herbert and Pollatos 2012).

Foundations: Trauma Processing

Trauma-specific treatments for children have blossomed over the last twenty-five years. Some of these treatments are comprehensive treatment approaches aimed at influencing the whole system around the child (e.g., family, school, community), such as Attachment, Regulation and Competency (ARC) (Blaustein and Kinniburgh 2019); whereas other treatments are focused more specifically on the trauma processing element of the healing process, such as Eye Movement Desensitization and Reprocessing (EMDR) (Gomez 2012; Tinker and Wilson 1999; van der Kolk et al. 2007) and Trauma-Focused Cognitive Behavioral Therapy (TF-CBT) (Cohen, Mannarino, and Deblinger 2012). Yet, trauma processing and meaning-making are common to most treatments for complexly traumatized children, and have been conceptualized and approached in a variety of ways. Essentially, the traumatic material needs to be addressed either explicitly (e.g., through exposure therapy, EMDR, or TF-CBT); through displacement and metaphor, as in play therapy (Gil 1991, 2006, 2017); or through bodily experience, as in Somatic Experiencing (Levine and Kline 2006; Payne, Levine, and Crane-Godreau 2015). Different children respond to different treatments based on developmental capacities, temperamental preferences, and level of family involvement. For example, young children who do not have fully developed language capacities will struggle with

TF-CBT and other narrative forms of trauma processing. Children who have a low tolerance for intense feelings will have trouble bearing the emotions necessary for EMDR or exposure treatments. Many traumatized children have not developed the abilities to symbolize and to be creative that are necessary to effectively use play therapy.

In order to understand trauma processing therapies, it is important to explore how traumatic material is expressed in treatment. The simplest form of expression is verbally narrated trauma material; this is easily recognized by the therapist. Reenactments constitute a second universally held way traumatic material becomes evident. However, reenactments take many forms. More symbolic forms include utilizing art materials, dolls, stuffed animals, stories, plays, or puppets. In the acting out of content, the therapist may play the role of perpetrator, caretaker, rescuer, or powerless bystander. Another form of reenactment is based on implicit memory and takes the form of behavioral reenactments (Terr 1990) and habitual and sporadic body movements, postures, tonal expressions, actions, sexualized behaviors (Ensink et al. 2019; Kendall-Tackett, Williams, and Finkelhor 1993), dissociative reactions (Macfie, Cicchetti, and Toth 2001; Silberg 2012), and relational reenactments (Beebe 2014; Fonagy, Gergely, and Target 2007; Lyons-Ruth 2016; Stern 1985; Tronick 2007; Tronick and Beeghly 2011). Without a sense of the context, these behavioral enactments by the child frequently go unrecognized. Instead they are often misidentified as acting out, aggression, oppositional behavior, depression, avoidance, or boredom.

If you consider a continuum from embodied to symbolic, most of the child trauma treatments available fall from the middle of the continuum to the symbolic end of the spectrum. They rely heavily on higher cortical functions such as receptive and expressive language, autobiographical memory, abstraction, and executive functions; i.e., inhibition, cause and effect, sequencing, working memory, planning, and cognitive flexibility. SMART was developed to expand the range of embodied trauma processing therapies. In other words, it was designed to target the somatic dysregulation of trauma with minimal dependence on verbal engagement. Thus, SMART aims to support expression and processing of implicit and preverbal trauma at the core of some children's dysregulation.

Somatic approaches to trauma therapy for adults have grown significantly over the last twenty years. Some of the therapies primarily used with traumatized adults include Somatic Experiencing (Levine 2010, 2015; Levine and Frederick 1997); Sensorimotor Psychotherapy (Ogden and Fisher 2015; Ogden and Minton 2000; Ogden, Minton, and Pain 2006); Psychoanalytical-Action-Related

Model (Vogt 2007); and Trauma-Informed Yoga (Emerson and Hopper 2011; van der Kolk et al. 2014). Although these approaches contributed significantly to the field, reflecting a growing acceptance of the body as central to trauma treatment, they have not focused on the developing child.

Trauma-informed treatments providing somatic regulation for children and adolescents include sports-based interventions such as Do the Good (DtG) (Bergholz, Stafford, and D'Andrea 2016; D'Andrea, Bergholz, et al. 2013) and dance and movement therapies (Goodill 1987; Harris 2007; Ho 2015; Kornblum and Halsten 2006; Truppi 2001). However, these treatments require basic social skills and emotion regulation in order to participate in a group activity. Adjunctive somatically based approaches include yoga (Spinazzola et al. 2011) and Equine Facilitated Therapy for Complex Trauma (Naste et al. 2018) and are best offered in conjunction with a trauma psychotherapy. Finally, Sensory Integration Occupational Therapy provides somatic regulation through impact on physiological arousal modulation (Reynolds, Lane, and Mullen 2015; Reynolds et al. 2015) but does not specifically address trauma processing and attachment-building.

SMART (Warner et al. 2013) was designed as a somatically based treatment for children and adolescents to address Somatic Regulation and Trauma Processing utilizing activities able to support full bodily expression, high intensity, labile emotional expression, and sensory seeking behavior. Thus, children can be treated for their dysregulation and social struggles in SMART rather than be screened out for these symptoms.

To be clear, we feel it is vital to have a full range of treatments available for the variety of complex needs that traumatized children present, and thus, one end of the embodied to symbolic spectrum is not more important than the other. Children who can access approaches requiring higher levels of neurodevelopmental functioning are encouraged to utilize any of the treatments that are evidence-informed. However, when reenactments take the form of habitual and sporadic body movements, postures, and tonal expressions, combined with unpredictable actions and chronic explosive relational interactions, treatment needs to focus on arousal and bodily regulation without dependence on language or co-regulation. Painfully, these children seem to communicate their trauma narrative via their dysregulated behavior. Such reenactment behaviors can be enduring and resistant to change (Gaensbauer 2002, 2016). Those caring for such children frequently describe fatigue and vicarious traumatization due to this never-ending, looping pattern. This experience of expression without resolution was the primary impetus for the development of SMART.

Foundations: Attachment-Building

Attachment theory and its importance in human development began with the seminal work of John Bowlby (1969, 1973, 1980). Essentially, Bowlby highlighted how the primary caregiving relationship is critical to survival because of its impact on the formation of multiple areas of development, including arousal regulation, sense of self, and relational capacity. He hypothesized that the mechanism for this widespread impact was through internal working models that were based on the infant's experience of the early caregiving relationship. Ainsworth and her colleagues (1978) developed a categorization system to describe a child's attachment style based on this primary relationship that ranged from secure to insecure. Insecure was then broken down into resistant and avoidant subtypes. With this structure in place, attachment research blossomed.

In the 1980s, attachment research turned its focus to maltreated children (Crittenden 1985; Egeland and Sroufe 1981; Schneider-Rosen et al. 1985). Main and Solomon (1986) described a fourth type of insecure attachment, the disorganized subtype, which has become particularly relevant for traumatized children (Lyons-Ruth et al. 2006; Lyons-Ruth et al. 2016). This subtype is characterized by displaying both avoidant and aggressive relational strategies. It has been hypothesized that the dissociative process so common to trauma has led children to have to adapt their strategies based on a rapidly changing relational environment. In SMART, disorganized attachment has been a major challenge in treating traumatized children.

The neurobiology of attachment has also grown as a field starting with Harlow and his monkeys (Harlow and Zimmerman 1959). Harlow demonstrated how primary the attachment relationship to survival is when his monkeys chose a cloth-covered wire "mother" monkey over a wire one that dispensed food. Schore (2003, 2012) has written extensively about how the attachment relationship impacts developmental neurobiology. In 1996, the discovery of mirror neurons provided yet another mechanism for how the attachment relationship affects biology through intersubjectivity, empathy, and learning (Gallese et al. 1996).

More recently, the attachment field has focused on the neurological and psychological mechanisms of growth and development (Beebe and Lachmann 2014; Delafield-Butt and Trevarthen 2013; Fonagy, Gergely, and Target 2007; Stern 2018; Tronick 2007; Trevarthen and Delafield-Butt 2017). Trevarthen speaks of the rhythms of engagement between a mother and her child as critical to the development of consciousness (Trevarthen and Delafield-Butt 2017), while Beebe and Lachmann (2014) have elucidated many of the nonverbal forms of communication in this primary dyad. The importance of attachment in the development of arousal regulation, in particular, is essential to SMART. This early relationship is the original source of arousal regulation and the basis of not only future arousal regulation, but all of the areas of development that depend on a regulated system in order to grow and evolve.

The intergenerational transmission of abuse and neglect provides another line of research on how trauma is passed on through the attachment relationship. This research has focused on both the cycle of maltreatment, through which parents who were abused or neglected as children or adolescents are significantly more likely to abuse or neglect their own children, depending on such factors as type and timing of maltreatment and gender (Assink et al. 2018; Bartlett et al. 2017; Madigan et al. 2019; Thornberry et al. 2013), and the transmission of emotional themes, psychological defenses, and relational patterns (Felman and Laub 1992; Laub and Auerhahn 1993). Thus, it is critical to assess the caregivers' early childhood experiences in order to understand the effect on the child and family in the present.

Although many of our families are still intact after traumatic events have occurred, many are not. Adoption through kinship arrangements, domestic adoptions, and international adoptions are quite common for traumatized children and their families. Under these circumstances, attachment-building takes on some unique challenges in which the adoptive parents have to contend with the aftermath of the trauma and build a caregiving relationship when the child is older. Thus, the developmental needs are often at odds with the chronological age, which is confusing for both child and adult.

Many clinicians and researchers have recognized the importance of the attachment relationship and, thus, have developed treatments targeting the caregiving relationship (Hughes 2018; Lieberman and van Horn 2008). Some of these treatments have focused on the early years—e.g., Lieberman—whereas others have taken a more instructional approach—e.g., Parent–Child Interaction Therapy (PCIT) (Bagner and Eyberg 2007; Chaffin et al. 2011) and Theraplay (Booth and Jernberg 2010). In Dyadic Developmental Psychotherapy, Hughes has incorporated family therapy and psychodynamic principles to build the attachment relationship in families with traumatized children. Particularly, he emphasizes the attitudes of playfulness, acceptance, curiosity, and empathy to increase the intersubjectivity between the caregiver and child. All of these treatments have understood that in order to make a significant difference in children's lives, one has to address the caregiving relationship.

SMART has recognized the quintessential importance of attachment from the beginning, but our understanding of how to incorporate it into our treatment has evolved. Although we started with a focus on Somatic Regulation, the significant role of co-regulation was recognized from the start. As Trauma Processing emerged as a thread in our treatment model, the ways in which traumatic reenactments occur within the relationship were one of the main foci within this thread. However, we found that there was still more to be done in building the attachment with the caregiver. Attachment-Building forges new ways of connecting between caregivers and children, provides experiences of safety in relationship, and promotes play and mutual enjoyment.

PART 2

Tools and Skills

Introduction to Part 2: Tools of Regulation, Therapist Skills, and Video Reflection

The SMART technique is built on three legs: the multisensory Tools of Regulation, specialized Therapist Skills, and Video Reflection. As with any three-legged stool, if you lose one leg, the soundness of the whole becomes compromised. With three legs, this stool is sturdy and can support the complex treatment process. Chapter 3 elucidates the sensory motor tools available to the therapist, chapter 4 the skills that a SMART therapist will employ, and chapter 5 the use of Video Reflection to support the process. Throughout the text, Regulation Tools and Therapist Skills are capitalized to distinguish their special meaning to SMART treatment. In order to guide therapists as they navigate SMART, there are two important overarching structures: the SMART Spiral and the SMART Regulation Map. These two concepts provide the road map of treatment, while the tools, skills, and video are the specific methods to help you get there.

The SMART Spiral

As described in the Introduction, the SMART Spiral represents the evolution of our process and highlights the three main themes of SMART treatment: Somatic Regulation, Trauma Processing, and Attachment-Building (See Spiral: Insert 1). In the development of the model, Somatic Regulation took precedence as the greatest challenge in daily life and in therapy. We learned that if we followed the child's body, and scaffolded her attempts at regulation, Trauma Processing organically emerged in her play and nonverbal self-expression, or often in adolescents, in the quality of their verbal communication. We realized that the child bounced back and forth between the two processes within and across sessions. Later in the model development, we identified the many ways that the children and adults—whether therapist or caregiver—were creating new rhythms of engagement. These rhythms had greater predictability, reciprocity, and room for novelty and fun, thus building attachment capacity. We called this Attachment-Building, and added this thread to the Spiral. These therapeutic processes are threads throughout the treatment that intertwine in different ways for different children, across age, culture, race, ethnicity, socioeconomic status, sexual identity and orientation, religion, and environment. Treatment supports the child to develop a wider Window of Tolerance for sensations, affect and emotions, relationships, thoughts, memories, and other forms of experience. Over time, a stronger sense of self emerges and flourishes in the child.

The SMART Regulation Map

The SMART Regulation Map allows the therapist to Track psychological states and state shifts over time and helps to guide the therapist in decision-making (See SMART Regulation Map, Insert 3). The map contains three distinct states: the Integrated State and the two Traumatic States of Hyperarousal and Hypoarousal, along with two transitional areas we call the Fluid Zones. The Fluid Zones represent the more unstable, open time in which the child is available to build new capacity and to process traumatic learning. These moments in time offer important opportunities for therapeutic intervention and change.

This map was built on similar models noted in the literature (Ogden, Minton, and Pain 2006, 27; Siegel 1999, 253; Siegel 2012, 281–86) but was further developed for children and adolescents by the SMART team through observation of clinical recordings, and through a research video recording coding study in progress. (See Child State Descriptors, Inserts 4 and 5.)

The SMART Regulation Map shows the Traumatic States of Hyperarousal and Hypoarousal, and like the Modulation Model (Ogden and Fisher 2009; Ogden and Minton 2000; Ogden, Minton, and Pain 2006) captures both ends

SMART Regulation Map

Figure prepared by Elizabeth Warner, Anne Westcott, Alexandra Cook, and Heather Finn, 2019

The SMART Regulation Map

of the arousal spectrum. We call the state sometimes referred to as "optimal arousal" or being "in the Window of Tolerance" the "Integrated State," because it represents the nature of the child's best organization. We identify the two additional zones as High Intensity and Low Intensity Fluid Zones, which are important therapeutic working zones.

Integrated State

In the Integrated State, the child's thinking, feeling, and doing appear organized, coherent, and goal-oriented. Therapists witness children sustaining attention and intention, connection, curiosity, exploration, and mastery play. Children also show clear, observable feeling states and they have access to language, so that they may be able to put their feelings into words. Awareness of interoceptive body signals such as thirst, fatigue, or body temperature, and the ability to act on them, is evident. The Integrated State can easily be identified in session and on video recordings. Therapists generally feel present to the child and connected even when merely witnessing a child's activity.

SMART Regulation Map
Child Descriptors — Integrated State

Movement and Action	Body Awareness	Affects and Emotions
Energized and active or calm and alert body movement • Grounded, coordinated • Posture, arms, legs coordinated and organized around action • Directed, controlled, fluid	**Aware of body in space** • Uses visual/tactile information to navigate environment without bumping into people or objects • Adjusts pressure or intensity to activity	**Clear, readable affect and feelings** • Consistency across prosody of voice, facial expression, gestures • Matches activity or narrative
Organized actions • Shows plan, sequence, or follow-through in actions • Intent clear to others	**Shows interoceptive awareness** • Notices thirst, fatigue, body temperature, and other body signals; addresses needs • Aware of pain (e.g., headache), and physical sensations	**Voice tone and prosody are consistent with emotions being expressed** • May recognize and respond to emotions in others • May name own emotions
Aware and engaged with environment and others		
Physiology is in-sync with activity • Breathing heavier with exertion • Slower when relaxed		

SMART Regulation Map: Child Descriptors—Integrated State

Traumatic State of Hyperarousal

When children are in a Hyperaroused Traumatic State, they are often frenetic and out of touch with the therapist or caregiver. The way they move about the room lacks clear intention and is sometimes aggressive. They seem to be in sympathetic activation of the "flight-or-fight" fear state, and they convey this through hypervigilant, impulsive, or reactive behavior. High intensity affect may be reflected in a loud, unmodulated voice but without awareness of emotional states. Generally, judgment, reality testing, and a sense of time are not evident.

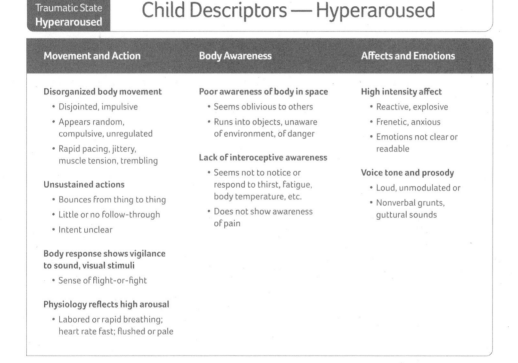

Traumatic State Hyperaroused	SMART Regulation Map Child Descriptors — Hyperaroused	
Movement and Action	**Body Awareness**	**Affects and Emotions**
Disorganized body movement	**Poor awareness of body in space**	**High intensity affect**
• Disjointed, impulsive	• Seems oblivious to others	• Reactive, explosive
• Appears random, compulsive, unregulated	• Runs into objects, unaware of environment, of danger	• Frenetic, anxious
• Rapid pacing, jittery, muscle tension, trembling	**Lack of interoceptive awareness**	• Emotions not clear or readable
Unsustained actions	• Seems not to notice or respond to thirst, fatigue, body temperature, etc.	**Voice tone and prosody**
• Bounces from thing to thing	• Does not show awareness of pain	• Loud, unmodulated or
• Little or no follow-through		• Nonverbal grunts, guttural sounds
• Intent unclear		
Body response shows vigilance to sound, visual stimuli		
• Sense of flight-or-fight		
Physiology reflects high arousal		
• Labored or rapid breathing; heart rate fast; flushed or pale		

SMART Regulation Map: Child Descriptors—Hyperaroused

Traumatic State of Hypoarousal

Children in a Hypoaroused Traumatic State are often experienced as unavailable, disconnected from those around them, from the environment, and from themselves. They may be spacey, lethargic, and/or collapsed. They may seem tired and sleepy, have trouble focusing, and move slowly, as if the whole body or parts of it are physiologically depressed. Therapists feel the disconnection and experience the withdrawal through averted eye gaze, turning their body away, and shutting the therapist out, as if overwhelmed. Often, the client's spacey demeanor reflects diffuse, undefined affect, as well as slowed thinking and language processing.

SMART Regulation Map
Child Descriptors — Hypoaroused

Traumatic State Hypoaroused

Movement and Action	Body Awareness	Affects and Emotions
Slowed body movements • Limp, flaccid, collapsed, immobilized, or frozen • Low energy, sleepy, spacey **Aimless behavior** • Little or no follow-through in actions; appears as effortful • Intent unclear **Disengaged from environment** • Passive, under-reactive • Oblivious to surroundings **Physiological depressed arousal** • Slowed responses • As if trying to wake up • Dizzy, shaky, wobbly when going from prone to standing	**Poor awareness of body in space** • Little or no evidence of noticing surroundings • Connections with others weak or nonexistent **Diminished interoceptive awareness** • Slowed awareness of internal state, body signals • Often aware of only part of body, not whole	**Low energy, diffuse affect** • Low emotional energy • Hopeless, helpless, or withdrawn • Engagement with others is an effort **Voice tone and prosody** • May be slowed, slurred • Verbal output diminished, trails off, or stopped

SMART Regulation Map: Child Descriptors—Hypoaroused

Fluid Zones: High Intensity and Low Intensity

The two Fluid Zones are therapeutic working zones of both High Intensity and Low Intensity arousal. They lie between hyperarousal and integration, and between hypoarousal and integration. These working zones capture the psychological states in which the child appears to be in a state of flux, an unstable system, which is therefore more open to change. At these times, the child seems more accessible and accepting of therapist gestures of help, scaffolding, or new experiments. It is in these moments that we tap into the client's capacity for growth by offering a lead toward regulating activity that helps them reorient to their surroundings. They may then experience a new sense of safety in their environment and in relationship, which further grounds them in the present. It is likely we are viewing in real time children's amazing neuroplasticity, reflected in behavioral plasticity, a key developmental mechanism to harness for growth and healing.

The therapist's "gut sense" that he still has some connection with his client is often the key indicator that the child is now in this more Fluid Zone. That connection may feel tenuous and vulnerable to change at any moment; however, the child is able to respond to contact, nonverbal or verbal, and guidance from the therapist. One clue that the child is in this Fluid Zone is that he waits for a therapist to move a mat for protection, or makes an effort to aim the ball when the therapist offers a "yes, and let's find a way that is also safe" approach. The body of an adolescent in a Low Intensity Fluid Zone may look shut down and collapsed, yet may still show signs of "reaching for" the therapist through bids, such as peeking out, tilting the head, grunting a response, or returning a ball rolled by the therapist with a small flick of the hand.

We feel it is crucial to highlight these Fluid Zones because they offer the opportunities for change in our clients. Over and over again, we witnessed children presenting at the edge of or beyond their Integrated State. At these times, when therapists offer co-regulation and scaffold with Tools of Regulation, new capacities emerge. If practiced, new habits of self-regulation develop, and over time a stronger sense of self emerges that is solidly grounded in the world.

Widening the Window of Tolerance

As the therapy unfolds and the different threads of the SMART Spiral are addressed, the child's psychological state-shifting smooths out. This process grows the child's tolerance for sensations, feelings, thoughts, memories, and relationships as they experience more time in an Integrated State. The SMART therapist will be able to identify the ways in which the client's Window of Tolerance expands in a single session as well as over time. This process is not linear; it may be rough and bumpy, or may stall. Developmental growth spurts bring instability but also opportunities for new skills. Unexpected life events or normal transitions may result in a sudden collapse of integration. However, overall, we routinely see a steady, if at times slow, march toward increased capacity when the young client is afforded opportunities for sensory motor engagement with an attuned therapist.

3

SMART TOOLS OF REGULATION

In this chapter, many examples of sensory motor play are given to illustrate for the reader the SMART tools—and corresponding equipment—our clients have creatively used. These examples come from watching the way children and adolescents in the SMART room naturally gravitate toward and use the equipment we have provided. Except when Tending to Safety or adding or adjusting an input to help a child better satiate a need for sensory input, the therapist is not prescribing what to do with the equipment as an occupational therapist might. The goals of SMART as a trauma psychotherapy and Sensory Integration Occupational Therapy differ, and as a consequence, the therapeutic processes diverge. Rather, we Follow the client's lead and have learned that much of the movement we witness is self-regulating for the child. For most of our clients who have had attachment disruptions, learning how to seek, accept, and benefit from help is part of the therapeutic work.

Many of the ways that children use the equipment (See Appendix: SMART Equipment Basics) incorporate several sensory inputs at once. However, the equipment is not the tool; the sensory inputs and motor outputs are the tools. The skill of identifying what form of sensory input is most regulating (and what may be dysregulating) distinguishes the SMART approach from the use of playgrounds and games of "hoops" that child and adolescent therapists have always used. Parsing these tools has helped us better guide children and teens in creating their own regulation toolbox and sharing those discoveries with their caregivers, teachers, and other helpers in their lives.

The Tools of Regulation are the following:

1. Tactile Inputs
2. Vestibular Inputs
3. Proprioceptive Inputs
4. Sensory Satiation
5. Combining Inputs
6. Rhythmicity
7. Safe Space

As the tools are described, we give examples from the clinic, the home, private practice offices, and residential treatment settings. In addition, considerations about how to co-regulate safely and how to use the equipment productively are elucidated (See Tools of Regulation, Insert 8).

The Movement Senses

Vestibular, proprioceptive, and tactile sensations together give us awareness of our bodies, our relationship to the environment, and our relationship to others, and a core sense of being (Lackner and DiZio 2005). When these three senses are working well together, we engage with the environment spontaneously, flexibly, and with vitality. We know where we are in relation to the world around us and in relation to others, and we can judge how to move through the environment safely. Children can feel safe in their bodies, the masters of their fate, and therefore, playful. A feeling of threat precludes play; in contrast, a felt sense of safety in the body allows for playfulness and positive affect. Adolescents hanging out on a local playground without adults around spontaneously connect with each other by touching and hugging, horsing around, and using the playground equipment while talking and laughing.

Ayres noted as far back as 1972 that "multisensory stimuli are more effective than messages from one modality only" (30). The multisensory integration of the Tactile, Vestibular, and Proprioceptive inputs supports *self-location* (a sense of where I am in the world and that I am located within my body), a *first-person perspective* (I see the world from me), *a sense of agency* (I am the author of my thoughts and actions), the experience of *mental groundedness and stability* (I feel my center of gravity grounding me), and a *continuous sense of self across time* (I have a sense of myself across time, with a past, present, and future). It is these functions that give us a core sense of being (Ionta et al. 2011; Lenggenhager, Smith, and Blanke 2006; Pfeiffer, Serino, and Blanke 2014).

TOOL 1: Tactile Inputs

*Touch is our most immediate and extensive interaction
with the world in which we live, but also a crucial agent
in the construction of our self-consciousness.*

—SERINO AND HAGGARD 2010, 234

Touch is the sense originating in the skin, the largest organ of the body and the primary contact boundary with the outer world. The tactile sensory system is complex with mechanoreceptors specialized for sensitivity to skin movement, motion against the skin, vibration, form and texture perception, skin stretch, temperature, pain, and pleasant touch, as well as fine discriminations of hot and cold, texture, and degrees of itch and pain. As a consequence of this complexity, touch experience contributes to and informs our psychological experience of ourselves and others as well as the environment of objects and the physical world.

The two types of tactile experience of interest to SMART are deep pressure and light or moderate touch, which can be quite varied. There are multiple different receptors that process variations of these Tactile Inputs to the skin (underscoring the overall importance of tactile sensation). In the SMART room, there are several pieces of equipment with which children and adolescents can access Tactile Input, including both the deep touch pressure and light or moderate levels of pressure. The therapist's role is to assess the child's seeking or avoiding of Tactile Inputs and consider ways to meet the need.

Deep Touch Pressure

For those children seeking deep pressure, weighted blankets of varying denominations provide a way to experiment with discovering the amount of deep pressure that feels just right. Two large foam-filled pillows or two couch cushions at home can provide a "deep pressure sandwich" that is one kind of calming pressure that many, but not all, people like. However, sometimes a child or adolescent will run and jump onto the large crash mats, landing frontally or on his back, just as he might do at home by running and flying onto a mattress. This creates a sudden, intense full-body pressure. Body socks made of spandex can provide a gentler full-body pressure. Hands and feet receive the pressure if the person is inside pushing out from the body. Young children may experience a similar full-body tactile "feel," with the added element of rhythmic Vestibular Input, when wrapped or swung in a large piece of spandex like in a hammock.

Tactile Input in body sock

A game called "peanut butter or jelly" is a playful way to offer choices of kinds of Tactile Input and provides an opportunity for the child to express where on the body and how she prefers the input. "Peanut butter," when a physioball is rolled up and down the body while the child is lying prone on a mat, offers dynamic deep pressure and tends to reduce arousal. "Jelly," gently bouncing a ball along the back, provides yet another form of Tactile Input, and one that tends to increase arousal and upregulate. In addition, in this game, the child can choose where on the body—torso, arms, or legs—to get the input. One child sought pressure on his head, too, and eventually enjoyed a head massage from his mother.

It is important with all of these activities to Follow the child's lead in a manner that feels comfortable. Some children will ask to have the blanket or cushion over the body with the head out, and others prefer to have the head covered. It is critical to ask the child how she wants the deep touch pressure applied or to allow her to direct it so that she has a sense of control over the touch experience. Traumatized children can regain or develop a sense of active control over their bodies in this way and thus have a healing experience of co-regulated touch.

At times, children may crave strong amounts of deep touch pressure, often surprisingly more than one would expect. Physically or sexually abused children, or those who have witnessed violence in the home, may not want the therapist to provide pressure but will still seek it by creating piles of equipment to crawl under. Or a child may crawl under the crash cushion and ask the therapist to place the weighted blanket and another crash cushion on top for more pressure. The therapist may need to apply some of her body weight to satiate the need. At these moments, it is essential that the therapist actively check in with the child. She may ask in the following ways: "How does this pressure feel?" "How is this for you?" "Would you like more … or less?" or "I am going to give some pressure. Give me a thumbs-down if you don't like it and thumbs-up when it is just right." The therapist should apply the pressure slowly so that the child has time to process his experience and respond. This method of collaboration allows the child to guide the discovery of the "just right" sensory input for regulation. It also allows room for the child to reject a particular input, which gives him a sense of control, expands his awareness of likes and dislikes, and creates greater attunement with the therapist. As one little boy said to his therapist afterward, "Thank you for going with what I said and not with what you want."

Moderate and Light Tactile Input

Play inside the sensory shaker provides a different kind of Tactile Input—a dynamic lighter touch—and is frequently sought by young children. In one clinic for younger children, the equipment is so popular, each SMART room has a ball pit large enough for children to tumble in, hide under the balls, and roll about. Another way of getting a moderate input is with the use of a blanket or large swath of spandex wrapped lightly around the child. For some children numbed to touch, a lighter Tactile Input awakens awareness of sensation, particularly if neglect experiences included a lack of sufficient touch and attention to the body. It may also provide the input over the entire body from head to toe, which is otherwise hard to obtain. In some cases, receiving this kind of Tactile Input increases tolerance for human touch and deep pressure.

Dynamic Tactile Input in the sensory shaker

Touch is a natural part of a child's play and is necessary for healthy development. As such, touch will occur in the SMART room by the very nature of the approach. Most often, touch is child-initiated or part of the play. Occasionally, when clinically relevant, the therapist may initiate a touch contact for a specific purpose. So the therapist needs to understand:

- How to use touch,

- How to communicate about it with the child and the parent, and

- How to adapt the approach when either the child's presentation or the institution does not allow for direct touch.

It is essential that the therapist is internally mindful and clear about her intention when using touch and, if asked, could articulate the function of the touch moment. Such functions may include ensuring physical safety, supporting or scaffolding an activity the child is doing, soothing or reassuring a struggling child, providing needed resistance in a proprioceptive activity, and participating in play. As part of the consent process, therapists inform caregivers that touch will happen in SMART and ask them to discuss their child's experiences and responses with regard to touch. Therapist-initiated touch is always an intervention that must be used cautiously and with clear purpose, given the possibility that the child could have a history of experiencing abusive or unwanted touch.

The equipment provides the therapist with more options for safely meeting a child's need for touch or physical contact during a session. When possible, the therapist also determines how to incorporate caregivers in providing needed touch experiences in a manner that will feel just right for their child. In some cases, this process occurs rapidly—such as when a boy, crashing into a crash mat, jumps onto his father's lap and is received in a playful, accepting way. In others, such as a sexually abused adopted girl, it is a long process of supporting her to find ways to get the touch she needs, first with the equipment and gradually with caregivers. For this girl, her in-home therapist showed her adoptive mother ways to use weighted blankets and couch cushions to meet her daughter's intense need, while learning how to establish comfortable boundaries for giving and receiving affection.

Most of the time, touch occurs in the context of the play and flows naturally; however, some children seek excessive or inappropriate touch that the therapist finds invasive or uncomfortable. It is critical that the therapist also feels safe physically, relationally, and emotionally. In these situations, the therapist has many tools available to meet the child's sensory need for regulation in addition to addressing the issue verbally. A therapist has the option to hold up a physioball or large cushion for the child to grasp, push against, or hug when support is needed. Beanbag chairs can be helpful for establishing boundaries, and equipment such as resistance bands might be used to help a child feel connected to the therapist without direct touch. Reviewing video with caregivers or a supervisor is also used to reflect on touch moments and to develop plans that support the child to experience touch in a comfortable, healthy manner and to promote positive attachment. Finally, in many cases, children become aware of their need and yearning for more physical connection and warmth in relationships with others, and the therapist may support that wish by naming it, and exploring with the caregiver and child how to fulfill that healthy human need while maintaining physical, emotional, and relational safety in the room.

TOOL 2: Vestibular Inputs

Vestibular Input is generated when we move our head, processing our relation to gravity and movement in three-dimensional space, thus functioning as the GPS of the brain. Movement of the head up and down such as when jumping or running back and forth, or rotating in different directions as in spinning, rolling, hanging upside down, or arcing when swinging or rocking, all stimulate the vestibular system. Depending on factors such as current state of arousal, developmental stage, and neurological impacts of trauma, the Vestibular Input that traumatized children seek can be up- or downregulating. Many children spontaneously seek this type of input through spinning in an office chair, doing somersaults, jumping on a trampoline, swinging, lying with their head hanging below the body off a couch or over a physioball, trying headstands, handstands, or cartwheels, or trying to balance. Ayres (Ayres and Robbins 2005, 43) regarded vestibular activity as "a 'framework' for the other aspects of our experience" and referred to the vestibular system as "the unifying system ... [that] forms the basic relationship of a person to gravity and the physical world" through which "all other types of sensation are processed." In this pivotal role, Vestibular Input "seems to 'prime' the entire nervous system to function effectively." We have noticed the important role in arousal regulation and in general behavioral organization that Vestibular Input plays for all ages of traumatized children when using the SMART room.

Vestibular Input for Downregulation

Vestibular Input for decreasing a state of arousal can be obtained most readily when the movement is rhythmic; for example, from rocking movements while prone over the Dolphin air pillow. Slow, steady rocking can produce a calming effect; a slow arcing back and forth also tends to be soothing, especially in contrast to spinning. Occasionally the spinning board is used to sit or lie on while the child pushes back and forth in slow, partial arcs rather than spins, and this has a downregulating effect. Steady rhythmic bouncing may also be calming and provides both Vestibular and Proprioceptive Input.

A full or partial head inversion produces what is called the "carotid sinus effect" that causes the child to move into a parasympathetic state, lowering heart rate and arousal. Children often spontaneously choose to lean over the physioball, Dolphin pillow, or the crash pillows, and rest with their head hanging down. At home, teens may lie on a couch with legs up against the back and head down over the edge and become quite relaxed.

Standing on a balance board, balance disc, or Duck Walker and tilting back and forth while talking and/or playing allows a child to have subtle amounts of Vestibular Input as he seeks his center of gravity; this can be grounding and bring him into the present.

Resting on the Dolphin air pillow with a weighted blanket

Finally, a staple of every playground is the swing. When a swing is available in a SMART room, many an adolescent has been able to engage in dialogue with her therapist in surprising and productive ways while gently swinging. Residential treatment centers can take advantage of outdoor space to provide this Vestibular Input for distressed and dysregulated children of all ages who need regulation opportunities several times in their day. Just as for babies there are home swings, designed by sensory integration companies. For small children, being swung in a large piece of spandex or in the sensory shaker by a caregivers and/or a therapist together can also provide this gentler Rhythmicity along with the comforting Tactile Input. In-home therapists have taken portable hammocks to home visits to provide this input and to show parents how it works.

Vestibular Input for Upregulation

Spinning provides more intense Vestibular Input. We have observed children who have experienced early neglect spontaneously seek strong Vestibular Input through spinning in an office chair. Although most adults find this overstimulating and may experience dizziness simply by watching a spinning child, we have found that many traumatized children will gravitate toward opportunities to spin on a spinning board or, for example, by twisting in a swing and letting it spin out. One boy, who reacted aggressively to caregiving by hitting, adapted tag to the SMART room by chasing and being chased in circles by his therapist. Running in circles, a less intense form of spinning, seemed to help him modulate his aggressive impulses in the context of physical and emotional closeness to a caring adult.

Therapist attuned to child spinning

In SMART, we follow the child's initiative to spin, viewing this choice as an effort to regulate and organize her body in space. In some cases, the child better orients herself to the surroundings when finished, and it leads to better arousal regulation and social engagement. However, the therapist should carefully monitor this input to prevent overstimulation and the systemic physiological responses that can result from too much spinning. Some traumatized children do not notice changes in their bodies, override the signals, or simply like the feeling of a loss of control. So it is important that the therapist Tracks the signs of arousal in the child and Tends to Safety as necessary. Children may also invent games, such as rolling in a tunnel or placing mats over the crash cushions and rolling down the ramp-like structure they create. If an in-home therapist must use the outdoors, rolling down a hill will be even more fun. Rolling, with the intense deep pressure added, can be upregulating and exciting. However, the deep pressure that is simultaneously received when rolling can keep a child within his Window of Tolerance when experiencing intense positive or negative emotions.

> Vestibular Input can be organizing and self-regulating; however, it also can be disorganizing and overarousing. Sensory Integration Occupational Therapists recommend stopping the child after ten spins, allowing the brain to process the input, and then, if the child wants to continue, reversing the direction of the spin. It is important to watch for flushing, nausea, headache, or other systemic reactions, and in such cases, the therapist can Tend to Safety by stopping and shifting activity. Be aware that systemic responses can occur up to six to eight hours after strong Vestibular Input. Caregivers can be guided to track the child's regulation after the therapy session.

Older children can jump on a Bosu ball or mini-trampoline to upregulate, especially if done more vigorously or during a game of catch. However, even an

eighteen-month-old, when provided with the right-size trampoline with bars to hold onto, will seek out jumping. This linear input challenges the gravitational part of the vestibular receptors, and yet does not induce such intense physiological responses as spinning; rather, it modulates the Vestibular Inputs effect. Furthermore, children and adolescents creatively find ways to make it more fun by increasing the physical challenge; for example, by jumping from a bench into the cushions, or when outside, climbing and jumping over a fence just to see if they can do it. The experience of mastery—the light in the eyes and a proud posture that says, "I can do it!"— is highly motivating. Therapists notice the grounding and organizing effect of these kinds of sensory motor activities.

Vestibular Input with Rhythmicity

Vestibular Input to Overcome Fears

Gravitational insecurity (May-Benson and Koomar 2007; May-Benson, Teasdale, and Gentil 2016) is a clinical phenomenon treated by Sensory Integration Occupational Therapists. They have identified the connection between an observed fear of falling and vestibular deficits, specifically in the otoliths, which are the gravity receptors. It may also be a problem of the integration of Proprioceptive Input, and/or postural insecurity. Gravitational insecurity is characterized by an intolerance for or discomfort with movement.

A boy who walked like a little old man—halting and cautious—experimented with falling in different ways into the pillows and gradually overcame his fear of falling in the SMART room. The following summer, he joyfully challenged himself to jump off a pier into the water and ride ponies while on vacation. A teenage girl, anxious about moving her body in any way, danced to music she loved with her therapist, and began to experiment with finding her balance and center of gravity in a pleasurable, relaxed way. A boy who often played a gopher close to the ground in the SMART room, stood up one day on a stepping stone and looked proudly down at his legs and noticed how they held him upright. Though currently physically healthy and strong, he had suffered from rickets as a malnourished toddler. All of these children benefited from OT services and were overcoming their fear of falling in playful ways in a SMART therapy.

Sensory Integration Occupational Therapy is often recommended for traumatized young children because an alert teacher or caregiver recognizes the sensory-based problems even before the impact of trauma is identified. In these cases, the two therapies complement each other well. In the above SMART cases, the two boys had already received occupational therapy services. However, in the SMART room, they overcame residual fears when creating playful challenges that addressed the impact of early trauma on their development. The teenage girl benefited from the specialized attention of the occupational therapist, who focused on treatment of the gravitational insecurity that had rigidified her responses to the ordinary demands of life.

TOOL 3: Proprioceptive Inputs

Opportunities to engage the muscles and joints afford the child Proprioceptive Input in endless ways. The proprioceptive sensory receptors reside in the muscles and joints throughout the body, so that many different kinds of movement and resistance can activate these receptors. This sensory information travels to the spinal column and provides information to the brain and consciousness about where parts of the body are in relation to each other so that even in the dark, one knows where one's arm or foot is. A body schema forms and transforms throughout life, from the infant's reaching and head lifting, to the complex activities of crawling, bike riding, and walking.

With increased effort of the muscles, more information increases body awareness, hence the usefulness of proprioceptive activity in the SMART room. Proprioceptive Input also tends to upregulate a child in a low-arousal state and downregulate a child in a high-arousal state, and is safe and therapeutically effective for most children. Children may seek this input in their lower body through the legs; in their upper body through the arms, shoulders, and torso; or through engagement of the whole body, including the entire core.

The intensity and effect can be varied by using different pieces of equipment and by adding other inputs. When added to Vestibular Input, Proprioceptive Input enhances the sense of location in space and of agency. When added to Tactile Inputs through dyadic play, Proprioceptive Input can increase engagement of the child with the therapist. When caregivers can learn how to access this tool, it can be very helpful for regulation at home or in school.

Sensory diets, prescribed by Sensory Integration Occupational Therapists, often utilize the need for strong Proprioceptive Input in order to help kids focus in school.

> A "sensory diet," a term coined by Patricia Wilbarger to refer to "the preferred sensorimotor experiences that help individuals function optimally within their environments" (Champagne and Stromberg 2004, 3). Just as you may jiggle your knee or chew gum to stay awake or soak in a hot tub to unwind, children need to engage in stabilizing, focusing activities, too. Those not able to "self-regulate" need to be taught how to do this. An occupational therapist who understands principles of sensory modulation and hypo- and hyperresponsiveness to sensory input can design such a plan for a child they have assessed.

We notice on video recordings what part of the body the child engages to seek the input: the whole body, the upper body through the arms, or the lower body through the legs. In some cases, a traumatized child may show an interesting "split" in which one part of the body seems engaged and another part seems limp or frozen. For example, one boy actively used his arms to toss a ball to the therapist, but upon reviewing video, his lower body appeared stuck to the ground. When the therapist pulled a mini-trampoline over, the boy jumped, engaging his lower body while continuing to throw the ball back and forth with the therapist. With fuller body engagement, his social engagement and verbal communication with the therapist increased as he jumped. Or for one adolescent girl, her whole body was inert on a mat, but with her eye gaze and a whistle, she engaged the therapist as she lifted her head slightly. This lack of integration of the full body is more easily observed on video and leads to individual-specific interventions to wake up and integrate the whole body in a way that feels safe to the client.

Whole Body. Crawling through a tunnel or squirming through piles of pillows provides complex Proprioceptive Input to all parts of the body and requires integration of the left and right sides and upper and lower body. Tug-of-war with a bike inner tube, a latex band, or a jump rope provides strong input to the upper and lower body. Lying prone over a large therapy ball and pushing back and forth from hands to feet give a gentler Proprioceptive Input as well as deep touch pressure to the full abdomen.

Launching from trampoline into crash cushion

One revved-up boy adeptly clung to the mini-trampoline that was leaning up against a wall, playing Spider-Man. He was receiving intense input to his muscles and joints throughout his body that he needed to downregulate. People will say, "They tired themselves out" with vigorous play; however, it is often more accurate to say that the child was able to regulate arousal more effectively. In this boy's case, he downregulated his hyperarousal to a more tolerable level but enjoyed a playful exuberance while his therapist admired his prowess.

Another strong ten-year-old boy liked to roll prone over the large yoga ball, and often sought out deep pressure to his abdomen. When he quickly tumbled off to the side, his parent noted that his core was weak. However, he continued to challenge himself, and when he allowed his parent to help him, he figured out how to use his whole body to balance and roll forward and back, smiling widely when he succeeded. This kind of spontaneous playful practicing also increased frustration tolerance as well as initiation and sustaining of goal-oriented behavior, core problems associated with DTD.

Lower Body. Jumping by bouncing on the Bosu ball or the mini-trampoline is a favorite way to get strong Proprioceptive Input to the lower body and legs. Sitting on a physioball while bouncing provides milder proprioception to the lower body. Games in which the therapist and child push their feet against each other's either in a bicycle movement or as a test of strength require no equipment and provide this same input with the important addition of building co-regulation.

Standing on a balance disc requires a person to intensely engage the proprioceptors in the feet, ankles, and calves as well as the full legs and core. The challenge of balancing, along with the proprioception required, quickly brings the child into present awareness of his body as he slows down and concentrates on staying upright. If he is not to fall, full attention to finding and maintaining a center of gravity is required.

Upper Body. Throwing or bouncing the large physioball back and forth provides Proprioceptive Input to the arms. One adolescent girl was self-conscious about her body and turned away from most of the equipment. However, she sat down on a physioball and gently bounced. The therapist mirrored her, and in a few moments, the girl picked up a weighted fitness ball and tossed it to the therapist. The therapist returned the ball, and as they tossed it back and forth, the girl surprised the therapist by talking about her experience of disappointment in her birth mother for the rest of the session. The game of catch with the weighted ball added intensity to the Proprioceptive Input to her arms and upper body and facilitated the "serve and return" of their dialogue.

When clinicians are able to identify the underlying proprioceptive experience that seems useful to the child, it then becomes possible to transfer this knowledge from the therapy room to the home. Clinicians can collaborate creatively with

Finding center of gravity on a Duck Walker

caregivers about the possible ways to employ everyday items to give similar inputs to the muscles and joints.

Deepening Basic Sensory Inputs

The opportunities in the SMART room for movement are key to arousal regulation. The actions, games, and play that are created recruit the Tactile, Vestibular, and Proprioceptive Inputs in unlimited ways. The therapist in this treatment method often must find ways to deepen or modulate the sensory inputs to facilitate arousal regulation and to increase the connection of child to caregiver or therapist. The following tools describe options for amplifying the power of the basic tools.

TOOL 4: Sensory Satiation

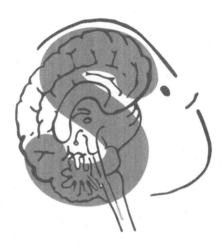

Sensory Satiation often occurs if a child can access sufficient sensory experiences in intensity, duration, and/or frequency to meet the neurological need resulting in more flexible emotional, cognitive, and motoric responses.

—WARNER, KOOMAR, AND WESTCOTT 2009

Children and teens often engage vigorously in an activity. Initially, psychotherapists, teachers, or caregivers may feel cautious about allowing a child to do an activity in a manner that increases the child's level of arousal, anticipating a loss of control. However, interrupting an activity prematurely may lead to frustration, just as running out of hot water in the middle of a shower would feel. In fact, providing opportunities for the child to experience sensory inputs at the level of intensity, duration, and frequency he seeks often helps him shift from a Traumatic State of dysregulation into a more Integrated State as his need for that motoric activity becomes sufficiently satiated. This experience is captured by the term "Sensory Satiation."

When a sensory need is satiated, clinicians often notice a corresponding shift in the child from social disengagement to greater interpersonal connection. Therapists report suddenly experiencing more connection with the child as if the social engagement system turned on again. There is more predictability, organization, and intention in the child's approach to an activity, and she shows a greater sense of self-location, where she is in the world and that she is located within her body. She may show greater awareness of internal sensory signals (interoception), and may notice a need to rest after vigorous play, or may notice that she is thirsty and ask to get a drink of water. In other instances, she may be able to notice an emotional feeling and identify and verbalize it. These shifts in state within session are the regulation process in action. As the child's states become more consistent, they set the stage for Attachment-Building and meaningful Trauma Processing.

Arousal Regulation or Loss of Control. A child may enter a therapy session agitated and hyperaroused due to a distressing event beforehand. Or he may start in what appears to be a fairly optimal state of arousal but then engage in an activity such as jumping into pillows that seems to rapidly heighten his arousal. The therapist may become concerned that the child will lose control or remain in too high a state of arousal. However, if the therapist sees that the child is safely conducting the activity and, with increasing repetitions, moves into a greater rhythm, choosing to sustain the activity will be to the benefit of the child. The end result is typically a return to an Integrated State.

Hypoarousal and Sensory Satiation. This concept of Sensory Satiation can also apply to a child who is in a low state of arousal. Hypoaroused children and adolescents may look depressed, sleepy, sad, or simply low energy. In this state, they respond best to gradual shifts in arousal through prolonged or more moderate sensory motor input.

> *A young teen, Darius, reported thinking he was paralyzed when he slipped into telling his therapist about a terrifying dream. The prosody of his speech slowed and his body posture shifted, signaling a shift from the Low Intensity Fluid Zone into a Hypoaroused Traumatic State. Although Darius loved to jump on the mini-trampoline, the therapist did not suggest it, knowing that a sudden*

strong sensory input can further physiologically dysregulate a person—just as getting up out of bed too quickly can make one dizzy. The therapist asked him to simply sit up on the Bosu ball. With the small amount of proprioception to his core muscles and Vestibular Input, Darius gradually returned to alertness. He reconnected with the therapist and asked to change the subject to his pet cat. As he told her about his nickname for the beloved cat, his voice changed, regaining a normal prosody and a warm tone.

When addressing Sensory Satiation for children and adolescents in a Hypo-aroused Traumatic State, the therapist's interventions must move at a slow and gentle pace. If the therapist responds with more intensity than can be tolerated, she will likely observe an increase in hypoarousal. This is in contrast to meeting Sensory Satiation needs for children experiencing hyperarousal, where the therapist attempts to provide enough input to meet the neurological need. Thus, the challenge for the therapist addressing Sensory Satiation lies in determining just the right *intensity, duration,* and/or *frequency* to gently support Sensory Satiation at any given time.

Need for Intensity. Some chronically hyperaroused children or teens may have a higher than usual need for intense sensory motor input. This may also be true when a client is particularly upset or angry at a given moment. The availability of equipment such as mini-trampolines, big crash mats, weighted blankets, and spinning boards allows therapists to assess for the level of intensity a child needs. For example, an adolescent in residential treatment would set up the four crash mats in the SMART room so that he could run and jump onto them with his full weight many times at the beginning of his session. The dynamic deep pressure he received to the full length of his body with the support of his therapist helped him to engage with the therapist. Often, after this activity, he would arrange the crash mats, settle in, and begin to talk to his therapist.

When a caregiver witnesses her child punching or kicking a piece of equipment, she might worry that the therapist is encouraging more aggression. Actually, allowing for safe regulatory activity in the session may create space for the therapist and child to collaborate and problem-solve: "When I am angry, how can I get my needs met in safer ways?" In many cases, children can better process events and solutions when calmer and more integrated. In some cases, the sensory need subsides when satiated.

The need for intensity of inputs often appears as compulsive activity or as anxious hyperactivity. When a therapist notices what the child is seeking, and provides opportunities in an activity or game that is fun, the child's behavior will become less frenetic, more predictable, more relational, and often more communicative.

Need for Duration. Through experience, we have learned that the duration of an activity may be much longer than adults would expect. However, if the adult can tolerate the amount of time needed, he will be rewarded by a more "put-together" child. One boy, who spent the first two years of his life in an orphanage, loved to have the physioball rolled on his back for up to twenty minutes. The newly SMART trained therapist discovered that he talked much more freely once he had enough of this pressure and spontaneously got up off the floor. Another young teenage boy jumped on the mini-trampoline for a total of twenty-five minutes, but after about the first ten, he began a long monologue about each of his family members and who he resembled, revealing his ability to think about and reflect on his identity. Once he was finished jumping, he continued his important self-reflection and asked the therapist when he would "see a shrink" with whom a client sat in a chair and just talked.

When to consider a Sensory Integration Occupational Therapy evaluation: For some children, a high need for input may indicate the presence of a sensory processing disorder. If a therapist does not see the need satiated, regardless of the amount of time allowed, intensity, or frequency for the activity, this can be a sign that the child has a sensory processing disorder and that occupational therapy assessment is indicated. The child may benefit from a greater variety of sensory integration equipment—e.g., suspended swings of different types, climbing apparatuses, planks, wedges, ladders, and other equipment—to provide ample opportunities for developing increasingly complex motor activities in order to effectively treat a sensory processing disorder. In such cases, a referral to an Ayres Sensory Integration® certified occupational therapist would be recommended for a diagnostic assessment, and if the assessment confirms the suspected problems, specialized occupational therapy treatment.

Need for Frequency. Sensory Satiation can also be provided by intermittent activities that may seem quite high in intensity. One young girl was very easily brought to a high state of arousal when discussing anything related to her family of origin. In school and at home, she would respond with behaviors others labeled aggressive, like striking out or knocking things off tables. In the SMART room, as her level of arousal was heightened, she would punch the Dolphin air pillow repeatedly. She could do this without having the therapist react with concern, and as she received the deep touch pressure and strong proprioception from this activity, she was able to quickly regroup and reengage with the therapist. This might occur several times in a session. But once her need for strong input to her muscles and joints was met, she was more available to problem-solve how to get her needs met in safer ways at school and at home.

TOOL 5: Combining Inputs

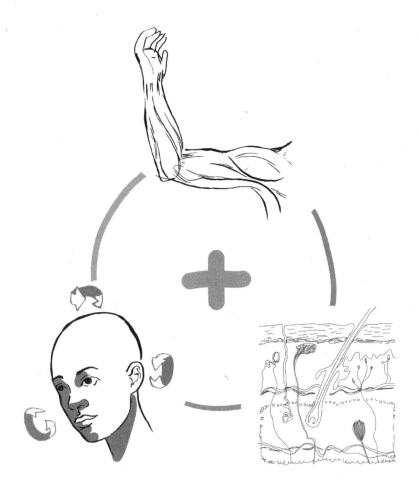

Some children seek more than one sensory input at a time for regulation—a multivitamin of sorts. Many activities naturally supply and integrate multiple inputs. For example, jumping on a trampoline or Bosu ball provides

Proprioceptive Input to the muscles and joints of the legs and Vestibular Input to the gravity receptors in the inner ear while bouncing up and down. Somersaults provide Vestibular and Proprioceptive Input, as well as dynamic deep pressure down the back, in one integrated series of movements. Rough-and-tumble play is a fantastic multivitamin of sensory motor inputs while building attachment with a parent or caregiver in the home or a therapist in the clinic and plays an important role in all mammalian early development (Scott and Panksepp 2003). Spontaneously, children add sensory inputs by increasing the exciting challenge of the game; e.g., adding a football pass to leaping into a crash mat.

Combination of balance, tactile, rhythm, and proprioception

In other cases, one may try an activity, such as placing a weighted blanket over the child, and discover that it is not sufficient to regulate the child. Sometimes the child may lead the therapist to what is truly desired by saying, "Put that blanket on me while I am lying on the Dolphin pillow; I want to rock with that on top of me." In other instances, a child cannot tell us what is desired, except by showing through actions. Some more hyperaroused and disorganized children may keep on the move and only briefly engage in activities that are offered. We have learned, in some cases, that they are seeking something but cannot figure out on their own how to effectively put it together—a kind of sensory seeking. With video recording of the session, a therapist carefully watching the child's movements will generate ideas about an action or a game to try in the next session that might include the combination of inputs the child seems to be seeking.

As noted above, Proprioceptive Input is a safe input and tends to ground the person quickly into awareness of his body in relation to the present challenge. If feeling drowsy or spacey, step up onto a balance disc, and you will suddenly notice your legs and feet as your muscles and joints work to balance. This property of Proprioceptive Input—bringing attention, focus, and awareness alive—can be instrumental in improving arousal regulation when added to most activities. It may be easy to add, for example, a tug-of-war with an old bike inner tube or a ball toss with a weighted ball, with the added benefit of including another person. Pushing or pulling using arms or legs also more fully engages the body to improve body awareness.

TOOL 6: Rhythmicity

Rhythm is an important tool that can facilitate or enhance arousal regulation by engaging the natural organization of the biological systems of the heart, the breath, and the wider nervous system (Feldman 2007 ; Koomar and Bundy 2002) and engaging the cerebellum, which is the seat of the coordination, timing, and adjustment of sensory motor actions (Stoodley and Schmahmann 2009). Rhythm can also increase the engagement of the child with the therapist. It creates order in the movement and thus in the child's behavior, and simultaneously it can regulate arousal such that the child can remain in an Integrated State while engaging with the adult. Furthermore, for some children who show limited capacity to tolerate positive feelings without losing control, Rhythmicity expands their tolerance for excitement, joy, and happiness as the intensity of the rhythm and play increases and subsides. Creating a rhythm in the interaction between therapist and child, in whatever form, is often a powerful tool in itself, both for internal regulation and co-regulation. When the rhythm is created together, the sense of attunement is automatically expanded.

Rhythms of engagement with other people often have never been developed in children with complex trauma. "Rhythms of engagement" is a term that we use to describe a natural dance in the interaction between people when in sync with each other. Ray Birdwhistell (1956, 1970), who created a field he called "kinesics" by viewing 16 mm film of human interaction slowed down, observed how "human beings are constantly engaged in adjustments to the presence and activities of other human beings" (Birdwhistell 1956, 143). Malloch (1999) recounts a "call and response" of a premature neonate and her father and refers to the dance as "communicative musicality" (36–37). Similarly, Beatrice Beebe and colleagues, with their microanalysis of infants and mothers, show the developing rhythms in facial expression, gaze, and body movements of mother and infant and the way the disturbances of attachment are created (Jaffe et al. 2001; Margolis et al. 2019). Although we can observe the disturbances in rhythms of our clients on video recordings, in SMART we are more curious about developing and co-creating new rhythms of engagement that will contribute to building a secure attachment.

In the case of traumatic experiences that happened after toddlerhood such as death of a parent or medical trauma, interpersonal rhythms that were established may have been disrupted. Hence, the use of rhythm is an essential tool for the goals of rebuilding safety in the attachment relationship. Introducing Rhythmicity to an activity serves the function of reliably enhancing co-regulation by increasing the engagement of the child, reducing the disorganization and unpredictability that make it difficult to Follow the child, and providing a structure when difficult material has to be addressed.

Rhythm for Arousal Modulation. Many games played with infants and young children use the repetition of rhythm and surprise as a structure in which the parent creates a rhythm, breaks the rhythm, and waits for a response before doing something that creates excitement. For example, holding the young child on her knees, the caregiver rhythmically bounces the baby while chanting in time: "Trot, trot to Boston. Trot, trot to Lynn. You better watch out or you might fall in …" and lets the young child drop a few inches between her knees while supporting him under the back, or by holding his hands. The caregiver repeats the game as many times as the infant laughs and, with a movement of his body, indicates he wants more.

The following illustration shows how the simple addition of a rhythm in a SMART session can decrease a child's hyperarousal and out-of-sync behavior.

A Hong Kong therapist struggled to follow a frenetic boy who ran about the room recklessly swinging a toy bat. Suddenly, he noticed a scooter board, pushed the mats out of the way, lay prone, and erratically pushed himself about with his hands. The therapist saw an opportunity to add Rhythmicity and began to clap her hands in a strong, steady beat. He responded by adjusting his pace to match her beat and as she varied her pace, he followed her rhythm. Slowly, he became more curious and experimental in what he was doing. Later, in SMART consultation, she and her colleagues watching the video recording could see how the boy intentionally and creatively explored various ways to use the scooter board for the rest of the session.

Along with his reduced arousal, his more organized behavior led to increased engagement with the therapist—an expansion of his tolerance for relationship—and more modulated affect.

Rhythmicity in the action creates predictability, simultaneously including the therapist into what the child is doing. Those children who are afraid of connection may break the pattern. But if the therapist can tolerate the break, pause for a moment, and then use the excitement of surprise to reintroduce the pattern, even the breaks can become part of the rhythm. This creates a dyadic game, thus improving the contact between therapist and child. Also, as the child is drawn into the excitement, she is learning to experience the high arousal of intense affect states such as frustration or excitement and then practicing modulation with each repetition of the game (Feldman 2006). This expands their Window of Tolerance for strong sensations and feelings in their bodies coupled with the immediate experience of modulation.

Rhythms of Engagement for Co-regulation Activities. In the SMART room, rhythms of engagement for co-regulation activities can begin in a fragmented or disjointed manner. This kind of activity is inherently unpredictable and makes it difficult for the therapist or caregiver to get in sync with the child. In some cases, children have never learned rhythms of engagement with others; and in other cases, they are traumatically activated by or avoiding greater engagement because they are afraid of getting physically or emotionally close to people. By noticing what a child is doing and creatively introducing some form of rhythm, a therapist can change the nature of the interaction. One therapist accomplished this by Following a young boy's attempts at drumming on the Bosu ball until the two were creating a catchy beat. Very quickly, the pair led and followed each other as if they had improvised music together before. Just as the infant both follows and leads the mother with voice and gesture in early communicative play (Malloch and Trevarthen 2009), the boy and therapist had created a musical rhythm that engaged them both in a nonverbal conversation.

Eye contact and face-to-face contact can inhibit social engagement for some children. At those times, oblique contact—so that the gaze is not upon each other but upon a distant point or a piece of equipment—can help. Having both therapist and child sit side by side on two therapy balls and bounce together in a steady and matched bounce brings the therapist and child into closer engagement, and can generate a shared sense of fun as they bounce higher and lower, but in rhythm with each other. When in sync with each other's pace, both can feel the attunement.

TOOL 7: Safe Space

Safe Space is a multipurpose tool that is used by clients in service of all three of the therapeutic processes: Somatic Regulation, Trauma Processing, and Attachment-Building. Repeated traumatic experiences engender a "felt sense of danger" in the body in reaction to the world, to caregivers, and to inner experience. The apparent paradox of trauma therapy is that the therapeutic relationship and space as a whole should be experienced as "safe enough," and yet a core long-term goal for traumatized children is to achieve a "felt sense of safety." SMART resolves this dilemma by providing a therapy space that affords the opportunity for the natural regulating sensory motor activity and proximity regulation that the body seeks when experiencing a sense of threat. That said, we observe the way in which a felt sense of safety is never fully achieved but is a dynamic process. It ebbs and flows and must be addressed over time in terms of physical safety, relational safety, and emotional safety discussed in depth in the next chapter.

SMART utilizes a tool called Safe Space to concretize creating safety. Building on the fact that children often like to create forts, cozy corners, or hideaways, and that children, and sometimes even adults with complex trauma in therapy hide under desks or in office closets, we provide movable gym mats, large pillows, crash mats, blankets, tents, and tunnels. In a traditional office setting, boundaries often need to be set on accessing such a space if there are computers, phones, or other adult-oriented furnishings that the child may come in contact with. In the SMART room, the child is given the opportunity to be creative with all of the furnishings to her benefit. With this equipment, both young children and teenagers create forts, houses, caves, or hiding spots. The child experiences a sense of agency—an important therapeutic element—when creating her own Safe Space versus simply hiding.

Child creates a personal Safe Space

In the practice of SMART, we observe that Safe Space can address all three threads of the SMART Spiral through enhancing Somatic Regulation and creating safety, facilitating Trauma Processing, and helping children regulate proximity with others to support Attachment-Building. In addition, the opportunity to initiate and sustain goal-directed behavior, a common difficulty for traumatized youth, is spontaneously addressed through Safe Space building.

Regulation and Creating Safety. Safe Spaces provide ways for the child to regulate by controlling light and sound stimuli that may feel overwhelming and by providing a feeling of containment with the physical boundaries of the equipment. One child used a tunnel to create a "groundhog game." She used blankets to block out all the light, popped her head out and in, and used her hand to hit different parts of the tunnel so the therapist could find her. Importantly, the Safe Space allows the child to experience control over the intensity of the interpersonal engagement by regulating eye contact and being seen, and providing a way to regulate social engagement by controlling the proximity to a caregiver or therapist. For children who have been physically or sexually abused, witnessed violence, or been bullied, such a space can help them feel safe by using physical boundaries and adjusting proximity to the adult.

Making a Safe Space is an opportunity for the child to create something just as he wants it. In the beginning, we had a tent that was premade; however, we discovered children prefer to make their own with whatever is at hand—mats, blankets, pillows, etc. Often, clients who have difficulty accepting help or tolerating frustration will spend a long time working on a Safe Space, getting it just right, tolerating the frustration when it doesn't work, changing it or reworking it to better stabilize, and asking for the help they need. The inability to initiate and sustain this kind of goal-directed behavior is a common symptom of Developmental Trauma Disorder (Spinazzola 2017) and yet, in this context, we witness the skills blossom as the child is given the time, tools, and opportunity to build something. Suddenly, their executive functions of inhibition, working memory, and cognitive flexibility kick into full gear in their drive to create their own Safe Space. The opportunity to create their Safe Space at their own pace, with an adult playing a supportive rather than directive role, appears to serve a self-regulatory function for children.

The use of Safe Space for Somatic Regulation can easily be transferred to home, and caregivers can learn to support the child to create their own Safe Space. One boy lying on a large soft cushion, who had learned to silently curl up his body in tiny spaces during many years in orphanages, imagined out loud a way that he would arrange his tent with a cushion like the one he lay on, a bookshelf, and a light, making it just as he would like it. The fast heartbeat and held breath he experienced while masterfully hiding in the SMART room changed to calm, comforting daydreaming out loud about a "safe space" for home. Use of this kind of Safe Space when a child tantrums or is fighting with siblings becomes a "time-in" rather than a "time-out" and can change everybody's understanding of what the child needs: an opportunity to regulate and to calm distress, rather than discipline, control, and isolation from others.

Trauma Processing. Frequently, Safe Spaces created by the child become the site of some form of Trauma Processing. One young boy had told his foster mother, "I hide scissors under my pillow in case I can't get away," reflecting his pervasive fear for his own safety. In his therapist's private practice office, which she had adapted for SMART, he spent an entire session patiently creating an elaborate fort. He then explored different ways to get away from a frightening situation rather than feel trapped.

When the therapist cannot see the child within a created Safe Space, checking in becomes doubly important to assess for freeze responses, dissociation, or flashbacks. One child suddenly froze when crawling into a small space and came out of this Traumatic State only when the therapist, after saying his name with no response, touched his back with her hand to help him reconnect to his therapist in the present moment. A man participating in a SMART training also froze when crawling through a blue tunnel. Only after the trainer encouraged him to come out and ground himself physically by changing his posture was he able to report that he had been caught in a flashback of a surfing accident that took place several decades earlier.

A single piece of equipment may be used to create a personal Safe Space. For example, one little girl who had been sexually abused was in In-Home Therapy with her adoptive parents. Her play was scattered and frenetic until she discovered the tunnel. She climbed inside, and standing up with the tunnel around her body from the neck down, her state immediately changed. The therapist could see the relaxation in her body when the tunnel provided a concrete interpersonal boundary. She suddenly began to make eye contact and verbally instructed her parents and therapist how to participate with her in the game she created. The sense of control that

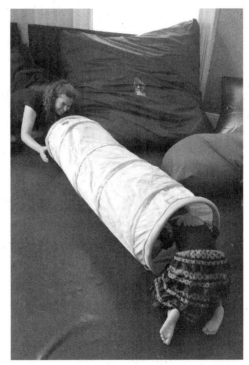

Tunnel for body boundaries, containment, safety

this boundary gave her—sorely lacking in her earlier life—helped her in working toward new ways of feeling safe and engaging with caregivers.

Attachment-Building. Many children with attachment losses and disruptions eagerly seek the chance to create a house or a home. One little boy's first houses were simply four walls made out of mats while his therapist helped to hold the walls up. Over the course of several sessions, he worked hard to create a roof that stayed up, as if to increase the protection he felt when in it, but the house remained sterile and empty inside. Eventually, he asked his foster mother to hand him comforts like pillows, little rugs, and a stuffed animal and then invited her in. The creative transformations in this process signaled the difference between traumatic play and traumatic reworking. His foster mother, who eventually adopted him, could easily understand the evolution of his simple need for safety and protection to a need for comfort, warmth, and affection as the house became a home. His invitation to her to join him increased her feeling that she was indeed building closeness and connection with him— something that seemed impossible at the beginning of therapy.

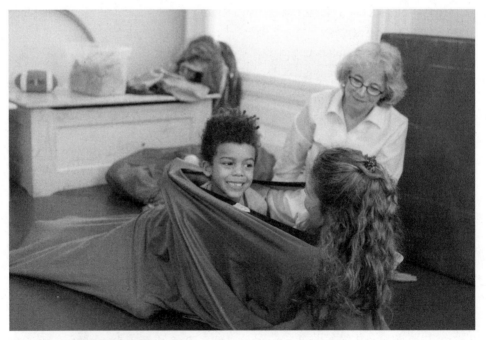

Attachment-Building in a body sock

4

SMART
THERAPIST SKILLS

Origins of the SMART Therapist Skills

Eight core SMART Therapist Skills have emerged since 2009 out of our accumulated experiences across many clients, clinicians, and settings. These skills developed out of practicing SMART in our offices, providing hundreds of consultations, and watching and reflecting on many hours of clinical video recordings. Sensorimotor Psychotherapy (Ogden, Minton, and Pain 2006), an adult model of somatically based treatment for trauma, informed our initial Therapist Skills (Warner et al. 2013; Warner, Spinazzola et al. 2014). However, after ten years of practice with children in the SMART room, we asked SMART therapists to name for us everything they did, concretely, in their SMART child and adolescent therapies and to be as specific as they could. Out of this list of sixty actions, we then asked ten general therapists to sort and cluster the actions that "hung together." Among these were ones that we knew we did but had not named explicitly. Others were analogous to our original skills but were better described by the results of the naming and sorting process based on work with children and adolescents, rather than adapted from adult models. The skills naturally clustered into two categories: Skills Internal to the Therapist and Skills External to the Therapist. Some of the SMART

Therapist Skills will feel familiar and have much in common with sound child therapy practice; others are quite unique. When we employ these skills within a SMART framework, in a room specially designed to afford opportunities for varied sensory inputs and a camera to make Video Reflection possible, we see amazing creativity, profound change, and emerging capacity in our young clients.

Eight SMART Therapist Skills

The eight SMART Therapist Skills are

1. Tending to Safety
2. Tracking Out and Tracking In
3. Choice Points
4. Embodied Attuning
5. Following
6. Full Participation
7. Leading
8. Verbal Scaffolding

The first skill, Tending to Safety, is an overarching skill. Tracking Out and Tracking In and Choice Points we regard as internal skills because they take place within the therapist. Skills four through eight are considered external because they can be observed and reflected upon through video review, whereas the internal skills are hard to discern, yet crucially important to effectiveness. All the skills aim to support children's enhanced regulation capacity, reduce their traumatic symptoms, and improve their attachment (See Therapist Skills, Insert 8).

Before presenting the eight Therapist Skills in order, it is important to acknowledge the contribution of the unique construction of a SMART treatment room to the successful use of these skills. The room design invites more physical engagement from the child compared with a traditional therapy space. Much thought, care, and consultation from Sensory Integration specialists helped us create this special place where opportunities to address physical, relational, and emotional safety with children emerge organically. Children learn best through experimentation (Koomar and Hughes 2011). By exploring the SMART tools with an attuned adult, traumatized children repeatedly explore their own and others' sense of "unsafe" and "safe."

SKILL 1: Tending to Safety

The first skill, Tending to Safety, is an overarching skill because feeling safe is a fundamental need for all people impacted by trauma (Herman 1992). Although most trauma treatments address safety-building early in therapy, SMART views Tending to Safety as an ongoing and active process of helping children experience a "felt sense of safety" in their bodies. SMART also recognizes that a felt sense of *physical* safety is necessary for building a feeling of safety in *relationship*. When children feel safe enough within relationship, they can then begin to explore their own internal world, thus creating feelings of *emotional* safety. The SMART room provides a rich array of opportunities to address safety in the physical realm, by inviting physical activities and interactions between the child, caregivers, the therapist, and the tools. By Tending to Safety in the physical realm, the therapist opens up possibilities for addressing safety on the relational and emotional levels.

Physical Safety. SMART treatment begins with Tending to Safety in the physical domain by ensuring that equipment such as mats and cushions is available in the room and that limited breakable objects are present. The thoughtful design of the room supports the therapist to safely scaffold children's physical movements and to facilitate the sensory and motor inputs they seek. SMART helps the child, caregiver, and therapist experience success as each participates within the treatment space. The therapist first Tends to Safety by being explicit about engaging with the space and equipment in a way that does not hurt anyone in the room. The therapist's focus is to find a way to say yes to the child's play while collaboratively working with the child to find ways to play that are "safe enough." Thus, the therapeutic stance is, "Yes, how can we try out your idea so that it will feel fun and no one gets hurt?"

If regulated enough, the child is invited to collaborate with the therapist and consider what equipment may be needed or adjustments made to safely follow the child's lead. For example, a child looking to partake in vigorous play may first be invited to look around the room and notice the distance of walls or location of bench corners. The child might be asked to consider whether a mat or cushion could cover the specific area to increase safety and support while continuing the play. When a child is heading into a Traumatic State, the therapist will model Tending to Safety by using equipment to enhance safety while succinctly narrating the action to the child. Over the course of SMART treatment, we find that children typically begin to internalize the importance of keeping their own bodies safe, and spontaneously will set up mats and cushions around the room in advance to support the action or input they seek.

Tending to physical Safety by placing mats over walls and crash cushions on ground

We encourage all therapists we train to hold in mind that "safety" is not static, nor does "safety" have a fully definable threshold; rather, it is dynamic and contingent. It lies on a continuum between high and low levels of risk, and it is inherent in how we experiment and learn through mistakes. For example, when a child learns to ride a bike, she may fall and skin her knee; however, falling is necessary to develop the degree of balance and coordination needed to master the task. The risk of injury may be reduced when the caregiver has the child wear a helmet and pads, and practice on grass rather than cement. SMART aims to create a place safe enough for the child to take risks in a manner that allows her to fully explore, discover, learn, and heal.

Relational Safety. While working to create a felt sense of physical safety in SMART, therapists often encounter ways in which a child struggles to experience a sense of safety in relationship with others. These challenges often manifest in the SMART room as relational reenactments (Bromberg 2011) of past interpersonal trauma. The affordance of the space and embodied nature of SMART can bring relational reenactments to the forefront of treatment and make them accessible for reworking. These experiences can feel very present for all involved, and the degree to which a therapist, child, or caregiver experiences a felt sense of safety within the room ebbs and flows over the course of a session and throughout a treatment.

> *Seven-year-old Isaac's early developmental experiences were significant for neglect, separation from his biological mother, and death of one of his adoptive parents. In SMART he presented with a disorganized attachment pattern when interacting with his current adoptive mother. Observed behaviors included reaching out and using a toddler tone of voice to get his mother's attention, followed by a sudden forceful head-butt to her chest when she reached back in response. Isaac also engaged in this disorganized pattern with his therapist in treatment. After she validated his vulnerable emotional response to a recent doctor appointment, Isaac responded by walking behind the therapist and forcefully throwing a large physioball at the back of her head.*

Although this reenactment led to a decrease in felt safety for all present in the room at that moment, it was also helpful for this reenactment to occur within the context of the treatment environment so that it could be reworked. By Tending to Safety, using the SMART Regulation Tools and Video Reflection, the therapist explored this child's challenges with experiencing vulnerability, being seen, and navigating relational closeness and distance through a variety of means. Slowly, over time, his tolerance for staying regulated when in relationship widened, thus increasing his capacity for relational safety and connection with caring adults.

> *Over the course of treatment, Isaac started initiating games of tag with his therapist in session. While running in large circles, Isaac and his therapist laughed and playfully took turns trying to tag each other. They identified where and how each person felt comfortable being tagged, and attention was given to respecting individual differences. With time, Isaac invited his mother to join the game, and exploration of touch and reaching could occur in a way that was new for both. By Tending to relational Safety through this child-initiated play, the therapist helped Isaac develop a greater tolerance for feelings of vulnerability (getting tagged) and for closeness or distance in relationships.*

Tending to relational Safety through familiar games

To build relational safety, it is important that SMART therapists tend to their own felt sense of safety in the room. The therapist's stance when Tending to relational Safety in a SMART room is "How can we try out your idea so that it feels safe for both you and me?" Each therapist will have her own comfort level with the interactions, revealing her own individual Window of Tolerance. The therapist's Window of Tolerance may also change during a course of therapy, as personal experiences such as pregnancy, injury, or illness will affect her own tolerance for different kinds of activities as well as her experience of the child.

SMART therapists Track their own internal sense of safety and can choose to explicitly or implicitly tend to their sense of safety. For example, a therapist might say, "I am going to put this mat in front of me, so I feel safe in this game." If therapists do not attend to their own safety, it reduces their ability to remain regulated and present to the needs of the child. In addition, this modeling gives children permission to attend to their own sense of safety, and explicit interventions provide concrete examples of how to communicate about bodily and emotional needs to others. Most importantly, it supports the child in negotiating safety in relationship.

Emotional/Internal Safety. A primary goal of trauma treatment is to develop the capacity to safely experience, tolerate, and identify internal experiences, especially strong emotions, as they arise. SMART treatment often elicits emotions, somatic experiences, and memories associated with the child's internal world that become expressed in a fully embodied way. The child's experience is felt intensely by all in the room and becomes more available for expression and integration in session. By utilizing Regulation Tools that engage the child's full body, the SMART therapist works to increase the child's sense of internal safety, and the ability to notice and feel "big" emotions without entering into a Traumatic State of activation.

> *Gerry, a fifteen-year-old adolescent, seemed upset as he walked into his SMART therapy session. He started to bounce a large physioball with intensity. He denied feeling angry, and was unable to verbalize his internal experience to his therapist. Tending to emotional Safety, the therapist wondered out loud if Gerry could bounce the ball to match what he was feeling inside. Gerry vigorously bounced the ball, and after it hit the ceiling several times, his therapist immediately "got" the intensity of his feelings and supported this form of emotional expression.*

Through this sensory motor action and connection with the therapist, Gerry's tolerance for his internal experience began to expand, thereby helping him feel more capable of experiencing, noticing, and expressing his intense emotions.

Due to the embodied nature of SMART, the intensity of the emotional experience felt in the room has the potential to heighten both the therapist's understanding of the client as well as feelings of vulnerability. As one experienced play therapist observed, working with a child in the SMART room felt akin to entering into the child's sand tray. Once "in the tray," the therapist experiences the felt sense of the child's world rather than witnessing it through displacement. It is therefore necessary in Tending to emotional Safety for therapists to be aware of their own emotional Window of Tolerance and Track their own arousal while working with a child who is struggling with intense feelings. SMART therapists are also encouraged to discover and use regulatory tools in session that help them feel grounded and present while Tending to Safety with their clients.

Skills Internal to the Therapist

SKILL 2: *Tracking Out and Tracking In*

Tracking is when we "listen, observe, and sense with our whole self the present moment experience" (Ogden, Minton, and Pain 2006). This unique kind of paying attention is how the SMART therapist Tracks the experience of the child he is working with, as well as his own internal experience as the therapist. Because children are still developing their language skills, they express themselves largely in their actions and body language. The therapist needs to become a skilled observer of this form of communication. Additionally, therapists can turn this special kind of paying attention inward, to better use their own internal experience to inform the therapeutic process. Tracking Out helps in quickly recognizing expressions of dysregulation, trauma memory, and attachment disruptions in clients, which is, after all, where the sequelae of trauma lives. Tracking In ensures that the SMART therapist attends to her own internal sensations, feelings, thoughts, and memories while working with the child, in order to self-regulate and to learn to use this information as a guidepost to what is happening in the therapy. The ability to Track In and Track Out is significantly enhanced by the use of Video Reflection, which will be discussed more fully in chapter 5.

   Tracking Out. Tracking Out is the process of learning to observe and describe a child's presentation without judgment, meaning-making, or interpretation. This skill entails an open curious stance, and an intentional commitment to attend to all the child's forms of expression. The SMART therapist will observe the child's posture, movements, actions, object of eye gaze, facial expressions, and bodily tension. She will feel the child's energy, intensity, rhythms, or discordance. She will hear the tone, prosody, inflection, and emotion in his voice. She will sense the child's intensity through bodily movements. She will see and feel the closeness and distance both spatially between her body and the child's, as well as emotionally, in withdrawal, connection, or intrusion. The therapist Tracks what the child gravitates toward spontaneously and what he avoids in the room. She will observe changes in the child across time, use of inputs, different attachment relationships, and the length of a session. Tracking Out is essential to all active skills and provides a foundation for our ability to Follow the child's lead.

Often therapists prioritize the child's words and verbal story and find it can be challenging to develop the explicit ability to Track all forms of the child's expression. Essentially, this is an observational skill rather than one of making inferences or interpretations. When sound did not work during a video review, one SMART consultant fumbled upon a simple way to gain stronger access to this unique kind of listening. He turned off the sound and simply watched the child and the therapist. Therapists benefit from reducing their attention to the verbal output and increasing their attention to the child's nonverbal, embodied forms of communicating. When doing so, it becomes easier to notice information gathered implicitly via nonverbal and right-brain processes. The experience in the consult room that day was akin to how one's hearing heightens in the dark to offset the lack of sight.

Tracking In. Tracking In is the process of noticing and sensing what is happening in ourselves as we relate to the child. When turning attention inward, the therapists can notice their own inner body experience, including tensions, sensations, emotions, and arousal levels, as well as breath and impulses to move toward or to pull away. One can tune into one's thoughts, becoming aware of judgments, meaning-making, memories of previous sessions, or the child's history. The therapists may notice memories or associations from their own life. Strong emotions may overtake a therapist, which can be powerful and disturbing during embodied Trauma Processing, or soft and quiet when experiencing a moment of deep connection with a child.

Over time, Tracking Out and Tracking In may reveal patterns in the child's behavior, emotions, or thinking. By reviewing cases with video, the therapist hones Tracking skills and develops refined assessments for each client. Curiously, using this process of Tracking on a regular basis can increase therapists' awareness about their own patterns; i.e., what arises in the therapist that is unique and informative about a particular child and what is universal across clients. It is important for therapists to distinguish what may be coming from their own histories and what is a reflection of or reaction to the child's experience.

There are truly no limits to what one can Track in the child or therapist. Although Tracking In is a conscious skill, it is not possible or expected that the therapist will make explicit Choices regarding all that they Track. Decision-making and actions about what to do next in therapy rely on a rapid-fire process of sorting and selecting through all the information available. This occurs quickly and, in many cases, below the level of explicit awareness.

Tracking is a fundamental skill that shifts the therapist's primary focus from what children have to say to what children have to show about their trauma story. SMART focuses on the way children show their story through actions and full-body play, because memories of trauma and attachment disruption experiences are stored deeply within implicit and bodily memory.

SKILL 3: Choice Points

Choice Points arise at the moment when a therapist pauses to decide what to do next. These "pause" moments naturally occur during the session. Sometimes a therapist may intentionally slow down the pace of the session to figure out in which direction to go. At other times, the therapist may make a quick and rapid decision to address a safety concern. During Choice Points, the SMART therapist synthesizes information gained from Tracking in the moment, with his vast fund of prior knowledge about the child, along with current treatment goals. The sources of data are both conscious and subconscious, coming from our explicit and implicit information systems. This integrative skill typically occurs spontaneously and rests on the two prior skills, Tending to Safety and Tracking Out and Tracking In.

Overall, the therapist will utilize Choice Points to support various treatment goals, including building attunement and curiosity, tending to a felt sense of safety, collaborating, increasing regulation capacity, processing traumatic material, and supporting attachment needs. At Choice Points, the therapist may ask herself, "How does this interaction feel in this moment?" "Is this child with me, or do I feel disconnected from the child?" "Can I seem to reach the child?" "Does it feel like we are working together?" The therapist may also incorporate explicit information such as where the child is on the SMART Regulation Map, known triggers, known Regulation Tools, and time left in the session, as well as specific session agendas and the child's overall treatment plan.

As an embodied therapy, SMART emphasizes learning from experience. Each Choice Point leads to either an action or a nonaction on the therapist's part. It is crucial that the therapist be attentive to the child's response at these moments. Frequently, the SMART therapist may Track increased dysregulation in response to a Choice Point made in treatment, revealing a possible misattunement by the therapist. These moments of misattunement are to be expected in treatment and often are the most fruitful moments in a session. Such interchanges between child and therapist create fertile ground for relational repair. Following misses with repair promotes the development of resilience (Tronick 2007) and a sense of relational safety, both of which are crucial for traumatized children.

Pausing at a Choice Point can be brief, because things often happen fast in a SMART room. The pacing of the child may require the therapist to make quick decisions, rapidly drawing from fast thinking, intuition, and subconscious systems (Kahneman 2015). This is one reason why Video Reflection is essential to SMART. In SMART therapy, many Choice Points are specific to the child and repeat from session to session, revealing places or processes where the child struggles. Video Reflection, expanded upon in the next chapter, helps the therapist study the results of the different directions taken at these repetitive moments of challenge for the child.

Skills External to the Therapist

SKILL 4: Embodied Attuning

Embodied Attuning captures the process of matching the "vitality dynamics" of the other person to create the experience of being in sync with the other (Stern 2018). This skill expands on the concept of mirroring first presented by Winnicott (1967) and more recently studied via mirror neurons in the brain (Iacoboni 2008; Rizzolatti and Sinigaglia 2008). Daniel Hughes (2018) highlighted in his demonstration films the way the therapist does not match the affect of the child's intensity; rather, he aims to match the tone and prosody captured in the expression. The SMART space allows the therapist to engage his whole body to connect and to get in sync with the child. By intentionally utilizing body posture, movement quality, intensity, proximity, tension patterns, and actions, as well as eye gaze, voice, facial expression, and affect, the therapist can convey a powerful sense of deep understanding to the child. This skill expands the therapist's repertoire to include the broader nonverbal communication with the child and to gain a greater window into the child's felt experience.

In one example of Embodied Attuning, a young child jumps vigorously on a trampoline in a SMART room while his therapist jumps in rhythm alongside him. Suddenly, the child leaps into a pile of cushions, and upon landing, lets out a satisfied sigh. The therapist joins the child, sits on the floor, and releases a sigh in response. Through Embodied Attuning, the therapist hopes to communicate to the child that his experiences are meaningful and welcome, and can be shared with another. The child receives powerful nonverbal information through observing an adult physically reflect his experience. This therapist-reflected information promotes the child's developing capacity for awareness of his own experience in the SMART room.

It is important to note that some children impacted by developmental trauma can feel overwhelmed by shame or fear to have their experience so fully seen and reflected by another. "Are you copying me?" is a typical question for some of these children. For many children who have survived abusive experiences, it was more adaptive to fly under the radar, avoiding notice by adults. If the therapist sees that mirroring interventions seem to lead the child into greater dysregulation, she can use Embodied Attuning to explore whether responses that reduce connection, such as backing away, shrinking the size of her movements, or averting eye gaze, reduce arousal and shift the child's state.

Ten-year-old Ricardo consistently disengaged each time his mother asked him to look at her when she was speaking during SMART family therapy sessions. Tracking that the parent and child seemed out of sync, Ricardo's therapist suggested that the mother experiment with varying proximity and eye gaze with her son to find out if it might impact the felt sense of connection between them. When the mother allowed Ricardo more physical distance and tolerated his rolling on a physioball behind an upright gym mat, it seemed to help him tolerate the conversation. The mat created a visual barrier that enabled Ricardo to modulate eye contact with others in the room. Despite the lack of eye contact, the conversation deepened and Ricardo's mother began to realize that her son had not been ignoring her, but needed to reduce the intensity of relational contact to tolerate staying in conversation. With time, the mother's improved Embodied Attuning supported greater understanding and more sustained conversations between her and the son.

Ruptures in attunement are part of the therapeutic process and are essential for children to learn about themselves and others. The child's attachment and sense of self grow within the mutual process of repeatedly discovering what repairs the relationship when a rupture has occurred. Ultimately, the therapist aims to stay with the child by responding to the behavioral shifts in a manner that allows for enough in-sync periods to sustain therapeutic engagement. As these rhythms of connection, rupture, and reconnection between the child and therapist are established, co-regulation becomes increasingly possible, and with it, healing.

Emotional safety created using mats to modulate intensity of relational contact

SKILL 5: *Following*

Following represents an active process in which the therapist supports exploration and discovery initiated and led by the child. This is an essential skill in SMART and can be surprisingly challenging to acquire. Through experience, we have learned to trust the inner wisdom of the body in expressing the problem and, with support, finding what it needs to heal.

Following incorporates both Tracking of and Embodied Attuning to the child's lead and pace. This skill is analogous to the powerful role Following plays in infant–parent communication. Infant researchers have demonstrated the way in which the very young infant can lead the parent via pre-linguistic sounds, movement, gesture, and facial expression while the parent Follows, and out of this the dyadic dance of attachment in which the parent sometimes leads, communication and connection develop (Bateson 1979; Daniel and Trevarthen 2017; Provenzi et al. 2018; Condon and Sander 1974; Stern 2008).

As the therapist Follows the child's lead, the focus is on fully supporting the child as director of her play. Staying attuned and curious about the child's intent, the therapist provides scaffolding to support success. Following allows the therapist to tune in fully to all the child's means of communication in the hopes that this will improve the therapist's capacity to scaffold new growth in a manner that can be received by the child. This core skill reveals our conviction, based on clinical experience, that the child holds wisdom about her own needs.

By Following the child, the therapist discovers what sensory inputs the child naturally gravitates toward and avoids, and what experiences tend to be up- or downregulating. This co-regulatory process helps the child discover, through his own experimentation, just the right level of intensity or frequency of the input desired. By becoming director of one's own play, the child experiences mastery and agency, both internally and interpersonally. As the study of developmental trauma is showing (Ford et al. 2018), the ability to initiate and sustain goal-directed behavior, which is the essence of agency, is impaired. Interpersonal victimization and attachment disruptions deprive children of essential experiences of embodied and relational agency that are critical experiences for healthy development, capacity for relationships, and self-regulation.

Nathan, a highly active five-year-old boy, repeatedly attempted to climb to the top of a large cushion leaning against the SMART room wall. Aware that this activity would provide significant Proprioceptive Input and milder Vestibular Input, both helpful for supporting an Integrated State, the therapist decided to Follow. Holding the cushion steady to scaffold his efforts to climb the wall, the therapist offered plenty of room and time for Nathan to engage in this activity to his satisfaction. This stance allowed Nathan to experience the input more intensely, and improved the likelihood of success. Nathan repeatedly ran, jumped, scrambled, failed, slid to the bottom, and tried again. After several attempts, he succeeded. As he balanced on top of the "wall," Nathan appeared more regulated and proudly surveyed his accomplishment from up on high.

Ultimately, a cardinal rule for the SMART therapist is to intentionally Follow the child's lead whenever possible. The therapist utilizes Following when the child initiates play and is within the Window of Tolerance, or when the child is in a Fluid Zone, in order to build regulatory capacity or master a new experience. It is also important for the therapist to Follow when a child seeks decreased engagement and to adjust the pace of the session accordingly. By Tracking the progression of play across a session or over several sessions, the therapist Follows as long as the play does not appear to be unsafe or caught in an unresolved looping pattern, typically associated with increasing dysregulation. In conclusion, the most helpful rule of thumb for the SMART therapist is "When in doubt, Follow."

SKILL 6: Full Participation

Perhaps the skill that differentiates SMART the most from most play therapies is the ability to fully participate in an embodied manner. Not only does this skill, Full Participation, amplify one's attunement, it intensifies the therapist's experience of being present, thus opening up a whole new source of understanding of the child. Full Participation entails the adult joining the child by engaging fully in playing games, taking on a role in embodied trauma enactments, or exploring regulatory inputs. This kind of involvement transmits a more intense, direct experience to the therapist than is commonly felt in other child play therapies. One must be comfortable moving one's body, tolerating being a beginner or "not yet competent," and not knowing where the session is headed. Full Participation calls on the therapist to take an exploratory, curious, spontaneous, and fully embodied stance.

Full Participation will take the therapist into the child's experience. Listening to a child describe hiding in her closet, frightened as she hears fighting, or having her show you with a small doll in a dollhouse does not compare to having the child make a small fort, go in it herself, and ask you to yell loud, unpleasant words from the outside. Being asked to go into the small fort, curl up as small as you can, and then being berated by the child brings the child's experience home—into the gut and the heart. The emotion, imagery, and bodily experience evoked by the play bring the therapist incredibly close to the child's felt trauma. The transmission of the "story" via this embodied communication is hard to describe in words, but can leave one with a feeling of having the story downloaded into one's own being. When used clinically, this transmission instantly changes the therapist's attunement. It generates a felt sense of "getting" the child and, in the child, of "feeling gotten."

Therapist Fully Participating in embodied dramatic play

SKILL 7: Leading

Leading occurs when the therapist guides the child or the activity either non-verbally or verbally. Similar to the lead when dancing the tango, there is a sense of being "in control" for the leader, in contrast to the sense of needing to "go along with" as the follower. In the dyadic dance of SMART, the therapist is thoughtful about selecting when to Lead, as Leading has significant potential to obscure the child's embodied communication. When the therapist does Lead, it is with the intention of guiding the child's unfolding process for a clear clinical purpose. Some children strongly resist the Lead of the therapist and need to keep rigid control, making reciprocity impossible. As trust grows through active engagement, the child tends to develop increasing flexibility in responding to the therapist's Leading and Following.

As in all therapies, there are times in SMART when the therapist must Lead. Early in treatment, therapists use Leading to orient a child to the room, to a new piece of equipment, or to the time remaining in the session. Therapists Lead when they provide psychoeducation to the child or family about how our bodies work, about trauma, or about regulation. However, most commonly, Leading is used at three specific times: (1) to Tend to Safety, (2) to introduce new possibilities to support the child's growth, or (3) to slow down and enhance important moments of attachment or mastery.

Tending to Safety calls for the greatest use of Leading. Even during these moments, the therapist Leads in a less directive, more collaborative manner with the hope of making the child aware of the natural risks around him and exploring safer ways to accomplish his aims. For example, when one young boy wished to jump off the storage bench and dive into the crash cushions, his therapist first took the Lead by asking him to pause with her words and a finger gesture. She pointed to the edge of the cushions, bringing his attention to places where the stuffing was thin. The child could take this information in, and following the therapist's Lead, happily dove several times into the middle of the cushions, safely giving himself strong multisensory input.

Leading may also take the form of setting limits during moments when a child's actions could result in harm to self or others. When limits need to be set in SMART, the therapist simultaneously considers alternate ways to support the child in meeting a particular need. This may be done collaboratively, if the child is within the Window of Tolerance or operating in the Fluid Zone. If the child is in a Traumatic State, the therapist can offer an alternate Regulation Tool. In the following example, an impulsive and affectively dysregulated six-year-old girl wanted to whip small weighted beanbags at her therapist. The therapist Led by stopping the activity, removing any heavy beanbags from the room, and then collaborated with the child to find something she could throw at the therapist safely. Together, the pair developed a game of dodgeball with a soft Nerf ball, creating tension, excitement, and competition. Leading by Tending to Safety, the therapist supported the young girl to create a game where she could experience, explore, and learn to modulate her high arousal impulses and aggression via play with a safe person.

The therapist also Leads during moments when new possibilities need to be introduced to support the child's growth in treatment. This type of Leading frequently takes the form of nonverbal scaffolding to assist the child to accomplish what she wishes to do. Leading through nonverbal scaffolding may be as simple as an extension of the therapist's hand to offer support or balance while the child seeks out a challenge. Alternatively, the therapist may demonstrate, with her own body, a way to approach a novel task that supports the child to experience success.

SMART therapists may also use verbal forms of Leading to support growth in treatment by guiding the child's focus to try something new, highlighting something notable about the child's present moment experience, or giving explicit directions during a session. This is a wonderful example of how Therapist Skills can overlap—in this case Leading and Verbal Scaffolding; they are not mutually exclusive.

After working in the SMART room for several months, twelve-year-old Alice identified that jumping on a trampoline and kicking a large physioball were two activities that helped her feel "calm." In one family session, Alice's mother raised a concern that Alice was refusing to complete homework after school.

Alice suddenly stood up and began to pace around the room, an early sign of dysregulation. The therapist chose to Lead by picking up the trampoline and placing it near Alice in the room. The goal of this intervention was to reinforce Alice's emerging ability to use Proprioceptive Input to regulate intense feelings. Alice was receptive to this nonverbal invitation, and proceeded to jump throughout her check-in with her mother. During this time, Alice seemed more able to listen to her mother's concerns, and to briefly share her own thoughts about homework without shutting down or becoming destructive. Following this discussion, Alice's therapist used verbal Leading to highlight her growth in treatment by labeling her successful use of a SMART tool to help her engage in a challenging discussion with her mother.

Lastly, SMART therapists may use Leading to slow down and enhance important moments of attachment or mastery that occur during treatment. To integrate any newly developing capacity, a child must first recognize that change is occurring, and take the time to register the effect of this change. The therapist can facilitate this noticing by bringing a child's or family's attention to the new area for growth. For example, when five-year-old Nathan finally climbed to the top of the cushions in the SMART room, his therapist used Leading to help this otherwise impulsive young boy to slow down and take in his accomplishment by inviting him to "pause and take in the view from on top." In follow-up sessions with Alice and her mother, the therapist used Leading to support Attachment-Building and invited mother and daughter to jump rope together in session. During this intervention, the therapist took time and care to highlight moments of collaboration, cooperation, and fun within the relationship.

In SMART, we prioritize learning through embodied experiences first, and then employ questions to promote reflection and integration through higher-order language and cognitive processes after the experience. Over the course of our work, we have seen repeated examples of a child's full-body play and movements demonstrating aspects of his trauma story. Leading with questions and conversation can constrict or stop the child's spontaneous communication, as well as impede the therapist from Tracking the child's nonverbal, full-body story. While many child therapists are familiar with Leading by asking reflective questions, in SMART, we consider this to be a unique skill called Verbal Scaffolding, discussed below. We have found it useful to differentiate verbal questions and conversation from other ways a therapist can Lead.

Leading is de-emphasized in SMART, because overuse of this skill can prevent children from discovering their own expression or experience of self. SMART was carefully created to interrupt the way repetitive traumatic and stressful experiences override children's sense of agency, and ownership and control of their bodies. The SMART room, tools, and skills are built to reconnect children to their bodies in space, to their likes and dislikes, and to experiences of agency, mastery, competence, and pleasure. To nurture these lost connections via the experiences in the SMART room, children need to explore, experiment, fail, try again, try alternatives, and repeat these experiences over and over again. Leading must be used sparingly to ensure that the therapist is supporting the child's unfolding process of knowing herself.

As we developed SMART, we Led a little and we Followed a lot. What unfolded inspired our deep respect and admiration for these children. They shared their creative solutions to current problems, revealed their ingenious adaptations and solutions to tough situations, and constructed powerful life narratives.

SKILL 8: Verbal Scaffolding

SMART is designed to foster expression of traumatic memory and disrupted attachment memory via the bodily experiences, the more available "language" in which these experiences are stored. Verbal Scaffolding is used to bring this body-based expression into language so it can be reflected on, made sense of, and integrated.

Verbal Scaffolding occurs when the therapist employs language with the child to achieve a particular therapeutic goal. Language is kept simple, and developmentally appropriate words are chosen for the age and state of the child. Sentences and questions are kept short so as not to flood the state-based language processing, working memory, or attention spans of traumatized children. Learning to highlight key words is part of the skill. Verbal Scaffolding has four particular goals: (1) to increase the child's awareness of and ability to communicate about his body state, (2) to reflect salient elements back to the child, thus increasing the child's attention to those elements, (3) to sustain a child's processing and connection when headed into a Traumatic State, and (4) to amplify positive states or events in the SMART room.

First, Verbal Scaffolding is used to increase the children's awareness of their own bodily sensations and their ability to communicate their states to others. For many children, a compromised attachment environment derailed this relationally fostered regulatory capacity (Streeck-Fischer and van der Kolk 2000). SMART addresses this need by using language, provided by the therapist, to help the child notice and identify his basic bodily experiences in the SMART room. The therapist begins by verbally noticing the child's sensory and movement experiences. For example, while a child is jumping on a trampoline, the therapist may ask, "How does jumping feel to your body?" The therapist can provide further scaffolding by offering a verbal menu of options to the child. For example, a therapist might wonder out loud if jumping makes the child feel excited or calm. Additionally, the therapist may deepen the child's ability to notice where he may experience certain emotions or sensations in his body. With repetition and time, the child begins to acquire the vocabulary and ability to describe his own experience: "Jumping makes me feel excited in my belly!"

Verbal Scaffolding also includes questions to the child in session to support greater awareness of choices. For example, at the beginning of therapy when a child surveys the SMART room, the therapist may ask, "What looks good to you today?" Or for a child who is shy or easily overwhelmed, the therapist may provide a short list of options: "Would you like to try the trampoline or the cushions?" Or as the session ends, the therapist may Verbally Scaffold with a reminder of the time: "We have ten minutes left. What do you want to use to help you get ready to go home?" These types of questions promote awareness of a choice and of preferences.

Second, we use Verbal Scaffolding to describe or reflect back salient elements of the child's experience that the therapist hopes to highlight or amplify in treatment. Depending on the treatment goal, the therapist may choose a particular moment to bring the child's attention to a body sensation, to deepen into a particular feeling, or to stay with a newly emerging ability. As Daniel Siegel writes, "Where attention goes, neural firing flows, and neural connection grows" (Siegel 2018, 19). The goal of this form of Verbal Scaffolding is to increase the children's curiosity about their own experience by providing information or feedback regarding a moment that the therapist has Tracked in session. Here are some simple examples from real sessions:

"You're really hanging in there trying to balance."

"Your body seems a little amped now."

"Looks like you really enjoy jumping."

"Big smile on your face as you play!"

"You seem a little edgy today."

This skill is not unique to SMART but is drawn from the concept of "making contact" or "contact statements" common to many other therapeutic methods (Gestalt Therapy: Perls, Hefferline, and Goodman 1951; Accelerated Experiential Dynamic Psychotherapy [AEDP]: Fosha 2000; Sensorimotor Psychotherapy: Ogden, Minton, and Pain 2006; Hakomi: Kurtz 2007; Dyadic Developmental Psychotherapy [DDP]: Hughes 2018; and Somatic Experiencing: Levine 2015). Such statements are short and direct, and do not ask a question. Instead, the therapist uses a tentative tone, or a qualifier, that allows the child to safely accept or refute the statement.

Third, Verbal Scaffolding is a way to support and encourage children to regulate themselves in order to remain in the Fluid Zone and stay engaged and connected. Statements such as "Really working hard here," "Let's try it together," "You almost got it," or "Seems like you have a plan of how you want this to go" can be enough to help a frustrated child continue to try. These examples each reveal how Verbal Scaffolding is used to increase a child's tolerance for more difficult feelings associated with effortfulness such as frustration, embarrassment, shame, or fearfulness in the face of failure.

Fourth, Verbal Scaffolding is used to amplify and expand positive moments in the therapy, particularly connected to events where the child displayed mastery, competence, or positive attachment affects. Examples may include:

"It's fun to play with you."

"Feels good to jump so high."

"Your dances are getting so creative."

"Seems you're really enjoying the music."

"Fun to feel how strong your body is."

Verbal Scaffolding to a relational moment can amplify the intensity:

"You love your mom, huh?"

"I can see how much your dad is enjoying watching you."

"Your daughter listens so well to your instructions."

"Looks like you enjoy her hug."

"It can feel so good just to cuddle together."

"You asked Dad for help, and look what you did!"

Not surprisingly, Verbal Scaffolding that amplifies the positive can be a delicate process for traumatized children, as so many of them have limited capacity to tolerate positive affects, as well as negative affects, within a relationship without dismantling the moment (Levy and Orlans 2014). This simple SMART skill of Verbal Scaffolding, to amplify positive states while carefully Tracking Out for the child's regulation, allows the therapist to titrate the intensity to the child's Window of Tolerance and to address these symptoms of attachment disorganization: a yearning for and fear of closeness.

Over time and with frequent use, therapists acquire greater and greater ease with these eight skills. When these skills are employed in a carefully designed room filled with inviting playful Tools of Regulation, children engage and move, discovering their bodies in space, their likes and dislikes, seeming to locate themselves in the world. In the next chapter, we look at the role of Video Reflection in supporting therapists' acquisition and integration of SMART Regulation Tools and Therapist Skills.

5

SMART AND THE USE OF VIDEO REFLECTION

There is precedence in the field of psychotherapy for use of film. Film micro-analysis opened up the study of the body in movement (Birdwhistell 1970), the world of communication between infants and their mothers (Beebe 2014; Fonagy, Sleed, and Baradon 2016; Lyons-Ruth 2006; Stern 2004; Tronick 2007), and the science of families and couples (Gottman and Gottman 2017). We hope the use of video recording for SMART treatment opens new possi-bilities to treat trauma, dissociation, and dysregulation in children, adolescents, and families.

When SMART was first developed, we were determined to find the uni-versal tools and skills effective across therapists in treating highly dysregulated children, so we video recorded many different therapists and clients in various settings. Because SMART places primacy on the nonverbal and bodily indica-tors of regulation and traumatic memory, we could not rely only on therapist recall to see and feel what was happening in the treatment room. Further, it was clear from many years of experience that therapists frequently have their hands full making it through an entire session Tending to the physical, relational, and emotional Safety as well as the regulation needs of all present in the room. This often left little room for nuanced recall of content. Video Reflection proved essential to identify common tools, skills, and processes in the therapy.

It was not until writing this book that we began to fully understand the essen-tial role Video Reflection serves in SMART. Physicists recognize that observing an experiment introduces a new variable, thus changing the outcome. Similarly,

SMART treatment is shaped by the process of observing and reflecting via team review in order to work with the moment-to-moment, nonverbal embodied communication, the language of early development and the imprint of trauma.

A Three-Step Process:
Observe, Hypothesize, and Reflect

Video recording supports the therapist and the treatment in several ways. Video allows the therapist to become immersed in the therapy session with the assurance they can look later at moments of import. Video recording provides a large quantity of data to the therapist unavailable in any other way. Finally, one can review video through multiple lenses to formulate what is happening within sessions and across the course of treatment.

SMART Video Reflection unfolds in a three-step process. First, from a third-person perspective, one observes the child, the interaction, the therapeutic process, and oneself, obtaining new information and noticing patterns. Information discovered may include state changes, actions in the body, emerging embodied play narratives, forms of co-regulation, and rhythms of engagement. This parallels what any coach does when breaking down video of an upcoming opponent in preparation for a match or any artist in listening to or watching a recording of their performance to refine the work. Second, with the luxury of the time offered by the pause button, one can *hypothesize,* alone or with the team, about what might be unfolding. Third, upon *reflection,* the therapist can layer known information about the child's history, age of important experiences, and nature of trauma exposures. Often, questions arise spontaneously that reveal gaps in known history. These steps lead to fuller ongoing assessment and more effective and efficient treatment planning.

Video Reflection provides information about the three treatment processes of Somatic Regulation, Trauma Processing, and Attachment-Building. Moreover, it provides feedback on successes and failures of regulation interventions. Therapists can identify implicit trauma themes and embodied trauma narratives via Video Reflection. With this knowledge, the therapist is better able to recognize and respond to subtle indicators of trauma content the next time it emerges in session. When outside the action of Full Participation, it becomes easier to recognize attachment patterns and consider new ways to create rhythms to grow the child's capacity to accept co-regulation.

Observing, hypothesizing, and reflecting flow naturally into refining the treatment plan. Therapists think of different Regulation Tools to offer the child or plan new responses to difficult behaviors when those Choice Points arise. Therapists may adjust which caregivers are in the room, at what point, and for how long. Many therapists formulate new treatment targets, and go about collecting missing information, such as age of a loss or move, nature of the trauma, or medical history. Video Reflection employed across a longer treatment reveals the unfolding of growth and development along the SMART Spiral over time. We feel this is very important, as traumatized children make major gains that are frequently overshadowed by the challenges of daily life or the next developmental task.

Clinical Skill Development

The therapist particularly benefits from Video Reflection in developing the skills of Tracking In, Tracking Out, and Embodied Attuning. Video Reflection provides another opportunity to practice Tracking; it allows the therapist to slow down, reflect, and more consciously review all the data they Tracked implicitly and all the knowledge they drew on in that moment to make the Choice. Often, with the time and distance to reflect offered by video, therapists are able to identify and verbalize the data that fed their "intuition," gaining greater confidence in themselves and the process. Video Reflection sharpens the therapist's Tracking eye for a specific child, making them more nimble and attuned in future sessions to subtler signs of shifts in the child.

Video Reflection supports therapists in developing the skill of Embodied Attuning. It allows the therapist to observe moments of being in and out of sync with the child. By slowing down and rewinding video of an interaction, the therapist can determine which embodied actions appear to disrupt attunement and, even more important, which appear to foster repair. For example, upon video review, one therapist observed a pattern in which the child took a step back each time the therapist moved toward her. Once conscious of this response pattern, the therapist became more mindful of maintaining her physical distance. This observation resulted in a simple adjustment that fostered increased sustained connection between the therapist and child in future sessions.

For a therapist who wants to become more confident using SMART, Video Reflection facilitates faster skill development and refinement, especially when done in the environment of a SMART consultation group. In the context of a group of therapists, one can see a greater range of diverse therapist styles in action, and generate new ideas from viewing each other's successes and challenges. Emotional and relational safety among therapists is established through a collaborative consultation process in which curiosity is emphasized and observational skill, rather than evaluation, is encouraged. Video Reflection in the group is aimed toward generating questions or hypotheses that help the therapist Follow the child's process more closely, and scaffold more than Lead or instruct. Therapists find that the variety of observations offered by group members enriches and deepens their understanding of their client and the work. This leads naturally to even greater curiosity that supports the therapist through the hard work of trauma treatment.

Use of Video Recording with Caregivers

With careful consideration, sharing video recording clips with families can be extremely powerful and provides an opportunity for them to see their child with a little more distance. Video clips are carefully selected to help caregivers to see their strengths and areas of challenge, and to feel more competent, successful, and understood. Video review accompanied by psychoeducation promotes caregiver skill at reading and making sense of their child's embodied communication. With increased understanding, parents are better able to plan their responses to regulate their child. Review with caregivers can promote attachment by highlighting overlooked bonding gestures on the part of their child. Video affords an opportunity to look at escalating patterns of interaction and then to pause, reflect, and consider. This process increases caregivers' self-reflection, often generating motivation for their own regulation work.

Special Considerations with Video Recording

SMART developers recommend carefully assessing when video recording is inappropriate and developing guidelines relevant to the setting in which you work. Situations in which recording may be ruled out are those in which future legal proceedings are anticipated, including, but not limited to, custody disputes, termination of parental rights, high-conflict divorce, and criminal investigation. In some cases, prospective referrals may refuse to be recorded. It is then up to the SMART therapist to determine if that would make the referral categorically inappropriate for SMART or if the client may benefit from SMART without video. If choosing the second option, a treating therapist should utilize Video Reflection with his other SMART cases so as to ensure his own skill development and fidelity to the model. However, the power and effectiveness of video as a therapy tool make it well worth assessing and addressing any resistance by clients or automatic opposition by administration.

This closing example illustrates how the three legs of the stool—Video Reflection, Therapist Skills, and Regulation Tools—support treatment assessment and planning, development of skills for therapists, and the differential application of the model. In Video Reflection, a tall male therapist observed himself taking off his sweater due to the heat in the room. As he watched, he noticed his client suddenly freeze, followed by physical capitulation, presenting a body posture of submission. In session, he had missed this sudden state shift in his client; however, because he was able to note the child's response when observing video, the therapist chose to Lead in order to Tend to relational Safety and introduced a way to create a Safe Space by using the gym mats to build a boundary between them. This tool was utilized for many therapy sessions to help the boy relax in his body and stay present with both his therapist and his caregiver.

PART 3

Components of Assessment and Treatment

6

ASSESSMENT AND TREATMENT

The beginning of SMART treatment is quite similar to that of any good trauma treatment: it starts with a solid assessment of the child and family. Some of the essential components include evaluating exposure to trauma and neglect, current symptoms and manifestations of trauma and dissociation, and placement history, in addition to developmental, medical, educational, and social history.

In assessing traumatic exposure, it is important to ask about acts of interpersonal violence, such as physical abuse and sexual abuse; types of psychological and emotional maltreatment, such as peer bullying and parental verbal abuse, as well as inquiring about areas of neglect, such as physical neglect, emotional neglect, and medical neglect. Exposures to domestic as well as community violence also can have traumatic impact on children. It is critical to understand these events in context and with detail, because when trauma surfaces in the play, the clinician will want to be able to recognize it. For example, setting up a Safe Space that looks like a crib in the therapy session may take on a greater level of significance.

Another component of assessment is the level of current symptomatology and manifestations in everyday life. What is getting in the child's way? How often? In what contexts? This is where the treatment will begin, because the child and family need some level of stability in their lives before they will feel safe enough to do more processing work. We use the DTD framework to evaluate areas of symptoms; namely, affective dysregulation and dissociation, somatic dysregulation, behavioral dysregulation, and disruptions in relationships and sense of self. In addition, we map these symptoms onto a developmental framework, so that we can understand where the child is stuck, in what developmental time period, and in what area of dysfunction.

Next it is important to fill in the historical context. Developmental history includes getting specifics about particular milestones such as language, motor, and elimination progression. The therapist should obtain significant medical history of both the child and the family. Educational history includes both cognitive and academic strengths and challenges, as well as social development with friends at school and outside of school. A therapist should also look for areas of competence and mastery, such as any extracurricular sports, artistic, or musical activities.

For a truly comprehensive assessment, the child's caregivers should also be evaluated for significant moments in their histories around attachment, discipline, and trauma. The caregivers' histories inform them as parents both consciously and implicitly. Having noted the importance of getting this information, we also acknowledge that this can be the hardest information to address. Some caregivers want to see treatment as only about their child, not them, whereas others may be reluctant to address their parenting challenges for various reasons. It is a difficult dance to convey the respect we have for their own struggles while trying to pay attention to areas of potential concern.

Lastly, we want to see the child and caregivers together to assess the qualities of attachment style, the parenting strengths and challenges, and the extent of co-regulation versus co-dysregulation. Sometimes the relationship between child and caregiver has a calming effect, and sometimes it leads to hyperarousal, and other times it leads to shutdown. Moreover, these can all happen within the same relationship but under different circumstances. For example, a child and father may be able to play a friendly game of basketball and truly enjoy each other's company. Yet, when the subject of school grades comes up, the child might either shut down and turn away or become hyper and unfocused. In another example, a mother might be so focused on talking to the clinician that the child acts up to get attention, but when the child then falls and gets hurt, the mother is right there comforting and providing what the child needs.

When beginning assessment in SMART, the therapist adopts a curious stance, seeing her role as that of an investigator and the SMART room as a kind of "lab" in which to learn as much as possible about the child's current regulatory strategies and attachment patterns. In SMART, there are three primary perspectives on the child and family from which to gather information: that of observer/witness, experiential participant, and video viewer/reflector. Throughout this chapter, we will discuss how each perspective offers unique information to be integrated into assessment and treatment.

During the exploratory phase, the therapist relies heavily on three SMART Therapist Skills: Tending to Safety, Tracking Out and Tracking In, and Following the child's lead. Upon introducing a child to the SMART room, the therapist takes a nondirective approach, inviting the child to explore the space by offering a wide range of equipment and activities for the child to consider. The therapist does not give instructions to the child regarding how to engage with the equipment but may offer a range of possibilities that allows for the child to invent something completely novel. The therapist carefully Tracks how the child explores (or does not explore) the room and uses the skill of Following to observe what tools or sensory inputs the child may gravitate toward, avoid, or quickly discard after a brief period of engagement. The therapist is careful to allow for and support the child's natural unfolding of his experience prior to initiating any form of intervention, unless safety is at risk. The goal is for the therapist to gain a deeper understanding of the child, and to support the child in having the felt sense of being understood by the therapist on a fully embodied level.

It is critical to introduce the caregivers to the SMART framework and approach before starting treatment. During the initial adult meeting, we take the caregiver(s) into the SMART room to orient them to the space and to the tools, and to share about the process that takes place in the room. This also allows the therapist to Track and assess the caregivers' comfort in their bodies and their curiosity about the tools. Caregivers may come with a preconception about therapy that is based on talking about problems and fixing problematic behavior. SMART requires explicit discussion with caregivers about the role of physical play in supporting Somatic Regulation, Trauma Processing, and Attachment-Building activities. During intake it is important to emphasize working collaboratively with caregivers as partners for healing.

This chapter will describe assessment and treatment within each strand of the SMART Spiral: Somatic Regulation, Trauma Processing, and Attachment-Building. Each point will be illustrated through case examples. We will discuss different ways to generalize the strategies developed in treatment to the rest of the child's world, including home and school.

Somatic Regulation Thread
Assessment

Assessing and developing a child's capacity for Somatic Regulation are foundational to the SMART approach. When first engaging with a child in SMART, the therapist assesses regulatory capacity in three areas: (1) patterns of arousal level, (2) use of sensory motor inputs, and (3) use of regulatory strategies—auto-regulation, co-regulation, or self-regulation (Warner, Cook et al. 2014). During the initial assessment period, the therapist aims to develop a beginning understanding of the child's natural means for organizing and regulating experiences in the present moment. Through this process, therapists enhance their clinical understanding of a child's regulatory challenges and strengths, to generate treatment interventions that support a child's capacity to shift states more flexibly. In this way, very early on, treatment focuses on expanding the child's Window of Tolerance and ability to integrate a wider range of internal and external experiences.

Child's Arousal Level. The SMART Regulation Map (see Insert 3) and the Child State Descriptors (see Inserts 4 and 5) provide a visual aid to help therapists assess a child's arousal level, and to Track state shifts across time. While Tracking Out and Tracking In, therapists look for physical indicators that suggest where the child is functioning across a continuum: (1) Hyperaroused Traumatic State, (2) High Intensity Fluid Zone, (3) Integrated State, (4) Low Intensity Fluid Zone, or (5) Hypoaroused Traumatic State.

The process of assessing the child's arousal level begins from the moment of greeting and continues throughout the session. Tracking for observable indicators of arousal, such as how the child moves through the room, her posture and muscle tone, quality of vocalizations and prosody, and level of eye contact, can provide valuable information regarding a child's state in a particular moment. The therapist also considers the child's tolerance for sensation, emotion, cognition, and relationship, while noticing any experiences or sensory motor inputs that observably shift the child's state. Learning to accurately assess a child's state in the moment is essential to determining effective interventions that will facilitate each child's unique regulation needs.

The Fluid Zones are the arousal levels where the deepest work and change occur. In the High Intensity Fluid Zone, a child presents with increased arousal, but is also able to access the therapeutic relationship enough to avoid entering into a Hyperaroused Traumatic State. For example, a fifteen-year-old boy, just suspended from school, forcefully bounces a ball so vehemently that it hits the ceiling. When his therapist checks in, the boy briefly makes eye contact and loudly states, "I hate everyone today!" The therapist assesses that this youth is in the High Intensity Fluid Zone upon observing that he is able to stay connected to a high intensity experience and to the therapeutic relationship. In the Low Intensity Fluid Zone, a child presents with low arousal, but can still utilize the therapeutic relationship to avoid entering a Hypoaroused Traumatic State. For example, a depressed twelve-year-old girl lay curled up on a beanbag chair, avoiding eye contact, but was able to roll a weighted ball back and forth with her therapist and notice feeling "sad." When these youth are in the Fluid Zones, the therapist may explore more deeply the sensations, emotions, and thoughts associated with their experience.

Therapists will witness a range of presentations when assessing children in SMART. Some children consistently enter treatment in a dysregulated state and become more regulated as they engage sensory motor inputs, whereas others demonstrate frequent state shifts in response to internal and external stimuli. By Tracking observable indicators signaling a change in arousal, and precipitants that lead to state shifts, the therapist finds guides to support later treatment planning. In the following example, eleven-year-old Tasha begins her treatment session in a well-regulated state, but experiences a sudden state shift in reaction to an unexpected event:

Tasha moves about the SMART room, focused and eager to build an obstacle course. Confident, she has an idea in mind of how she wants to set up the equipment. Tasha asks her therapist for help with setting up mats to crawl through. The therapist follows her lead, however, the mats collapse unexpectedly. Tasha forcefully kicks over the remaining mats, throws a physioball, and refuses to respond to the therapist's attempts to engage her verbally or with eye contact.

Initially, the therapist assesses that Tasha is in an Integrated State by Tracking the intentional and organized way she moves her body, her planful thinking, and her ability to seek out support as needed. However, the state shift is sudden and feels surprising for all involved. Tasha's therapist observes a rapid increase in Tasha's arousal, level of aggression, and relational disengagement. These indicators suggest that Tasha is now functioning in a Hyperaroused Traumatic State. Later, in the Treatment section, we will see how the therapist addresses what has happened.

When a child experiences a sudden state shift, a therapist may feel surprised, particularly when he felt in sync with the child just moments before. It is important that the therapist pause to Track In and self-regulate first, in order to remain attentive to the physical, relational, and emotional safety in session and curious about the child's experience. This may be as simple as taking a deep breath in the moment, and wondering, "What just happened?" The therapist can utilize the SMART Regulation Map, along with knowledge of the child, as a guide for choosing what to do next. It is also extremely beneficial to review video after such sessions to more carefully Track the early indicators of changes in the child's arousal level and precipitants to a state shift. Watching video recordings of a state shift makes it easier to hold a curious stance and to reflect on what occurred.

Sensory Motor Systems and Inputs. A second component of assessment is identifying the types of sensory motor input a child seeks, how he uses his body to explore that input, and how much is needed to effectively regulate arousal. Tracking Out, the therapist identifies regulating inputs, rather than specific pieces of equipment, that will support generalization to a variety of settings. For example, a child who needs Vestibular Input to regulate may access this input by using a hammock in the SMART room, swings during school recess, and sitting in a rocking chair with his parent at home.

Be curious about the way a child uses her body while engaging in an activity and look for any patterns in action. Children's ways of engaging sensory motor inputs are typically not conscious at the beginning of treatment; however, their patterns often are indicators of possible pathways for regulation. For example, one child may seek a significant amount of Proprioceptive Input by engaging her arms and hands through pulling and throwing, whereas another child utilizes his legs by jumping or kicking. In contrast, another child may seek the same input in more subtle ways by squeezing a fidget ball or shaking her leg. Additionally, a child who is hypoaroused may seek proprioception by rolling a weighted ball between her hands in a slow, gentle manner.

These individual variations become important later in treatment when helping children learn to regulate their body intentionally. Finally, assessing the degree of intensity, duration, and frequency with which a child engages in a sensory activity, to achieve Sensory Satiation, is essential for supporting Somatic Regulation. A therapist can tell that a somatic need has been satiated when a child's state seems better organized. The child may let out a satisfied sigh or may be finished and ready to transition to something new.

Auto-Regulation, Co-regulation, or Self-Regulation. A third component to assess is how a child may use himself or others to regulate in a particular moment. The SMART model focuses on three categories of regulation: auto-regulation, co-regulation, and self-regulation. Each strategy is equally important; all are necessary to support regulation.

Auto-regulation is a means of self-soothing that occurs with little to no conscious awareness. Human beings are biologically endowed with this capacity, which develops prior to birth. Rhythmic movements, such as thumb sucking in the womb, are one of our earliest means of auto-regulation. Following birth, auto-regulation can be seen in an infant's use of gaze aversion, a child's rocking and humming, or an adolescent's tendency to jiggle his leg. We rely on this basic, unconscious strategy to reduce internal arousal or block out external stimuli when other forms of regulation are not available.

Co-regulation, as the name suggests, is an interactive process where human beings regulate within the context of relationship. Infants are born needing attuned caregivers who establish predictable rhythms that attend to their needs for warmth, nourishment, sleep, and soothing distress. As children's basic needs are reliably met, they learn to internalize these experiences for themselves, thus supporting their own capacity for self-regulation.

Self-regulation is the ability to regulate oneself, sometimes intentionally and sometimes spontaneously, in either the presence or the absence of a caregiver. The ability to self-regulate comprises skills developed through repeated experiences of effective co-regulation and of attuned interactions with a caregiver. For example, in SMART, a child who has jumped vigorously on the trampoline for part of the session may learn to recognize his thirst and ask to get a drink of water. Or a child may learn to seek support from a parent as a way to recover when feelings are hurt by a friend. Thus, the child can experience high levels of arousal or emotion and manage to regulate by drawing upon her rich history of embodied and remembered effective co-regulatory experiences with a caregiver.

The SMART therapist intentionally assesses the effect of relationships on a child's arousal level both inside and outside of treatment. Focus is placed on Tracking Out to determine whether connection seems regulating or dysregulating for the child. Can the child accept soothing or ask for help when he is feeling frustrated or overwhelmed? Does the child reject an offer of support or appear afraid and avoidant of relationship? Some children may engage independently with the equipment as if they were alone in the room, despite having their therapist or caregiver present. Others may seek help in an overly dependent fashion, despite demonstrating the ability to complete tasks on their own. A fundamental assessment question therefore focuses on understanding whether a child can effectively and flexibly access and utilize co-regulatory and self-regulatory strategies to manage shifting arousal levels, or whether he is limited to just using auto-regulatory methods.

The child's relational regulation strategies may differ by caregiver or by emotional state. It may be that a child easily accepts support and co-regulation from one caregiver but relies more heavily on self- or auto-regulatory strategies with another. Similarly, a child may be more comfortable sharing certain emotions (e.g., anger, disappointment, or joy) with one caregiver rather than the other.

The therapist must also be cognizant of her own regulation patterns within relationships, and mindful of ways in which they may intersect with the child's regulatory strategies. For example, a therapist who is most comfortable with co-regulation may unintentionally dysregulate a child by moving in too closely to help. The therapist can also assess and help parents or caregivers become more aware of their own patterns of relational engagement and how these may match up with their child's. For example, a child who benefits from co-regulation may feel rejected and become dysregulated in response to a parent who values independence and encourages self-regulation strategies. Sometimes an adjustment as simple as changing physical proximity during a challenging moment can make a difference in the outcome. Video Reflection proves crucial for therapists to gain a clear understanding of how relational experiences are regulating for a child and to reflect on their own habitual attachment patterns.

Treatment

The treatment process for building Somatic Regulation weaves knowledge gained through ongoing assessment by observing children across time with moment-to-moment Tracking of their responses to therapeutic intervention. The focus of treatment within the Somatic Regulation thread centers on four main goals: (1) expanding the Window of Tolerance, (2) developing a regulation toolbox, (3) increasing the effectiveness of co-regulation, and (4) enhancing experiences of mastery by increasing self-regulation through independent use of Regulation Tools. The therapist strives to scaffold the child's full-body exploration of inputs and discovery of what feels regulating. Through this process, children are invited to notice their internal experience and what changes how they feel inside. Determining "what I like" or "what I don't like" and learning "what helps when I have big feelings" are foundational for developing self-regulation. As the child's awareness grows, the therapist encourages him to practice utilizing identified Regulation Tools with intention. Frequent repetition of this experience, over time, allows the child to become more confident in his ability to recover from distress, and to handle big feelings as they arise.

Expanding the Window of Tolerance. A primary goal of every SMART treatment is to increase the child's ability to tolerate a full range of sensations, feelings, thoughts, and memories as they occur in the present moment. Treatment interventions that build these capacities by working in the Fluid Zone expand the child's Window of Tolerance. The therapist will Track Out for shifts in arousal state, both in session and across time, using the SMART Regulation Map to inform therapeutic Choice Points.

For a child within an Integrated State, the therapist prioritizes the skill of Following as a primary treatment intervention. As long as the child's actions and desires are safe enough, the therapist Follows the child's lead and supports the experience as it unfolds naturally. This therapeutic stance communicates trust in the child's inherent drive toward healing and growth. It also places primacy on the children learning to listen to their own bodies' internal wisdom, an underdeveloped capacity for children impacted by trauma, and necessary for building self-regulation.

The Fluid Zones, occurring at both edges of the Window of Tolerance, are where SMART therapists can effect the most change. When in these zones, a child is able to experience high or low intensity arousal while also being able to access needed support to preclude repetitive traumatic reexperiencing. Therapeutic interventions focus on widening the Window of Tolerance when the child is in a Fluid Zone by scaffolding experiences that promote regulation, helping the child connect to internal experiences, processing traumatic content as it arises, and building rhythms of engagement. As with the development of any new skill, children who are learning to regulate intense arousal will become dysregulated, but the therapist is there to help.

When a child moves beyond the Fluid Zone into a Traumatic State, the therapist prioritizes Somatic Regulation, focusing solely on returning the child to a more Integrated State. Often, this involves a shift in the therapeutic stance from Following to Leading. A primary goal in supporting regulation for a child in a Hyperaroused Traumatic State is to find a safe way for the child to fully express, explore, and ultimately satiate the sensory seeking. Children in this state often need sustained and intense sensory motor input to regulate; moreover, they can become dysregulated by verbal engagement or by efforts to problem-solve.

When Tasha became frustrated and hyperaroused following the collapse of her obstacle course, her therapist noticed Tasha using her arms and legs to throw and kick objects in the room. Hypothesizing that proprioception through her hands and feet may represent Tasha's attempt to regulate her internal state, the therapist placed a soft cushion against the opposite side of the room and invited Tasha to throw and kick the physioball at it as hard as she wanted, for as long as she needed. Tasha engaged in this activity for the next fifteen minutes, gradually showing increased playfulness and Rhythmicity in relationship with her therapist over the duration of that time.

The young girl obtains full-body Proprioceptive Input while maintaining physical and relational safety by kicking a physioball at a Dolphin air pillow

By holding the frame that children's behavior often represents an attempt to meet a regulatory need, Tasha's therapist was able to stay grounded and curious about the way Tasha used her body when hyperaroused. This perspective invited exploration of new ways that Proprioceptive Input could be used as a possible Regulation Tool. The therapist was careful to ensure that Tasha had enough time to engage the inputs with enough intensity to support Sensory Satiation. Tasha, feeling understood, followed her therapist's Lead, and began to experiment with safer ways to use her arms and legs to regulate overwhelming feelings and sensations. As Tasha returned to a more Integrated State, she reestablished connection with her therapist, and with the feeling of confidence she experienced prior to becoming overwhelmed.

Alternatively, a child who presents in a Hypoaroused Traumatic State in session is often attempting to regulate by avoiding or decreasing distressing internal or external sensory stimuli. This child will typically appear sleepy, numb, shut down, and disengaged. In these moments, the therapist Tracks Out for subtle sensory inputs, or small movements that may indicate a potential pathway toward increasing arousal and engagement.

> *Upon learning her mother missed their weekly visit, Samantha, a sixteen-year-old in residential treatment, lay down limply on a beanbag, averted her gaze, and began rubbing the fabric covering of the beanbag with her fingers. Tracking Samantha's continual hand movement, her therapist Led by rolling a ball gently toward Samantha's hand. Samantha returned the ball, showing the smallest increase in energy. After a few minutes of silent, back-and-forth ball rolling, Samantha spontaneously stated, "I want to go home." The therapist kept the rhythmic ball game going and noted Samantha appeared more present and connected. As Samantha's arousal state shifted from hypoarousal into the Fluid Zone, the therapist continued the rhythmic game to support regulation during a challenging discussion about home.*

Samantha's therapist focused on inviting small, gentle movements to support a slow transition out of the Hypoaroused Traumatic State and into the Fluid Zone. A paced intervention is needed in this state to prevent the youth from becoming further dysregulated.

When the client is hypoaroused, milder inputs, gradually applied, allow the body to adjust slowly. A measured return to an Integrated State allows the autonomic nervous system to adjust physiological activity throughout the body at a more tolerable pace. Heart rate variability, or the flexibility of response of the heart rate, respiration, and blood pressure to stressors, is thus being trained to more smoothly adjust.

Creativity and curiosity are two essential components for helping a child regulate arousal. Dysregulated children frequently require tools to be offered in a variety of ways before discovering what is helpful. Tracking when an intervention does not improve regulation is just as important as when interventions are successful. These moments are *not* mistakes, but rather useful information about a child's unique regulatory needs to aid in creating an individualized regulation toolbox.

Developing a Regulation Toolbox. A SMART regulation toolbox is a knowledge bank of the sensory motor inputs that regulate a particular child. The child, therapist, and caregiver collaborate to find tools that co-regulate and that the child can use for self-regulation. Children are more able to expand their Window of Tolerance when they become aware of what sensory motor experiences help them to feel better. As the therapist and child each learn what inputs are up- or downregulating for the child, this information can be used to create an individualized regulation toolbox. The purpose of this toolbox is, first, to help the child identify and successfully access inputs that are regulating in session, and then, to teach caregivers at home and within the community how they can best facilitate the child's expansion of his regulatory capacity outside of session. Over time, the child learns to use these skills independently to self-regulate.

During a course of treatment, the therapist and child explore and play together in the SMART room. A primary therapeutic goal is to experiment with and identify different sensory and motor inputs that regulate. The child is invited to notice what experiences she likes or dislikes, and how playing with different types of equipment impacts energy and emotion. For example, a child may begin to notice having "calm energy" when walking on a balance beam, and feeling more "excited" while bouncing on a trampoline. Or she may find she is scared when standing on a tippy pile of equipment, but if she stabilizes the pile, feels safe again. The therapist also helps the child attend to somatic cues accompanying the present state, such as body temperature and breathing, and even heart rate if that is helpful or interesting to the child. As the child begins to notice connections between preferred inputs and shifts in how he feels, the child can intentionally use a particular tool, or combination of tools, to support self-regulation.

To build the regulation toolbox, the therapist collaborates with the child to discover how best to capture the child's felt experience of different arousal states (see Child State Descriptors, Inserts 4 and 5). Children commonly choose imagery or symbols that represent an interest or something unique about themselves. For example, John, a train-loving seven-year-old boy, created a regulation toolbox that depicted hyperarousal as "bullet train energy" and hypoarousal as "steam engine energy." Over the course of treatment, he discovered that pulling on a resistance band for tug-of-war was one way to downregulate "bullet train energy" and upregulate his "steam engine energy." Similarly, after experiencing effective co-regulation with her therapist, Samantha, an adolescent, discovered that she could use Rhythmicity independently to self-regulate in her room by gently bouncing on a physioball to the rhythm of her favorite music. Once the child has created such a toolbox, it can be shared with caregivers or other adults to explore ways to adapt these Regulation Tools for home and school.

Increasing the Effectiveness of Co-regulation. Through the assessment process, the therapist gains a clearer picture of how the child regulates in response to relationship while in session. An important treatment goal is to widen the child's capacity for co-regulation, which underlies the development of effective self-regulation. This may include encouraging the child to ask for help when needed, or to accept soothing and comfort when overwhelmed. Although the work of Attachment-Building will be explored in depth later in this chapter, it is important to name the intersection of relationship with regulation in treatment here.

The Therapist Skills of Tending to Safety, Following, Embodied Attuning, and Full Participation create an environment in which a child can learn to feel safe enough in relationship to accept co-regulation. Priority is placed on communicating deep respect for the child's experience by moving at the child's pace and joining her in a fully embodied way. Rather than relying on limit-setting or redirection to address safety and regulation needs, the SMART therapist invites the child to collaborate by Tending to relational Safety: "How can we try out your idea so that it's safe (for you and me)?" Such experiences often provide an important foundation for widening the child's tolerance for co-regulation with an adult.

As the child begins to widen his tolerance for accepting help and care, the therapist identifies what type of relational experiences feel tolerable versus triggering. For example, the therapist may explore the impact of proximity and distance on the child's sense of safety. Another therapist may experiment with creating rhythms with a child or adolescent (e.g., through drumming, ball tossing, clapping, or call-and-response games) and observe the impact of being in sync versus out of sync. Attending to moments that lead to increased connection, as well as to ruptures that require repair, is equally important to widening the child's tolerance for relationship.

Building Mastery. Children often initiate actions or create games that increase the level of challenge as regulatory capacity increases, thus building a sense of mastery. Through the sensory motor activity in the SMART room, the child is able to attain a core sense of being—an awareness of himself, of where he is in space, of what he is doing, and of how he got there. It is important for the therapist to encourage the child to pause, notice, and take time to integrate these moments of growth, and to strengthen the child's self-awareness and sense of accomplishment. For example, an impulsive four-year-old boy, who typically avoided seeking help, chose to ask his mother for a boost in order to climb to the top of a pile of mats. When the boy achieved his goal, the therapist used Verbal Scaffolding to highlight his request for help and to enhance his experience: "Wow, look how high you climbed when you got Mom's help! Take a look around while you are up there!" As he stood up on top and looked about him, noticing his therapist and his mom watching him, he felt strong and able to balance, and this experience gave him a core sense of being.

Older children and adolescents also gain a sense of mastery by discovering that they have the power to change how they feel through the intentional use of self-regulation tools. In SMART, our goal is not just to decrease a child's dysregulation, but to promote positive, fully embodied experiences of being present, of knowing where he is in his world, and of knowing himself as an agent of his own experience. These small moments build the child's sense of self and resiliency over time.

Generalizing to the Child's Life. With knowledge gained from the SMART room of Regulation Tools, new solutions to difficult problems can be developed and generalized to life in the family, the school, and the community. Parent consultation time can galvanize the process of generalization, but often children find their way to what they need. Younger children, and youth who are highly dysregulated, often benefit from having a supportive adult present who can help them use Regulation Tools at home or while in the community.

Adolescents often independently use their tools for self-regulation. Specifically, Samantha and her therapist collaborated with milieu staff to ensure that Samantha had access to a physioball in her room and at school. Similarly, youth at home request equipment that works for them.

> John's mother spent a full session with her son as he showed her how he regulated "steam engine" and "bullet train" energy using resistance bands. After session, his therapist provided psychoeducation to John's mother about the regulating function that Proprioceptive Input had for John. With this understanding, John's mother began inviting John to play tug-of-war with her during high-energy moments at home. Following an individualized educational plan (IEP) meeting at John's school, his teachers agreed to support John's need for proprioception by placing him in charge of passing out books in class and providing movement breaks. As John's regulation toolbox was adapted to life outside of session, his parents and educational support team each expressed feeling more connected to John and effective in their ability to provide him with needed support.

Once parents understand the regulating function, they can also suggest ideas for new Regulation Tools. Additionally, generalization of these tools to school life typically requires that parents or therapists advocate for their child with educational teams. The ease with which the Regulation Tools can be generalized to other parts of the child's life is one of the strengths of SMART.

Trauma Processing Thread

Assessment

The assessment of Trauma Processing follows a different path than in Somatic Regulation and Attachment-Building. Therapists must learn to *recognize* the expression of traumatic material, but also track the child's arousal level and state in order to assess whether the child is *re-experiencing* or *re-working* the trauma. Is the child in a Traumatic State or in a Fluid Zone and accessible to therapeutic support? Often, assessment and treatment are fully intertwined, and identification of the Trauma Processing occurs only after the processing work by the child is well under way. Through the practice of SMART, we have watched how trauma memory is embedded in body memory and is expressed spontaneously at the child's pace. The unique forms of Trauma Processing in this fully embodied treatment will provide the organizing principle of this section with assessment and treatment delineated for the reader through examples.

Two elements of Trauma Processing in SMART therapies repeatedly surprise therapists: the spontaneous expression and the level of intensity of traumatic material. The first aspect is the rapid and unprompted way in which the child expresses traumatic material in early individual sessions, as well as over the course of therapy. Because of the unexpected manifestation, the therapist does not formally assess for Trauma Processing at the beginning, but simply recognizes when it shows up in the therapy. In this way, it is different from assessment of Somatic Regulation or Attachment-Building. When reviewing video recordings of the treatment over time, therapists see how early in the course of the therapy trauma material was expressed and reworked without Leading by the caregiver or therapist. Often, the therapist has not recognized it as such because problems of regulation required more immediate attention. However, in looking back, the therapist can see how the themes first emerged. If the therapist has not interfered with or interrupted the play, but has Followed the child's lead, the traumatic expression and form of reworking reveal themselves. The body and mind together know how to seek healing from traumatic experiences.

The second element is the "experience-near" quality of the way the Trauma Processing impacts the child, caregiver, and therapist. The Full Participation of each person in the SMART room promotes a more intense experience of what is being processed, whether the trauma expression is through actions, games, embodied dramatic play, or language. Everyone "feels" the deepening and reworking of experience more profoundly and with a powerful sense of

"*Now* I understand what you experienced." This is what happened for young Dan and his family:

> *Dan, a robust four-year-old, experienced a two-month traumatic separation from his mother when his eight-year-old brother underwent an organ transplant. He "had little interest in growing up," in that he showed delayed toileting, difficulty using his words, struggles at transitions, rigid thinking, tantrums, and aggression. In his therapy with family members, he needed to find ways with each parent and his brother to repair the impact of separation by creating new rhythms of engagement that could console him and support him. That is what he found when he gained the courage to allow his mother to place him in the hammock to swing and rock him slowly back and forth. In the following session, he sought out the same inputs when his father rocked him in the hammock. A sweet poignancy, tinged with sadness and warmth, filled the room. Young Dan began to pipe up about how he had missed his brother, while the family talked about their experience of these hard times together. Dan and his parents had found a co-regulating activity to rebuild attachment. The healing journey had begun.*

It is important for therapists to recognize how and when a child is using regulatory inputs, even in a subtle way, to support a difficult conversation or to process traumatic material. One of the most consistent observations in SMART has been that as the child's Somatic Regulation increases, she spontaneously brings up thoughts, feelings, beliefs, or memories that need further processing in treatment. At that point, the work shifts from a primary focus on addressing regulation needs to weaving regulation work with Trauma Processing and Attachment-Building, with the goal of supporting the child to develop a more cohesive sense of self over time.

Treatment

Because the assessment and treatment processes are so intertwined for Trauma Processing, we will present examples of the various forms of traumatic expression in two parts; i.e., the assessment (or recognition) phase and then the treatment phase. By presenting the material this way, we hope to convey the experience of recognizing traumatic expression and then to offer strategies for working with the multiple ways that traumatic experiences can emerge.

Traumatic Expression: Embodied and Symbolic Forms

Broadly, there are **embodied** and **symbolic** forms of traumatic expression that therapists recognize and participate in within the context of SMART treatment. Both forms are important; however, in our experience, the embodied forms support fuller reworking, whereas purely symbolic forms often show up initially as repetitive or looping expressions that do not seem to change easily. When traumatic expression is fully embodied, the client actively engages the whole self, body and mind. Because the SMART room seems to afford the opportunity for more embodied forms of expression and reworking, we will spend more time describing the nature of embodied forms of Trauma Processing. That said, when both children and adolescents are given the opportunity to regulate their bodies through movement, they often express themselves symbolically. In particular, children create a hybrid form we call embodied dramatic play (Warner, Cook et al. 2014), and older adolescents often move into productive dialogue.

Embodied Forms of Traumatic Expression

In the SMART room, the opportunities afforded by the larger space, equipment, and the Full Participation of the therapist and caregiver allow for trauma expressions to emerge very quickly, in fully embodied ways. Trauma therapists variously call this "body memory," implicit memory, or procedural memory. These traumatic experiences include acts of abuse, neglect, and relational trauma, as well as medical trauma, witnessing frightening events, and other overwhelming experiences. There are several ways in which these types of traumatic experiences are encoded and expressed through embodied forms of engagement.

Posture and Body Memory. Therapists of the body such as Ogden (Ogden and Fisher 2015; Ogden, Minton, and Pain 2006), Levine (Levine and Frederick 1997), and Kepner (2001) and bodyworkers such as massage therapists, Reiki practitioners, craniosacral therapists, and trauma-sensitive yoga teachers (Emerson and Hopper 2011; Emerson 2015) have long noticed and described the way particular traumatic responses are held in the overall posture and the skeletal and muscular structure of the body. It is no different with children; the trauma is encoded in their bodies. However, children and teens can change their patterns more rapidly. Their readiness to move their bodies creates more opportunities for creative changes. For example, Darius, the young adolescent boy, while lying in a large cushion as he would in bed, slipped into deep hypoarousal when he recounted a nightmare in which he thought he was paralyzed. The therapist realized that his gesturing left arm had caught her attention as he described the dream, but she had missed the odd way his right side was completely inert. However, when simply asked to change posture by sitting up on a Bosu ball, Darius changed states—from a Traumatic to an Integrated State; simply by sitting up, there was a physiological change accompanied by a psychological state change. He then spontaneously asked to change the subject and talked about his beloved cat.

In another example, an adolescent girl's posture tells a story of her early life:

Assessment: *Colleagues watching a video recording with a residential treatment therapist in SMART consultation noticed a particular posture of an adolescent girl, Katja, and exclaimed, "She looks like a baby in a crib!" Upon replaying the few minutes of the recording, the therapist noticed that her client was indeed playing with her own hands and feet as an infant might, while lying on her back surrounded by pillows. While in the therapy session, the therapist had been attending to the flowing dialogue and the unexpected feeling of connection with Katja and missed the embodiment of her client expressing a younger state. This observation led to assessing Katja's regulatory state—which was quite integrated and present—and the quality of her communication with the therapist—which was more expansive and reciprocal than usual. She was clearly in a fully Integrated State.*

Treatment: *One of the fellow consultees watching the video recording asked for a reminder: what was the girl's early history? She had been in orphanage care during her earliest years. Group members then wondered aloud, "Was this a healthy reworking of the experience of early neglect of caregiver attention and attunement in this girl's history?" The consultees all observed that the way in which the girl and therapist were connecting looked like the creation of the early rhythms of engagement needed for a healthy attachment, yet were integrated with a more adolescent verbal expression of what was on her mind, reassuring the therapist of the effectiveness of what she and the client were doing together.*

This example demonstrates the organic process of traumatic expression and reworking. In a sense, the assessment occurred during the consultation *after* the treatment had successfully occurred without the therapist being fully aware of the nature of the work.

Through Katja's postural presentation, she showed herself in a younger state, and yet she was not emotionally regressed. Rather, her capacity to verbally communicate with the therapist was enhanced. She seemed to enact the experience of being alone in a crib but embody a different experience of needed connection with an adult by engaging with her therapist in age-relevant dialogue. It was as if Katja needed to rework the experience of deprivation of sufficient social engagement at an infant stage of life, in a full-body way, to embed the longed-for experience of connection in her body and her mind.

Actions. In many cases, traumatic material is embedded in an action or a behavior that shows up abruptly and that caregivers describe as perplexing, distressing, or mysterious. The therapist may feel caught off guard and confused by what just happened in the session. This is a tip-off either that some traumatic material is triggering the unexpected action, perhaps a freeze-flight-fight-fright behavior, or that it is showing up as an intrusion in the form of an action. In the following example, the treatment proceeded as the therapist supported the child's drive to engage in a certain form of sensory motor play. Only later was the Trauma Processing fully understood through assessment of the patterns and further inquiry with the parents.

> **Assessment:** *Isaiah became excessively clingy with his mother and refused to go to preschool—a form of separation anxiety. He played with friends but only in his own home. In watching him play, his mother reported an excessive caution in physical play, an unusual self-control when shoved by a friend, and hyperfocus on fantasy play with action figures in which "good guys" and "bad guys" repeatedly battled each other. In session, he gravitated to the big pillows and the Bosu ball and created many fun ways to jump and fall into the pillows, including being tossed by a parent.*

> **Treatment:** *In session, his mother Followed Isaiah's requests to let him fall into the pillows. Later, at home, he asked his father to toss him onto his parents' bed at home "like a sack of potatoes." His excitement gradually filled the room as he explored all the ways he could fall without getting hurt. Over the weeks, his mother reported his increasing bravery on the playground. He began play wrestling with his best friend and standing up to him when he felt pushed too far. One day, when the therapist described the odd way Isaiah retracted his hands in physical play, his father recounted a memory of how, as a toddler, his son had fallen into a campfire, had burned his wrists, and had to be rushed hours away to an emergency room. His mother's feelings of panic had persisted for a long time, until the wrists healed perfectly. The therapist and parents suddenly recognized that Isaiah's experience was embedded in his wrists with his hands retracted and unable to protect, defend, and support his body. With help, Isaiah learned to do wheelbarrows and discovered that he could use his hands to support, protect, and guide him as he fell. He also began to push against other kids in play. Only when he felt unafraid of falling and more robust was he able to separate from his mother and explore the world more freely.*

The basis for Isaiah's anxiety became clear only over time as we observed the sensory motor play that he repeatedly explored. The falling games that Isaiah created helped him recover from the frightening fall into the campfire. Only then could adults see the hand retraction and help him practice engaging his hands to develop the ability to protect himself and to gain full use of his body. When his mother fully participated in developing his increased physical and social resilience, she, too, could heal from this traumatic event. The therapist Following the child's lead and scaffolding the mother's support of his play moved Isaiah through his avoidance and anxiety to greater vitality, sense of agency, and a sense of himself as strong and able to defend himself.

Familiar Games. Children often create familiar games such as hide-and-seek, dodgeball, or monkey-in-the-middle. The therapist may find that familiar games provide much needed predictability and structure for a child who typically begins the session by jumping from activity to activity in a Hyperaroused Traumatic State. The mutual pleasure in the game is to be enjoyed and extended for as long as the child can tolerate the positive feelings and connection it brings. However, suddenly some unique feature of the game will catch the therapist by surprise, but it may be unclear: what does this mean? Staying "present" and active in the game may not give time to truly reflect, even when the therapist has a sense that something important has happened. In this case, both note-taking after the session and Video Reflection helped the therapist assess what the boy was expressing and slowly reworking.

> **Assessment:** *Dmitri was adopted at eight years of age after placement in several Russian orphanages, including one located in a war zone. He was referred to SMART by his first therapist for a trauma-oriented approach that could accommodate his behavioral and affect regulation challenges. He was a well-coordinated boy who quickly engaged the therapist with his vitality and sense of fun, qualities that fit well with his active adoptive parents. He could kick a soccer ball with skill, and yet early in SMART treatment, he chose to play hide-and-seek with each of his parents. But they expressed their frustration with this game, telling the therapist that he should talk about his experiences. Most striking to the therapist was the deft and clever way he hid himself in nooks and crannies and his utter stillness and silence that gave no clues to his whereabouts. Over many repetitions and sessions, Dmitri allowed the therapist to assist him in hiding rather than leave the room with the parent while he hid. He also began to make small sounds, thus communicating clues to his parent, who played along. In one instance, he even revealed how scared he was when he thought he couldn't breathe when he stuffed himself inside the cover of a Yogibo in which he chose to hide.*

Treatment: *When writing up notes after each session, the therapist was puzzled by the significance of the game for Dmitri and aware of the parents' impatience with this use of therapy time. She decided to ask him about it at an emotionally charged moment in the game. One day, Dmitri had curled up on an upper cabinet shelf, closed the doors, and remained utterly silent. When his relieved parent finally found him, the therapist exclaimed in genuine astonishment, "You are the most amazing hider I have ever seen in this room. How did you learn to do that?" Dmitri replied quietly, "When I stole candy at night."*

His father knew that he often went hungry and that onions were snacks for the
kids when food was scarce in the orphanage. The miserable circumstances and
the significant role that silence, stillness, and hiding played in survival were
brought home to the parent and therapist with deep poignancy, leading to a
fuller resonance with Dmitri's experience. This discovery became a truly shared
experience rather than one had in isolation.

Hiding was a survival defense but now was a traumatic reenactment. In the SMART room, it could now be embraced as a competency in the game of hide-and-seek. With the therapist's guidance, this became an opportunity for reworking and attachment-building, creating a new end to old trauma. Finding the hidden strength in children's behaviors is characteristic of the SMART approach (Westcott and Hu 2017). For Dmitri, reworking his fear of adult contact when doing something "wrong" occurred when he gave his parents clues to find him in his hiding spots over the course of sessions. It also led the therapist to new Choice Points, such as making being found a moment for affectionate reconnection. It was possible to neutralize the negative emotional valence and fear associated with hiding by enhancing and extending the shared fun, silliness, and pleasure in the game.

The immediate assessment that the child is functioning in a well-integrated state during a high-energy game is important. However, Video Reflection allows fuller assessment of questions particularly relevant to the client. Dodgeball is a popular game and prompts the therapist to ask what function it serves. For example: "I wonder if this is what it feels like when teachers are always asking him questions. Have I been asking him too many questions? I wonder if life at home has felt like this for him." Or, after a monkey-in-the-middle game: "Wow, she has *never* been able to include both parents at the same time in a game before. This is interesting!" In trauma therapy, the role of the game in processing challenging or traumatic experiences must always be considered.

Embodied Symbolic Form

Embodied Dramatic Play. Embodied dramatic play is a hybrid: it is both fully embodied and has symbolic content in narrative form. In SMART therapies, this is a form of Trauma Processing frequently used by children from the young age of eighteen months up through young teens. This form resembles a theatrical play in which the child creates the story as he goes. It depends on the willingness of adults to suspend reality and Fully Participate in the story. When the therapist or caregiver joins in this way, the child's inner drive to express a story becomes evident. As will be shown in the section on Attachment-Building and in the case studies, the inclusion of caregivers often helps to build the bonds of attachment by increasing the caregiver's understanding of the child's traumatic experience. When caregivers fully participate as actors, it often brings home the story with deep emotional resonance.

The play takes on the character of a small drama, with the child as playwright and director. Each person is an actor, often with action, intent, and feelings, or a witness, or simply an audience member. The child doesn't hesitate to correct or to insist that something be performed in a certain way. However, as long as adults are willing to Follow the child's lead, there is a flow to the story. Sometimes it lasts for one session and, in other cases, the story transforms over many sessions.

It is important that the therapist recognize the child's directives as the child's best effort to communicate something about his experience and not as controlling behavior. Therapists sometimes worry that the child will get lost in the play, act out, regress, or dissociate. However, typically the child is able to momentarily leave the drama. A therapist can test this by asking a question in her regular voice, or in a whisper. For example, if the child throws a blanket over the therapist's head to trap the monster, the therapist might ask, "How can we do this so I can breathe?" As long as the child feels that the play will continue, he shifts to a regular voice and alters what he does to make sure the therapist is okay.

If the child becomes aggressive, the test will be whether the child modulates the intensity or direction of his aggression if the therapist says, "Let's keep this play safe and make sure not to hurt each other." If the child cannot modulate, the therapist's job is to recognize a traumatic activation, step out of the play, and shift to regulating activities until the child is back in a more integrated and accessible state. Another challenge is when the therapist is asked to play a perpetrator-type character, presented in more detail in a case illustration in chapter 7. Often this is a necessary component for the child to process some element of her experience, but the therapist needs to maintain some distance from their "character." This can be done through frequent requests for direction from the child or Tending to Safety of the "actors" in the play.

Caregivers who do not follow directions are firmly told by the child what they should be doing. Those who cannot suspend their parental job of teaching manners or their reactions to the child's wish to control will require some consultation time to better understand the function of this play. This is a form of processing typical of a young developmental stage and an important vehicle to master fears and difficult experiences. More than one child has said to the adult in disbelief, "Don't you know this is just play?" Thus, the therapist is told that the child is aware of the theatrical nature of what he is doing.

In both of the following examples, young children very quickly create their own opportunity to work through what is troubling them, with the participation of willing parents:

> **Example of a very young child:** *Sam, a nineteen-month-old who had witnessed up close his father's aggression toward his mother, sobbed at daycare drop-off time. At home, he did not want to give up nursing, and sought his mother's breast every time he experienced the slightest distress. In a session with a toddler-size trampoline, a tunnel, and a pillow, he gravitated to jumping unsteadily on the little trampoline and playing peek-a-boo in the tunnel. In the second session, he dug into his mother's bag, pulled out her gloves and keys, put on the gloves as best he could, took her keys, and toddled toward the door, waving "bye, bye" as he pushed the door open to go out.*

> **Example of a three-year-old adopted girl:** *As for Sam, drop-off at preschool was a time of great distress and tantrums for Amy. In session in the SMART room, Amy became the teacher, and while jumping on a trampoline, told the "children"—her parents and therapist, whom she had instructed to sit on the floor— the schedule for the day. Amy then had each one, in turn, including the therapist, come to the door and greet her at reunion with a short hug. Amy then told each, "Go back to your problems." She continued as teacher through long sequences of jumping on the pillows with the three adults, who were compliant but laughed as they made mistakes and she corrected them.*

The ability to symbolize experience begins very early in development, and when given the SMART room as a stage, even the youngest can enact and rework their difficult experiences. With these children, the problem and solution emerge within the play, thus assessment and treatment are blended. Older, school-aged children create elaborate plays in which frightening hospital experiences are worked through, fears of intruders are mastered through play in the dark, or babies are born out of body socks into their adoptive parent's arms. The possibilities are endless, as archetypal as fairy tales, and yet as unique as each child's experience.

What Distinguishes Embodied Dramatic Play. The symbolic content of the play is fully embodied; the actors are the people in the room, and the actions, intentions, and feelings are not displaced onto small figures but are acted in the drama. Thus, it lies midway between symbolic displacement onto objects and embodied action. The symbolic content in this play expresses and communicates important experiences, feelings, and thoughts of the child, just as symbolic play with dolls or puppets may do. The engagement of the whole self—body, mind, and feelings—increases the potency of the play. The spontaneous emergence and expression of feelings in the play provide the opportunity to experience and then to modulate those feelings. It also allows for the feelings of fear to blossom and then to diminish through effective action and to be replaced by feelings of pride and strength, glee and relief, curiosity and surprise. The helplessness in the face of threat dissipates naturally as the child creates effective actions in the drama. Finally, therapists have noted the difference in intensity of their own experience in fully embodied play, as compared to manipulating a doll or puppet. The therapist resonates with the child more fully, feels herself to be more in tune and in sync, and thus gains a deeper understanding of the work the child is doing.

Symbolic Forms of Traumatic Expression

Fully symbolic forms of traumatic expression are familiar to child therapists trained in play therapies and are not unique to the SMART modality. These include puppet and dollhouse play; writing stories, poetry, and song; and art therapy. Some adolescents have found "rapping" to be a way to express a personal story through words with a musical rhythm. Or teens often begin by talking about a movie or a TV show but lead into parts of the story that bear some resemblance to parts of their experience. It is not unusual for English writing assignments to startle teachers with either explicit or oblique references to traumatic experiences. In addition, verbalizing autobiographical memory, dream descriptions, and telling about movies, YouTube videos, or books often reveal traumatic themes and preoccupations in symbolized forms. Many of these methods have long histories in therapeutic interventions of all kinds and are effective with some children. With some protocolized trauma treatments, these forms of expression can be used to help some older children and adolescents rework aspects of their experiences through narrative, writing, dreamwork, or psychodrama.

Generally speaking, SMART was developed for those children and teens with complex trauma whose arousal dysregulation disturbs their ability to think, symbolize, and stay connected to helpers. Those clients typically cannot reliably access cognitive or talk-based therapies. That said, when clients in SMART begin to sustain more regulated states, they begin to access symbolic methods of expression to communicate their experiences.

Over the course of SMART treatment, therapists may find that they are spending more time "just talking," particularly with adolescents. By stepping back to an observing stance or reflecting on video, therapists notice the ways that the client is regulating himself while talking. An adolescent may carry on an important dialogue that fully engages the therapist's attention. But watching video provides time to shift focus to what the client is doing. The client may be jumping on the trampoline, holding a big pillow on the stomach as she reclines on a Yogibo, gently kicking a ball back and forth with the therapist, or slowly swinging in the suspended swing while dragging her fingers across the floor the whole time. Many therapists have found that when they move into a standard office, thus withdrawing these tools, a decline in the child's capacity to talk occurs. It is only then that the quiet forms of self-regulation made possible by the SMART tools are fully appreciated and recognized for the ways they enhance the client's ability to communicate effectively about important experiences.

Bridging Home and Therapy

Sometimes caregivers describe symptoms such as nightmares or intrusions, which suggest the possibility of trauma-based thoughts, images, or body memories. Or parents witness disturbing repetitive symbolic play with action figures, dollhouse play, or stuffed animals, or drawings with the same theme over and over again, revealing traumatically based preoccupations. Most frequently, caregivers describe significant so-called behavioral problems with no obvious traumatic content. Once the therapist has seen the way the child is expressing traumatic material in session, it is important to explore with the caregiver these manifestations in the other twenty-three hours of his day.

It is often the expressions at home that most hurt caregiving relationships and, in extreme cases, may jeopardize school placements, foster placements, and even adoptive relationships. Reenactments, for instance, can be dangerous and are frightening to caregivers. It is critical to remember that these behaviors are the child's only way to communicate their experiences. Developing a parent's ability to reflect on the behavior may help them to self-regulate at these times rather than reacting too quickly. The skill of looking behind the behavior also helps when advocating for their child at the school and in community activities from a trauma-informed, rather than a purely behavioral, perspective.

Assessment of and discussion of trauma expressions at home coupled with what is seen in the therapy provide the ground for psychoeducation for parents through making clear links between behavior and traumatic experience, and understanding the distinction between reenactments and reworking. Working together with the therapist, caregivers can learn to help the child bring the Trauma Processing to therapy.

Attachment Expressions of Trauma

The last area of traumatic expression and reworking centers on how relational patterns are manifested. The forms of trauma expressions often show up both at home with parents and in relationships with adults, such as teachers. The problem is most effectively addressed with a parent in treatment; however, other caregivers can be counseled on ways to change their rhythm of engagement with the child based on what has been learned in therapy. The area overlaps with and leads into the third thread of Attachment-Building. In this section, we will focus on how traumatic attachment patterns emerge in session for processing.

Avoidant Engagement. Children with avoidant patterns often behave as if they do not need caregivers. Some children may precociously complete small tasks such as when a five-year-old makes a bed or carefully folds clothes, giving the message they do not need adults. In some cases, these children have parented younger siblings. Some avoid looking at adults, and yet others may behave as if clearly scared—keeping their distance, overinvesting in a sibling or peers, but rejecting all overtures for closeness from caregivers. They lack ways of engaging with caregivers and thwart attempts to connect. These children avoid co-regulation with caregivers, and auto-regulation has become the habitual way of regulating their internal state.

> **Assessment:** *Four-year-old Dan's constant motion around the room involved rough-and-tumble engagement with his brother, while seemingly unaware of his parents' attempts to tend to his general safety. The parents had concerns about the impact of the separations from them and changes in the home and caregivers while his brother was in the hospital. The way Dan threw himself about seemed as if he was constantly seeking stimulus and input to his body, yet he had no way to satisfy his hunger. This hyperaroused behavior reflected Dan's avoidance and challenge in knowing how to accept caregiver care and help.*

> **Treatment:** *Dan was continually curious, across sessions, about the suspended hammock, a tool that provides deep touch tactile pressure, Vestibular Input, and Rhythmicity, and promotes attachment experiences. In an important session, Dan, his brother, and his mother came. Dan sought the hammock, and his mother spontaneously picked him up and slid him in. He asked to be rocked, and his mother, with care and attention, began to rock him steadily. As a rhythm developed, he began to relax and allow himself to melt into the support and containment of the hammock. This marked the first time Dan settled and calmed in therapy. The next session, the therapist encouraged his father to lift Dan into the hammock, and, as Dan "melted" into the hammock as he had*

with his mother, his father gently swung him back and forth. Repeated many times, this activity gave the parent and child a way to explore a new rhythm of engagement in which his parents soothed and consoled him. This increased Dan's tolerance for and pleasure in his father's caretaking, healing the experience of "something is missing between us" by creating a new and easily practiced rhythm of engagement with each other.

Combining Inputs to support an Integrated State and build a secure attachment

The **SMART** Spiral

Widening Window of Tolerance

Somatic Regulation

Trauma Processing

Attachment Building

Image 1: SMART weaves the three threads of Somatic Regulation, Trauma Processing, and Attachment-Building in order to widen the child's Window of Tolerance for the full range of feelings, for physical sensations, for more connected relationships, and for being present in the moment.

Hierarchy of Development

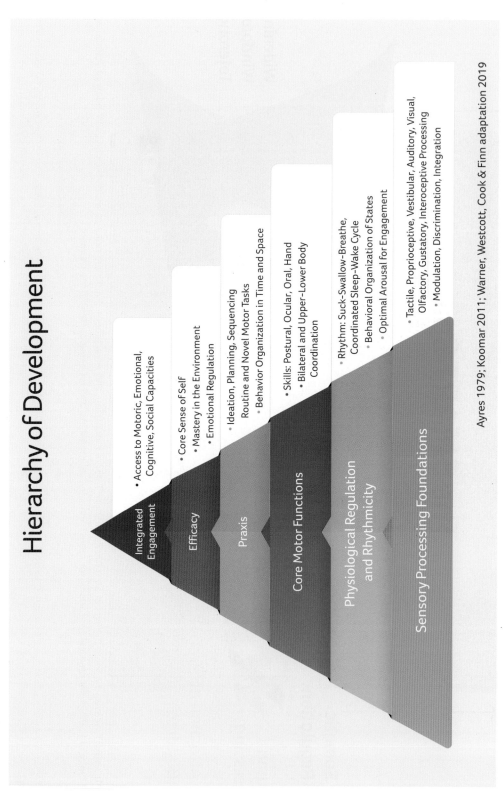

- Access to Motoric, Emotional, Cognitive, Social Capacities

Integrated Engagement

- Core Sense of Self
- Mastery in the Environment
- Emotional Regulation

Efficacy

- Ideation, Planning, Sequencing Routine and Novel Motor Tasks
- Behavior Organization in Time and Space

Praxis

- Skills: Postural, Ocular, Oral, Hand
- Bilateral and Upper-Lower Body Coordination

Core Motor Functions

- Rhythm: Suck-Swallow-Breathe, Coordinated Sleep-Wake Cycle
- Behavioral Organization of States
- Optimal Arousal for Engagement

Physiological Regulation and Rhythmicity

- Tactile, Proprioceptive, Vestibular, Auditory, Visual, Olfactory, Gustatory, Interoceptive Processing
- Modulation, Discrimination, Integration

Sensory Processing Foundations

Ayres 1979; Koomar 2011; Warner, Westcott, Cook & Finn adaptation 2019

Image 2: SMART treatment focuses on Sensory Processing Foundations, and Physiological Arousal and Rhythmicity in order to facilitate higher order Brain functioning. When the lower systems are functioning poorly due to trauma exposure, all higher systems are likely compromised.

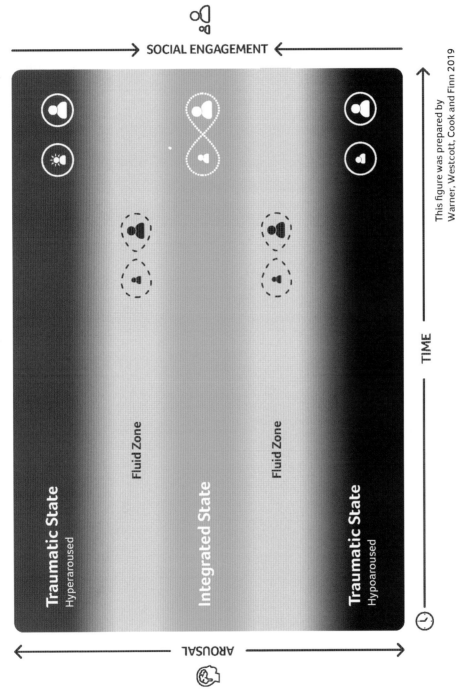

Image 3: The Regulation Map is designed to track children's level of arousal both in the moment and over time in order to guide the therapist's decision-making. Social engagement is an essential mechanism for understanding where a child is on the Map, particularly whether a child is in the Fluid Zone or entering one of the Traumatic States.

Movement and Action

Traumatic State: Hyperaroused	Integrated State	Traumatic State: Hyporaroused
Disorganized body movement • Disjointed, impulsive • Appears random, compulsive, unregulated • Rapid pacing, jittery, muscle tension, trembling	**Energized and active or calm and alert body movement** • Grounded, coordinated • Posture, arms, legs coordinated and organized around action • Directed, controlled, fluid	**Slowed body movements** • Limp, flaccid, collapsed, immobilized, or frozen • Low energy, sleepy, spacy
Unsustained actions • Bounces from thing to thing • Little or no follow through • Intent unclear	**Organized actions** • Shows plan, sequence, or follow through in actions • Intent clear to others	**Aimless behavior** • Little or no follow through in actions; appears as effortful • Intent unclear
Body response shows vigilance to sound, visual stimuli • Sense of flight-or-fight	**Aware and engaged with environment and others**	**Disengaged from environment,** • Passive, under-reactive • Oblivious to surroundings
Physiology reflects high arousal • Labored or rapid breathing; heart rate fast; flushed or pale	**Physiology is in-sync with activity** • Breathing heavier with exertion • Slower when relaxed	**Physiological depressed arousal** • Slowed responses • As if trying to wake up • Dizzy, shaky, wobbly when going from prone to standing

These charts were prepared by Elizabeth Warner and Anne Westcott, adapted from SMART coding study descriptors, 2019

Image 4: The SMART Child State Descriptors provide detailed lists of qualities characteristic of each state useful for tracking a child's arousal via observation in session and in video review. A child's presentation may not match every descriptor, however, a simple, quick assessment of the child's state in the moment indicates when to prioritize Somatic Regulation through the use of Regulation Tools and Therapist Skills.

Affects and Emotions

Traumatic State: Hyperaroused	Integrated State	Traumatic State: Hyporaroused
High intensity affect • Reactive, explosive • Frenetic, anxious • Emotions not clear or readable	**Clear, readable affect and feelings** • Consistency across prosody of voice, facial expression, gestures • Matches activity or narrative	**Low energy, diffuse affect** • Low emotional energy • Hopeless, helpless, or withdrawn • Engagement with others is an effort
Voice tone and prosody • Loud, unmodulated or • Non-verbal grunts, guttural sounds	**Voice tone and prosody is consistent with emotions being expressed** • May recognize and respond to emotions in others • May name own emotions	**Voice tone and prosody** • May be slowed, slurred • Verbal output diminished, trails off, or stopped

Body Awareness

Traumatic State: Hyperaroused	Integrated State	Traumatic State: Hyporaroused
Poor awareness of body in space • Seems oblivious to others • Runs into objects, unaware of environment, of danger	**Aware of body in space** • Uses visual/tactile information to navigate environment without bumping into people or objects • Adjusts pressure or intensity to activity	**Poor awareness of body in space** • Little or no evidence of noticing surroundings • Connections with others weak or non-existent
Lack of interoceptive awareness • Seems not to notice or respond to thirst, fatigue, body temperature, etc. • Does not show awareness of pain	**Shows interoceptive awareness** • Notices thirst, fatigue, body temperature, and other body signals; addresses needs • Aware of pain (e.g. headache), and physical sensations	**Diminished interoceptive awareness** • Slowed awareness of internal state, body signals • Often aware of only part of body, not whole

Image 5

Hierarchy of Development Brain Mapping

This figure offers a neurobiological account for the theoretical framework underlying sensory processing development. It is critical to note that all brain regions identified in each layer of the hierarchy work in tandem to facilitate Integrated Engagement.

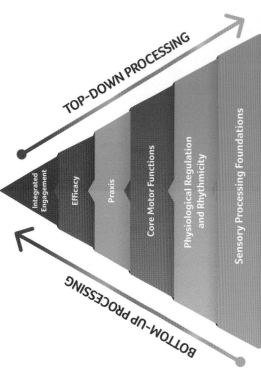

TOP-DOWN PROCESSING

BOTTOM-UP PROCESSING

- Integrated Engagement
- Efficacy
- Praxis
- Core Motor Functions
- Physiological Regulation and Rhythmicity
- Sensory Processing Foundations

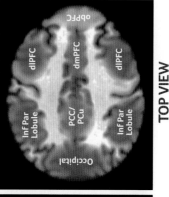

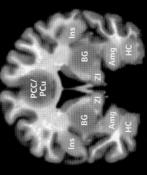

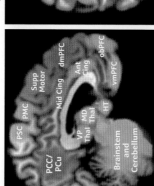

This figure was prepared by Ruth A. Lanius and Sherain Harricharan, 2019

BRAIN STEM

SIDE VIEW

FRONT VIEW

TOP VIEW

Image 6: Green CER (Cerebellum, SC/PAG (Superior Colliculus/Periaqueductal Gray), PPN (Pedunculopontine Nucleus), VTA (Ventral Tegmental Area), LC (Locus Coeruleus), VN (Vestibular Nuclei), ZI (Zona Incerta). **Orange** HT (Hypothalamus), Amg (Amygdala), MD Thal (Mediodorsal Thalamus). **Blue** BG (Basal Ganglia), Mid Cing (Mid Cingulate Cortex), Supp Motor (Supplementary Motor Area). **Pink** VP Thal (Ventral Posterior Thalamus), Ant Cing (Anterior Cingulate), Ins (Insula), vmPFC (Ventromedial Prefrontal Cortex), obPFC (Orbital Prefrontal Cortex), HC (Hippocampus), PMC = Primary Motor Cortex (Precentral Gyrus), PSC = Primary Somatosensory Cortex (Postcentral Gyrus). **Red** PCC/PCu (Posterior Cingulate Cortex/Precuneus), dmPFC (Dorsomedial Prefrontal Cortex). **Purple** dlPFC (Dorsolateral Prefrontal Cortex), Inf Par Lobule (Inferior Parietal Lobule), Occipital

Brain Stem

The brainstem receives sensory input from the internal body viscera and from the external outside world. It is thought to play a critical role in translating incoming sensory information to the cortex for multisensory integration.

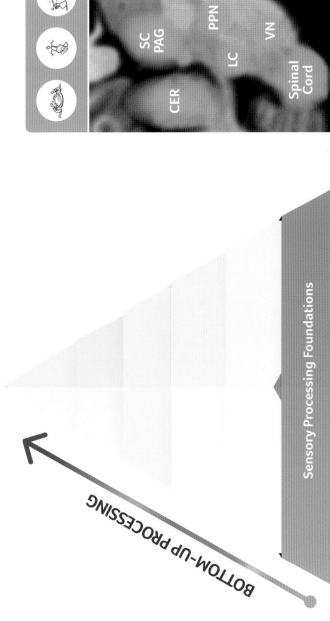

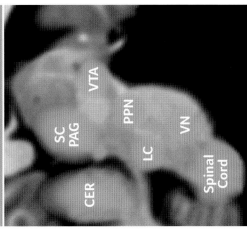

Image 7: CER (Cerebellum), SC/PAG (Superior Colliculus/Periaqueductal Gray), PPN (Pedunculopontine Nucleus), VTA (Ventral Tegmental Area), LC (Locus Coeruleus), VN (Vestibular Nuclei), Spinal Cord

This figure was prepared by Ruth A. Lanius and Sherain Harricharan, 2019

Regulation Tools

Tactile

Deep pressure or Light or Moderate touch

Vestibular

Spinning, Rolling, Arcing, Rocking, Swinging, Inverting, Balancing

Proprioceptive
Jumping, Running, Throwing, Pulling, Pushing, Bouncing

Sensory Satiation
Varying Intensity, Duration, and Frequency to get Satisfaction

Combining Inputs
Increases Sensory Input, Effect, and Challenge

Rhythmicity
Alone or together: bouncing, beating a drum, rocking, playing catch, clapping games

Safe Space
Containment Boundaries Mastery

www.smartmovespartners.com/downloads/tools

Therapist Skills

Tending to Safety

Physical Safety Relational Safety Emotional/Internal Safety

Choice Points

Synthesizing tracked information with treatment goals. Having alternative options

Full Participation
Total therapist engagement increases intensity, affect, and understanding

Verbal Scaffolding
Short simple language Checking in, Narrating, Wondering out loud, Asking a question, Offering a menu, Inviting

Tracking Out Tracking In

Out: observe child's reactions In: observe our own reactions

Embodied Attuning

Using the whole body to connect- Eye gaze, Posture, Muscle tone, Voice tone, Volume, and Prosody, Movement, Emotion, and Vitality

Following

Supporting the child's initiative When in doubt, Follow!

Leading

Orienting to Safety Expanding child's Window of Tolerance Enjoying mastery and success

www.smartmovespartners.com/downloads/skills

Image 8: Quick reference charts for Regulation Tools and Therapist Skills.

Anxious Engagement. Children with anxious attachment patterns are preoccupied by the whereabouts of their caregiver. Hypervigilance prevents them from exploring the world and separates them from peers as they worry about losing sight of or contact with their caregiver. Teens who are anxiously attached may "crowd" teachers or milieu counselors with their small needs or personal questions, or may even instigate connection and contact through provocative, annoying, or other forms of attention-grabbing behavior. They may be grasping at others to ease their internal agitation, a form of co-regulation that is often self-defeating because it overwhelms those who might help them.

An adolescent girl in residential treatment had experienced multiple separations in the first years of her life, and although she knew this was part of her life story, did not recognize how leaving people, even if for a few hours, triggered and dysregulated her.

> **Assessment:** *Trisha sought contact with milieu staff in her residential treatment center throughout her day, often without a clear need. Her lack of personal boundaries was a challenge to staff. She also looked for her therapist many times a day and was upset when she was told the therapist was busy. In some cases, she created a ruckus with staff or another student, insisting she see her therapist to help her calm down. In the SMART room during therapy, Trisha often asked the therapist many personal questions, and at times, would roll over the Dolphin air pillow into the therapist, who was sitting opposite her. This physical contact made the therapist uncomfortable.*

> **Treatment:** *In SMART consultation, fellow clinicians watched video recordings and observed the way Trisha anxiously watched her therapist while rapidly talking and rocking on a Dolphin pillow. She did not appear afraid of her therapist, but rather preoccupied with gaining her attention when she rolled over into the therapist. When a suggestion was made to mirror Trisha by also having a Dolphin pillow in front of her, the therapist visibly relaxed, and could more easily connect with her client. As the next session progressed, a playful rhythm of engagement developed as Trisha and the therapist both rocked back and forth, each on their own Dolphin pillow, and processed what it was like to be together in this new way.*

The physical boundary via the equipment provided an affirming, rather than shaming, way to be together while maintaining "personal space." Creative ways to use the equipment often can solve these problems in a way that relieves anxiety and promotes connection. Later in SMART treatment, while slowly rocking on the Dolphin pillow, Trisha was able to reflect on the link between her automatic reactions to disconnection from staff members and how she might have felt as a two-year-old when left by caregiving adults, thus engaging higher-order thinking to gain a sense of control.

Disorganized Engagement. This presentation is a common relational pattern in children who have experienced physical or sexual abuse. The child seeks connection with a caregiver, but then almost simultaneously experiences contact as a threat. An approach/avoidance or approach/aggression reaction naturally confuses caregivers when they move in to give care and suddenly are met with a "fight" response in the form of aggression or an angry or hostile rejection. A sense of the client's deep yearning for connection coupled with deep fear presses therapists to watch for creative ways of engaging that feel safe enough to the child yet widen their tolerance for connection.

> **Assessment:** *Jorge was removed from his mother's care when his infant twin succumbed to shaken baby syndrome at the hands of a partner. Jorge had extensive medical treatment at an early age for unrelated reasons. When Jorge went to live with his birth father, he was aggressive and showed "no interpersonal skills." Like Dan, he could play with and accept help from an older brother but could not accept being cared for by his father. In session, the therapist held up a large crash mat when Jorge began rapidly punching the air in the direction of his father with both fists; rather than hitting his father, he hit a soft mat. This allowed for the upper-body motor activity he sought, but in a way that Tended to the Safety of the boy and his father.*

> **Treatment:** *The therapist brought out a weighted blanket for deep pressure after observing Jorge jumping into the crash mat with a full-body landing. Jorge was fortunate because his father, although the object of his aggression, intuitively came over and gently and slowly wrapped the weighted blanket over the boy. He then lay down next to Jorge and Followed the boy's lead by pretending to sleep. He had sensitively entered his son's embodied dramatic play. Jorge relaxed under the blanket and mimicked snoring, and the father followed suit.*

Jorge initiated and the father joined this fully embodied experience, and thus he created a new way of feeling safe with and letting in care by his father. Had the father not so intuitively Followed the child's lead, the therapist might have checked in with the boy, and if he got a "thumbs-up," suggest that the father join. This game will be played many times in therapy and at home before it becomes part of the natural repertoire of Jorge's life. But it engages the organic processes of child development: the urge to play and to master the body, and to rework difficult experiences. This game importantly was a tool for Attachment-Building in which the father could participate.

The preceding vignettes illustrating traumatic attachment expression in this section show the way therapy can repair and then build more secure attachment through new rhythms of engagement. In the following section, the many rich ways that SMART offers for Attachment-Building will be more fully explored.

Attachment-Building Thread

Attachment-Building is growing the capacity to connect, to weather disruptions in those connections, and to repair them when damaged. When working with the Attachment-Building thread of the SMART Spiral, SMART focuses on increasing the child's capacity for healthy relationships, building successful rhythms of engagement between attachment figures and the child, and enhancing all members' confidence in their ability to negotiate ruptures. Children who have experienced severe neglect and multiple placements have a very limited sense of relationship. SMART aims to help these children update their mental models, replacing a sense that people come and go or are dangerous with a new model of people as safe, predictable, dependably helpful, and caregiving. This section will address (1) assessment of the caregivers, (2) assessment of the caregiver–child relationship and their readiness for attachment work, and (3) examples of activities and games to facilitate Attachment-Building and repair.

Assessment

Assessment of attachment starts at the moment of initial contact and continues throughout treatment, steadily informing the shape and trajectory of the unfolding process. Common questions to consider include whom to bring into the room and when, how to manage multiple Windows of Tolerance, and how to foster enough physical, relational, and emotional safety for each person involved. How does one engage caregivers who are central to the child's challenges and essential to the child's healing? Variations on these questions emerge in treatment as the Attachment-Building thread comes into focus.

Assessment begins with the caregiver in the room with the child whenever possible. The SMART room is designed to create greater safety and space so the therapist can step back and Track the interactive, dynamic flow between child and caregiver. Based on what is learned through observation, combined with information gained from Video Reflection and meetings with the caregiver, the therapist determines the initial treatment plan. Who will be involved in the SMART room, when, and how much? The balance of involvement is adjusted across time as regulation capacity grows and needs change.

The following information and tools can be adapted and combined to best fit the client, the family constellation, and the specifics of the clinical setting. The SMART process is flexible and may unfold in a different order, depending on the treatment setting (e.g., residential programs, schools, homes, etc.) and the people who are in the role of caregiver.

The main areas of assessment within the Attachment-Building thread are (1) the caregivers' Windows of Tolerance for arousal, emotion, and relationship, (2) the quality of the attachment, including the degree to which the caregiving relationship is regulating versus dysregulating, and (3) the rhythms of engagement.

Caregivers' Windows of Tolerance

Begin by assessing the caregivers' Windows of Tolerance with the child in the room in the present moment and over time. Whether the caregivers are biological parents, foster or adoptive parents, or caregivers in treatment programs, it is important to remember that being in close proximity for long periods of time with a child whose distress escalates quickly—or one who becomes aggressive or resists soothing—will inevitably impact a caregiver's arousal level. Attention to developing regulation capacity for caregiver and child, separately and together, is essential.

By the same token, the caregiver's ability to tolerate varying levels of arousal and affect will, in turn, affect the child's tolerance of these same things. Caregivers come with their own personal histories, including their own trauma and attachment issues on top of recent or current stressors. All of these things can influence their parenting and tolerance for different affects. When the child explores intense states and emotions outside of a caregiver's tolerance, a negative reaction on the part of the caregiver may reduce the caregiver's attunement and availability to the child. These patterns may show up as emotional avoidance that limits the child's opportunity to express and explore a wider range of emotions in therapy. When these dynamics occur, they must be addressed by working separately with the caregivers to help them understand how their child is communicating emotionally and how they can regulate themselves in the face of their child's experiences.

In parent consultation, the SMART therapist supports parents or caregivers in recognizing their own relational regulation strategies and how these intersect with their child's strategies, for better or worse. For example, a caregiver who values self-sufficiency and needs the child to function more independently may respond with irritation and frustration to a child who seeks co-regulation in what seems like a constant, needy manner. Mismatches like these often fuel dysregulation in the child.

When children are easily triggered and aggressive in relationships, caregivers may become guarded and emotionally distant. Some even speak of feeling victimized by their child. Caregivers can become fearful of the child and reactive. Caregivers may respond (1) punitively, with excessive limits, (2) passively, and powerless to hold a limit, or (3) by retreating or hiding; for example, by barricading themselves behind locked doors. Video Reflection proves crucial to understanding this complicated process. These attachment patterns, if unaddressed, may lead to disruptions in adoption and foster placements and should be a primary focus of treatment.

During therapy, the therapist temporarily takes on the role as caregiver. Consequently, the therapist's Window of Tolerance for affect and arousal will also influence the child's range of expression. Again, video review provides the therapist an opportunity to see and reflect on her own implicit patterns of engagement or avoidance more clearly. It allows the therapist to thoughtfully formulate interventions to enhance all three dyadic relationships—of child and therapist, therapist and caregiver, and, ultimately, child and caregiver.

Quality of Attachment: From Dysregulation to Co-regulation

In the Somatic Regulation thread, we discussed assessing the extent to which the caregiver relationship is more dysregulating than regulating. This question applies to the Attachment-Building thread as well. The child intuitively aims to create predictable patterns of connection with caregivers. Oddly, predictably negative patterns can be more regulating to a child than an unpredictable mix of positive and negative since predictability often proves to be more important than the quality of the connection (Gaensbauer 2016). Thus, the goal of Attachment-Building is to establish patterns of co-regulation that have a positive valence in order to build a foundational sense of safety and care in connection; this is often achieved through playfulness.

Attachment-Building in the caregiving relationship occurs at the shared edges of each member's tolerance. Working in the Fluid Zones, slightly beyond the comfort zones, promotes growth in both the caregiver and child. Therapists will need to nudge the caregiver and child to experiment, while providing regulation inputs and relational attunement to support their sustained efforts to explore new patterns of co-regulation.

Assessment includes considering the degree to which caregivers are able to attend to their child's needs, as opposed to focusing on their own needs. Therapists are encouraged to identify explicitly what may be interfering, such as a caregiver's own level of maturity, a personal trauma history, or current stressors, including illness, caring for others, systemic racism, unsafe living environments, or economic instability. A mutual understanding that reduces judgment can increase the likelihood of a successful collaboration between therapist and caregiver.

Furthermore, the treatment will progress more rapidly when caregivers demonstrate an ability to reflect on their own experience. The skill of self-reflection lays the groundwork for curiosity about the child's experience and increases awareness of the impact of the caregiver's emotional state on the child. When this skill is absent, the work is to develop the caregiver's capacity for self-reflection.

Dissociation on the part of a caregiver has a profound effect on their ability to be consistently available. As the caregiver shifts state, the child will often display corresponding state shifts. One could conceive of dissociative-state sharing between parent and child as a choreographed process of synchrony (Gaensbauer 2016; Trevarthen and Delafield-Butt 2017), but one that ultimately impedes the child's development. In cases where a caregiver is known at the outset of therapy to dissociate, therapists may explicitly address the impact of this process in parent consultation in order to collaboratively find ways to ground both child and parent. In other cases, more extensive evaluation of and treatment for the caregiver will be needed.

A final element of assessing the quality of the attachment relationship is evaluating how structured versus flexible a caregiver can be. Caregivers of all children need to be able to balance predictability with flexibility. Traumatized children's extreme variability in arousal, affect, and reactivity challenges this balance. The SMART room provides a unique learning lab to assess caregivers' habitual style of care.

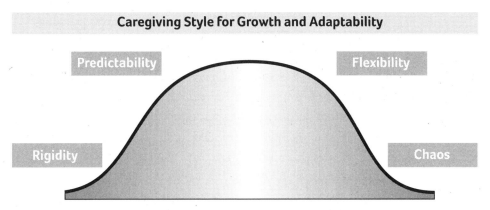

Caregiving Style for Growth and Adaptability

Predictability   Flexibility

Rigidity   Chaos

Caregiver capacity may vary across time, with present state, current life demands, stressors, and level of support

The Continuum of Caregiving Style shows the wide range from rigid to chaotic. The therapist tracks the verbal and nonverbal messages caregivers send their child as the child explores the tools. How are the caregivers guiding, managing, assisting, or supporting the child's exploration? Or are they instead interrupting the process? Do they scaffold with a "light touch" in support of the child's initiative and agency, or a "heavy hand," dampening this greater resourcefulness? When one set of expectations cannot be met, are they able to adjust and be open to other points of view? Parent and caregiver styles may vary due to outside stressors, fatigue, or cognitive load, and these shifts in response style when under stress are important to assess. Ultimately, predictable support helps ground the child, while flexibility in approach supports change and growth in development.

Rhythms of Engagement

Attachment processes are built on natural rhythms of connection and disconnection, also known as "call and response" or "serve and return" (Shonkoff and Bales 2011; Shonkoff et al. 2012). For most children in SMART treatment, these reciprocal rhythms have been severely disrupted. For these children, steady repetition of rhythms of engagement lays down expectancies of predictability and dependability. When a developing child experiences attunement from a caregiver, these processes become calming and reassuring. We venture to say these experiences help shape much of the neural wiring of a secure attachment (Beebe and Lachmann 2014; Hughes 2018; Schore 2003; Tronick 2007).

Assessment of rhythms of engagement involves tracking the rhythms in real time between child and caregiver as illustrated in this example:

A father and his nine-year-old son, Maahir, were playing basketball, shooting at a small hoop on the back of the door. Maahir initiated connection by tossing the ball and asking his father to play. The father rose from his chair slowly, appearing lethargic at first. He took a few shots at the basket as a wry smile appeared on his face. After one shot, he grabbed the ball before his son could retrieve it, and shot the ball. A small bit of keep-away began, and Maahir appeared excited and happy, but he also became more aggressive and competitive in his play. He was edging into the Fluid Zone. As quickly as the flash of playfulness on Dad's face appeared, it faded as he dropped back into his chair as if the air had gone out of him. He began to tell the clinician about his son's aggressive behaviors. The natural rhythm of turn-taking never materialized, and connection broke off. Maahir went back to shooting alone, his shoulders slumped and a scowl across his face.

This interruption of potential dyadic rhythms proved to be a repetitive pattern for this father–son pair. Encouraging them to collaboratively find and *maintain* rhythms of engagement became an ongoing focus for treatment.

Treatment

Attachment-Building begins by finding new rhythms of engagement between caregiver and child. It is an active, full-body form of relationship-building that facilitates Somatic Regulation while exploring new ways of being together. Naming what happens may assist the caregiver to hold the experience in mind, but sensory motor, embodied action with practice ensures that it becomes part of deeper procedural memory systems (Fogel 2009, 2011).

> **Assessment and Treatment:** *Tiffany had a history of an intense, rigid need to control, often banging her head on the floor when one of her parents did not do simple things in the order she wanted. Having weathered many of these fits that left her daughter bruised and her exhausted, the mother was vigilant in anticipation. Tiffany first explored the hammock swing, laughing and squealing with delight as she rocked back and forth receiving Vestibular and Tactile Input with Rhythmicity. At first the therapist sat at the end of the arc as the mother pushed Tiffany. Upon the therapist's Lead, the mother moved around front and sat next to the therapist. As Tiffany swung toward them, she began to reach for Mother's hands. At first, they hand-slapped each other at the peak of each long slow arc of the swing. As they established a rhythm, the youngster experimented with changing hands, faking a slap and then pulling her hand back, followed by establishing a new rhythm. She squealed with delight at the game, and her tone lost its controlling edge, becoming more playful. After a quiet suggestion from the therapist, the mother changed the hand-slapping pattern. Both the mother and therapist recognized this twist could nudge the child into the hyperaroused zone. Together, the therapist and mother watched carefully, wondering how Tiffany would respond. Instead of angry, bossy directives, Tiffany worked to follow the new pattern her mother had set. Her squeals of delight returned, and a sense of mastery won out as the pair established a new rhythm. They sustained this game for more than ten minutes, a very long time for this pair. In consultation later, the mother shared how much she took pleasure in this rare experience with her daughter. And we both reflected on the predictable rhythm of the swinging hammock to provide regulatory inputs for her daughter. It is likely these inputs supported her regulation to engage in and tolerate the fluidity of play.*

This vignette reveals how finding and sustaining Vestibular, Tactile, and Rhythmic Inputs combined with scaffolding helped to expand Tiffany's ability to learn through sensory motor play and increased the mother's pleasure and enjoyment with her daughter. Sustained moments like this one reveal the active nature of Attachment-Building.

Caregivers benefit from psychoeducational examples of how trauma, chronic stress, and separations from attachment figures disrupt the basic developmental functions. Therapists may need to explain how children learn through play, experimentation, mistakes, success, and fun. Attachment-Building takes repetition and active bodily engagement by both the child and adult. It is these moments of experience sprinkled through a child's day that address the impact of disruptions and build attachment capacity.

SMART treatment creates opportunities to explore full-body interactive rhythms individually as well as dyadically. Rhythmicity is important at the earliest level of neurodevelopment (Perry 2009; Perry and Dobson 2013). Rhythm games can be more passive, as in earliest infancy, such as when young Dan sought rocking from a caregiver in a suspension hammock. Attachment games like playing catch demand a partner and are wonderful serve-and-return games of reciprocity that require initiative and develop agency. As long as the adult is willing and able to maintain a "good enough" level of participation to scaffold the child for success, these games can be played at multiple levels of complexity in dyads or threesomes.

Activities That Build Attachment

The following activities and games have shown up spontaneously in many SMART therapies and promote healing in the preverbal sensory motor dialogue, the child's first language, between children of all ages and their caregiver.

Swinging and Being Swung by Adults. This activity, often accompanied by songs or lullabies, provides essential stimulus to the developing vestibular system and generates basic trust as predictability of actions is paired with calming effects. Swings help the child to receive inputs from the caregiver regardless of the child's age.

Rocking. As caregivers learn to match their rocking to the child's pace, they soothe and calm the child effectively. Gentle arcing side to side on a spinning board has a similar effect. At home, rocking chairs or just sitting in a parent's lap and rocking can provide this bonding experience.

Balancing. Balancing activities provide opportunities for exploring the reliability of the caregiver by reaching for a hand to balance and then letting go to balance solo. Balancing activities also assist with overcoming fear that help will not be there when the child needs it, and support work with both avoidant and anxious styles.

Deep Touch Pressure. When touch experience was contaminated by separations, neglect, or frightened or frightening touch, the equipment opens up the experience of touch pressure that can be expanded to caregiver touch as the child's Window of Tolerance expands.

Jumping and Diving into Cushions. This activity offers ways to explore one's body and risk-taking with supervision and protection, as needed, for safety. The child explores moving away from and coming back to the caregiver, and enjoying being witnessed by a caregiver.

Ball Play. Playing with balls facilitates experiences of "me and you," of reciprocity, and of getting in sync, falling out, and getting back in sync, the very nature of attachment processes (Tronick 2007).

Games That Build Attachment

The following games, frequently initiated by children, involve greater use of symbolism, language, and narrative structure. Therapists may feel relieved when these higher-order games emerge, feeling the therapy is getting traction. We find that these more complex, higher-order games emerge after a period of time in the session engaging in more basic sensory motor activities, or later in treatment when a steady theme is being addressed week to week.

Fort-Building. The spaces are elaborately built, with and without adult help, and themes of being "in" and "out" unfold. These games reconnect the child to her own agency, give her control over her space, and encourage proximity to another. In addition, the constructed "home" allows for exploration of themes of danger and actions of protection and can provide needed space in regulating the connection with caregivers.

Hide-and-Seek. This classic game addresses the panic and fear of abandonment, of not being found, or worse, of not being wanted or searched for. In some cases, hiding may trigger traumatic memories, requiring the therapist to help the child ground and reconnect to the present. Often, children seek mastery of these worries and fears through this game.

Dodgeball/Chase. These games bring excitement, with a high level of arousal and suspense, yet no danger from the adult: "Can you get me?" "Can I get you?" Experiencing these high-arousal states in play, whether with the therapist or the caregiver, without hijacking into a state of fear or destructive aggression, expands the child's Window of Tolerance.

Embodied Dramatic Play. There are many variations of embodied dramatic play that surface in the SMART room. Some of the most common themes related to building attachment are birthing games, scary games with bad guys, monsters, or villains, rescue games, or baby animal games. These games transmit the child's trauma story to the caregiver and support the child in building trust, on both a visceral as well as a cognitive level.

These activities with the caregiver and/or the therapist give everyone a full-body Attachment-Building experience. The activities spontaneously unfold during play, often emerging out of the use of the Regulation Tools. A game or activity might occur only once or may repeat for many sessions. By using Video Reflection, the therapist can choose how they use themselves in the room, with the aim to develop rhythms of engagement that build a sense of safety and pleasure in the child–caregiver relationship.

Caregiver Consultation

While parent consultation is vital in all child therapies, in SMART it is vital in order to facilitate understanding of this body-based therapy in communication that is often nonverbal. Consultation time allows the therapist and caregiver to make explicit connections about what unfolded in sessions, to draw insights, and gives room for the caregiver to share and reflect on their own experience. The caregiver and therapist may view carefully selected sections of video to foster further curiosity and reflection about the child. With planning and preparation during consultations, caregivers may then join sessions endowed with a deeper understanding of what the sensory motor play conveys.

The therapist needs to consult with the parent or caregiver regularly to create and maintain a strong therapeutic alliance. Building relational and emotional safety and a collaborative problem-solving approach in the therapist–caregiver relationship parallels the work with the child and requires time with the caregiver outside the child's therapy hour. This "adult time" provides opportunities to keep the therapist aware of current key events, to build parental self-regulation skills, to promote curiosity about the child's underlying needs while developing a greater understanding of the impact of trauma, and to explain and reinforce the value of attachment-promoting games or activities in therapy. Finally, learning to ponder together how best to raise the child cements the feeling of "we are on this journey together" for as long as needed.

Trauma in the Present Relationship

As noted earlier, the parent may develop patterns of avoidance or, in some instances, develop their own emotional reactivity when the child becomes highly dysregulated, is physically or emotionally aggressive, or experiences a significant state shift. The therapist needs to refocus on Somatic Regulation and Tending to Safety; but at moments like this, it may be necessary to have the caregiver reduce involvement, perhaps even leaving the room for a while.

> *Julia, age ten, had repeatedly hit, scratched, pinched, and bit her father in session, and became agitated during a conversation. As she was heading into a Hyperaroused Traumatic State, the therapist and the father anticipated her lash outward. In past sessions, she would try to nestle her head under his chin; however, her father would still be smarting from the hit, not ready to repair. A plan was created: if her father felt he was about to be hurt by her, he could wait in the waiting room while the therapist and Julia worked with her distress. The therapist said, "Dad is going to wait out in the other room while you and I find a way to cool down." This plan protected the relationship while working with this youngster's inability to regulate her aggression. Over time, even the youngster began to anticipate heading out of her window and would ask her father to leave when she felt herself escalating.*

The therapist reaches out to a caregiver in a separate meeting or phone call to unpack these moments and interrupt the potential for feelings of shame or anger in caregivers. Returning to basic Somatic Regulation is necessary when aggression occurs. It is important to verbalize explicitly that space is being taken to regulate big feelings and to care for the relationship, not to reject, to abandon, or to punish. If parents can do so, they are encouraged to name their own need for a time-out breather. In either case, the therapist moves quickly to Regulation Tools.

Attachment-Building supports processing and resolving traumatic memory. Safety and support in relationship to the therapist and to the caregiver provide a solid foundation needed to address traumatic memories. In some cases, the support system must be built before Trauma Processing emerges, and in others, Trauma Processing together rebuilds the foundation of secure attachment. If the caregiver was unable to protect the child, a rupture in the trust with the caregiver may need to be addressed. If the caregiver was a cause of the trauma or injury, active repair and apology will be essential. At times in SMART, we see children create embodied Trauma Processing play in which the caregiver is assigned to play the role of exactly what was missing.

Reenactments. If the caregiver was not in the child's life at the time of the original chronic trauma, it is common to find the caregiver unwittingly engaged in reenactments of the original violation, albeit at a lesser level. These reenactments communicate the child's early traumatic attachment experience but interfere with development of solid connections with current caregivers. Although these reenactments harbor significant risk, they are also fertile ground for reworking the original trauma to a new outcome in the current attachment relationship. Collaborative reflection on the session content leads to a more profound understanding in caregivers of the child's past and present experience in the world. With this understanding, the therapist and caregiver return to the SMART room more available and flexible to explore and experiment with the child to find new patterns, actions, and interactions supporting relationship.

Conclusion

Maahir and his father continued to explore rhythms of engagement over the course of therapy. They discovered that he loved to be rocked and spun in the silk hammock swing, and he sought out high intensity games of basketball and reveled in rough-and-tumble games of wrestle with his dad in the Yogibo. Often, after time with these Regulation Tools, he absentmindedly would grab the spinning board or wobble cushion and plop down for a long, fierce game of *Life* or *Pay Day*. As the father grew to understand his son's need for lots of Vestibular and Proprioceptive Input, their time together became more predictable and enjoyable for both of them. Laughter and smiles would fill the room, and Maahir would snuggle up next to his father to enjoy the warmth and connection.

PART 4

Embodied Treatment
in Action

Introduction to the Case Studies

Each of the following three chapters describes a single SMART treatment over a number of years as the therapist, child, and caregivers transitioned from periods of crisis into more sustained, careful work of trauma therapy. These case studies were chosen to illustrate examples of SMART treatments across the developmental span from toddlerhood to late adolescence. The first case started when Andy was two years old, the second when Emilio was seven years old, and the third when Alexis was ten years old. The latter two participated in different treatment modalities before starting in SMART.

In each case, the treatment began when the child and family were in crisis because of significant problems stemming from affect and behavioral dysregulation. The presenting problems seriously impacted the caregiver's ability to effectively parent. Each child's history was unique, and yet similar, in that they had experienced complex interpersonal trauma that impacted development across several domains, as therapists would discover. For these reasons, SMART was the chosen modality, and caregivers agreed to participate in the work.

The SMART Spiral evolved out of following many treatments over time. The common thread for these three treatments, like many other SMART cases we have studied, is the way in which Somatic Regulation work was foundational. Attention to regulation remained vital throughout, and to a lesser degree as therapy progressed. However, the focus and timing of the way in which Trauma Processing and Attachment-Building were woven in varied in each case in interesting ways.

Finally, by way of introduction, the three therapist-authors, each a member of the SMART development team, are different in personal style and professional background. We hope these three voices speak for the myriad of therapists' voices that we have seen, heard, and supported since 2009, therapists from many different mental health traditions, with different forms of training and styles, all trained and grounded in the principles of SMART.

7

FINDING A HOME

Andy's Treatment from
Two Years Nine Months to Ten Years Old

ELIZABETH WARNER

This case of a young boy who entered treatment, his first therapy at age two years nine months, will illustrate the interweave among the three therapeutic processes central in SMART: Somatic Regulation, Attachment-Building, and Trauma Processing.

For Andy, the initial pressing problem was extreme behavioral dysregulation that made it hard to keep him safe. This case study will show how using the Regulation Tools advanced two goals: Somatic Regulation and Attachment-Building. With these tools, the child's chronic hyperarousal calmed, and the caregiver could more effectively parent. Also, the caregiver and child could develop their new rhythms of engagement through active play, and this allowed a mutual bond to grow between them. Trauma Processing spontaneously emerged in therapy, and most often, Andy's caregiver fully participated in the games and embodied dramatic play that Andy created for reworking the intrusions that beset him. The work on co-regulation laid the foundation for self-regulation that eventually was sufficient for him to end his SMART therapy, and utilize a standard therapy that uses talking and cognitive behavioral strategies.

When Andy was two and a half, his life took a drastic turn. He had wandered off from his sleeping mother and was found by a Good Samaritan by the side of a highway playing with his toy cars. Andy was removed from his mother's care and placed with extended family—a kinship placement—on an emergency basis. Years later, in therapy, when he could formulate thoughts and connect to feelings about this event, he angrily stated to his adoptive mother and his therapist, "Why didn't [my mother] take me to Dunkin' Donuts? I could have been killed!" This terrible insight characterized his intelligence and exemplified one form of Trauma Processing. However, he had already walked a long road to get to this painful realization.

History of Complex Trauma

Andy was born on methadone, and after his birth, he had to stay in the neonatal intensive care unit for several weeks to withdraw from the drug. One mother on methadone described her baby's withdrawal from methadone like this: "He acted like it was painful to be touched, he cried a lot, he shook. It is something you don't want to see your baby go through," a representative portrayal of neonatal drug withdrawal (Hudak and Tan 2012). Andy's mother and father had ongoing problems with substances. Although Andy's mother loved him, she was too immature to raise him. When he was with his parents, he was materially taken care of but was exposed to drug use and frightening events that later showed up in therapy in preoccupations and drawings. His mother often left him in the care of a grandparent. He was hyperactive, and they contained him in a playpen as a way to keep him safe from the accidents to which his reckless behavior exposed him within the home. He did not have names for his grandparents at the time, and this fact would come to mind later when it became apparent that he had developed little to no evidence of an attachment with others.

After being found by the side of the road, Andy was fortunate to be placed immediately in a kinship foster family. Although he did not know them at all, he looked as if he had not a care in the world as he walked from the social worker's car up the driveway, pulling his little suitcase.

When Andy was placed with this new family at two and a half years old, he lost the world he knew. For a toddler, the total change in people and house encompasses the sounds, smells, sight, and feel of the physical environment, the tone of the emotional and physical caregiving, the timbre and prosody of the caregiver voices, the amount of talking to him, and the rhythms and routines of the day and night as they had lived them.

With limited capacity for cognitive meaning-making at this young age, the substitution of one environment for another is experienced primarily at a physiological, sensory, and motoric level. Only a child habituated to constant change could have walked up the driveway to a new home looking as if he had not a care in the world. In a context of good enough caregiving, such separation and loss trigger the panic system (Panksepp and Biven 2012; Scott and Panksepp 2003), an affective neurobiological response in mammals designed to support the survival of the young by signaling the parent to return. For Andy, it took a couple of weeks before he realized what had happened.

When in his mother's care, there were times that she was not psychologically present due to ongoing struggles with addiction and the nature of her relationship with his father. Andy witnessed domestic violence between them, including one person choking another and an attempt to run the father over with a car. Parents who are preoccupied with fighting with each other are, by definition, not attuned to the needs of a child. In one instance of neglectful care, there was an accidental house fire that endangered Andy's life.

Andy was not able to make meaning of these kinds of events, but they registered in his body, suddenly elevating his arousal in terror. This kind of exposure to frightening incidents established "triggers" in his implicit memory system that showed up later in his life and in therapy. He was expelled from a preschool when he tried to choke another child. His fear of choking also showed up in therapy one day when his foster mother admonished him, "Be careful. You might choke on too many cookies." In response, Andy angrily shoved her away. He was hypersensitive to the sounds of fire alarms and fire trucks and drew many pictures of fires in houses and rescue vehicles.

"Any Port in the Storm": Developmental Trauma Disorder

In the beginning, Andy was cheerful and sweet. There was no evidence that anything bad had happened to him. His foster mother, Diana, said, "It was as if any port in the storm" was good enough. However, as the weeks went on, he showed many signs of developmental trauma. He could not sit still, even to watch TV (attentional dysregulation), but was soothed by his pacifier. She took him to his pediatrician, who found that he had a "smoker's cough," presumably from secondhand smoke. The pediatrician's recommendations made at birth for early intervention services had not been followed. His behavioral and emotional dysregulation was extreme and, within months, she realized that Andy had been traumatized and began to search for help.

Life at home was very difficult because Andy was always on the go, running from one end of the house to the other. He related to everyone with the same indiscriminate intensity, showing a slight preference for the foster father. He had tantrums, flailed, hit, and kicked, particularly with Diana, and was described as "helter-skelter." He would run around crashing into his bed and showed none of the early socialization one would expect. Most disturbing to adults, he sometimes laughed when someone else was hurt. Language was delayed, he was not toilet trained, and he showed no apparent attachment behavior.

On the preschool Child Behavior Checklist (Achenbach and Rescorla 2000) filled out by Diana, there were clinically significant elevations on the following subscales: Attention Problems, Withdrawn, Aggressive Problems, Emotionally Reactive, and Somatic Complaints. The pattern of endorsements suggested a potential *DSM* diagnosis of Pervasive Developmental Disorder, and Andy was in the borderline clinical range for Attention-Deficit/Hyperactivity Disorder and Oppositional Defiant Disorder. Furthermore, patterns of both hyporesponsiveness (e.g., to pain, and to his name being called) and hyperresponsiveness (e.g., to sounds, in his case to sirens, and avoidance of touch) and sensory seeking (e.g., strong seeking of sensory motor input), as reflected on the Sensory Processing Measure (Parham et al. 2010), were similar to patterns found in autistic children. And yet the history of neglect and exposure to many frightening experiences suggested the etiology was complex trauma. In addition to his pervasive hyperarousal, Andy had an acoustic startle response—both prototypical symptoms of PTSD—that made his whole body shake when he heard the elevator in the clinic building.

Somatic Regulation

"Helter-Skelter"

In the clinic waiting room before his first treatment session in the SMART room, Andy seemed blind to Diana's extended hand when she offered to hold his toy car while he went to the bathroom. Although this behavior was similar to that of autistic children, an avoidant attachment was a more helpful framework given his history. Andy came into the SMART room with both of his foster parents, Diana and Bill, and the participation of both proved to be necessary. In the matted room, he heedlessly ran about like an inflated balloon let loose. His movement was frenetic and disorganized. When he stubbed his toe against the corner of a bench, only a reflexive flinch suggested an intact neurology, but he showed no awareness of pain. He jumped and ran about without clear intention and showed no awareness of his body in space. He approached equipment such as pillows, the balance beam, and gym mats as if he wanted to try something, but quickly moved on. Eventually, he seemed to want to roll down a ramp, like rolling down a hill. But he could not organize his body into a successful roll; furthermore, he did not look to any of the three adults for help. It was no wonder Diana felt so ineffective most of the time.

This "helter-skelter" presentation, much like what the foster parents described occurred at home, suggested a high degree of hyperarousal that did not abate. The constant movement seemed to be a form of auto-regulation. With the exception of a pacifier, nothing seemed to calm or soothe him. He sought no contact with others, nor was he able to organize what he was doing sufficiently to regulate his arousal system naturally through the sensory motor systems. He needed help but did not approach or communicate with the adults in the room; thus, he did not show any skills of co-regulation.

In one of the first sessions, Andy, who had an expressive language delay, surprised us when he said the word "ramp" several times. We propped up one end of a gym mat on the big pillows to create an incline, but Andy could not figure out how to organize his body to roll down. We tried to help by physically laying him across the top, but he tumbled off the edge like a little bowling ball. After he had made several failed attempts, I took a large stuffed teddy bear, stretched out the legs, and rolled it down. Andy watched intently and, all at once, with the physical scaffolding of an adult assisting him to do what he was seeking, he stretched out his body and rolled down. With excitement, he ran around to do it again … and again and again. Thus was invented a way for him to get some of the sensory motor input he was seeking. Because his caregivers could now see how to help him, rolling down the ramp became a game of co-regulation.

Andy also gravitated to the tunnel, and together we discovered that he liked to be rolled in it; he said it was like a "cement mixer" or a "washing machine." This rolling play—which gave him the same strong Vestibular Input and deep pressure Tactile Input to the whole length of his body that he seemed to be seeking on the ramp—was regulating for him. With that input, and because he wanted to keep the game going and needed help, he became more organized, predictable, and engaged with others.

In a similar way, we found that he loved to swing in the sensory shaker, a big nylon bag full of small plastic balls like those used in a "ball pit." When first presented with this equipment, he dumped the small plastic balls all over the floor and heedlessly ran about the room, slipping and falling recklessly. For a moment, there was a sense of chaos and disorder—perhaps what his life had felt like at various times—and I worried about keeping him safe. However, when I watched Andy more dispassionately, he again seemed hungry for sensory input all over his small body. He did not like deep pressure from weighted blankets or pillows. How was I to provide Tactile Input to his whole body at the moderate level of pressure that he liked? How were we to provide the vestibular movement that he craved, and the intensity of Proprioceptive Input to his muscles and joints, all at once? Dr. Jane Koomar, our Sensory Integration Occupational Therapist expert, visited a session to help me figure out what to do. After watching Andy, she pulled out the sensory shaker, and opened it in an inviting way. He got in, wriggled around, and seemed to relish the feeling of the balls pressing against his body. Then she asked him if we could swing it, and he nodded. As we sang "Row, Row, Row Your Boat," we lifted the bag with him in it and swung him back and forth, gently landing him in the pillows. He looked up at us from inside the bag with expectancy and asked for more, reminding us to drop him in the pillows. This new rhythm in the game calmed his chronic hyperarousal, and he shifted into a more optimal state of alertness and connection. He needed the caregiver to keep the game going, and he learned to ask for help, a small step in building an attachment to his caregiver.

Swinging in the sensory shaker was a game that Diana, Andy, and I played many times over the next few years, establishing a new rhythm of engagement. This game provided a more effective co-regulatory role for his foster mother,

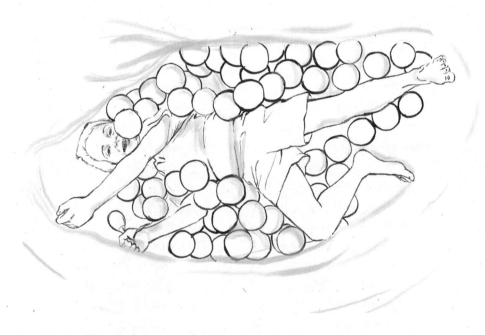

Sensory shaker balls providing light touch and dynamic pressure to child, the bag providing containment and body boundary

whom he often had otherwise rejected. Eventually he sought out, of his own accord, the "ball bag" in times of upset, general dysregulation, or heightened arousal, and asked us to swing him and toss him into the pillows. This initiative on his part showed some early steps toward self-regulation by seeking out the input he needed. And importantly, these simple requests helped his mother to feel connected and effective as his caregiver.

Rough-and-Tumble Play: A Multivitamin of Necessary Nutrients

Throughout the first year of Andy's life in his new home, his foster father, Bill, provided an enriched daily diet of sensory motor inputs and connection that Andy needed to develop and thrive. Fortuitously, Bill was laid off from his job just at the time that Andy came to live with the family. Every day, Bill took him to the playground to swing, climb, and play chase-me games. When the weather turned cold, he "wrestled" with Andy on the floor, a form of rough-and-tumble play that he remembered from his own childhood and from raising his older son to young adulthood. When asked to reflect on the role of this play, Bill replied that it had been fun for both of them and helped them to bond in those early days when Andy otherwise avoided close contact. Initially, Bill made the invitation to wrestle, but before long, Andy sought it out himself.

"Wrestling" and playground play provided a lot of Vestibular, Proprioceptive, and Tactile Input with the intensity, duration, and frequency Andy was seeking. Including another person in this kind of sensory motor play also gave Andy practice in having a physical connection with a caring adult. According to Jaak Panksepp (2008; Panksepp and Biven 2012; Scott and Panksepp 2003), mammalian young universally and joyfully seek rough-and-tumble play, and through this kind of play develop the social-emotional part of the neocortex involved in impulse control, or inhibition. In addition, a feeling of one's body, and body boundaries in relation to another person, develops, a necessary foundation for body awareness.

"That's My Foot!"

In the SMART room, therapists, children, and caregivers take off their shoes and socks in order to ensure greater Tactile Input to the soles of the feet; it also is a way to increase grounding in the environment. For Andy, being barefoot helped develop the body awareness that he was lacking. When he stubbed his toe or banged his shin, I always took a moment to notice it and knocked on what he had hit (e.g., the corner of a bench) to orient him to what had happened. I encouraged his foster mom to check his "boo-boo" to help him to stop and localize the sensation in his body, and then to connect it with what had happened. This was also an opportunity to build in caregiving from a special adult.

I pulled out a structure called a Swiss Cheese Board (Miller and Eller-Miller 1989) that was designed to help autistic children slow down and pay attention to their bodies in space. Andy eagerly stepped up and walked across, looking down to place his feet.

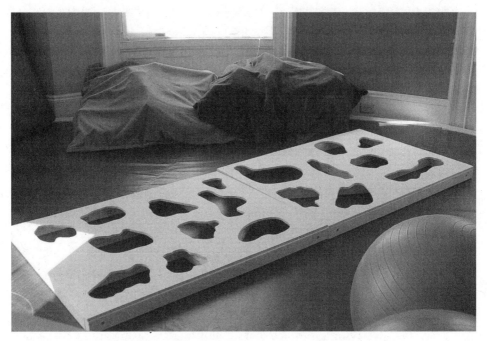

Finding my feet on a Swiss Cheese Board

He could not run recklessly but had to look down and notice where he stepped to avoid "falling" in the holes. This structure was raised off the floor and afforded the opportunity to integrate Vestibular Inputs and visual information by carefully negotiating this foot puzzle. Over time, Andy expanded this game by creating his own obstacle courses of increasing challenge by using stepping stones, pillows, a balance beam, a Bosu ball, a tunnel—anything that made it interesting to him but required him to pay attention to where his feet went so as to avoid what he called the "hot lava" below. He often asked his foster mother and therapist to try his obstacle course and watched with interest as we balanced on the beam or jumped from the Bosu ball to the pillow. Later still, he drew pictures of the obstacle course, a map of the floor that showed increased spatial awareness and perspective in his environment. As this drawing showed, his improved awareness of body sensations and of his body in space helped to build his cognition.

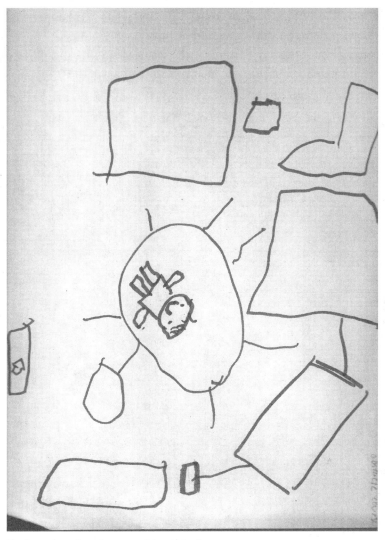

Finding where I am in space: My obstacle course

One day after a long period of regulatory play, rolling down the ramp and play in the sensory shaker, he dumped all the balls out on the floor, sat down against the wall, told Diana and Bill to sit on either side of him, and told me to sit facing them but at a distance. He wanted lots of blankets covering the legs of the three of them, and all the balls underneath the blankets. As he and his foster parents enjoyed this sudden creation of a new family scene, he suddenly wiggled his foot hidden underneath the blanket and giggled, "That's my foot!" Not only had his foot hidden under the blanket truly come alive for him, but he seemed to experience Diana and Bill's place in his world. With increased regulation and body awareness, he began to find a path to an attachment to his foster parents; as he made himself a family, his body awareness increased. As we would see over time, the ability to regulate through this sensory motor play seemed to set the stage for Andy to engage more readily with his foster parents, and in turn, Diana and Bill felt they could help him with strategies that seemed to work.

Attachment-Building

As Andy played in the SMART room, his foster parents began to experience a connection to him. Bill's rough-and-tumble play continued at home, and now the family had co-created games they could play together; through this play, a nascent attachment bond formed. Eventually, Bill returned to work and Diana took over the therapy, giving us a chance to build a mutual bond between Andy and her. Andy always started his sessions with large doses of regulation play, but he began to add ideas that referenced family—symbolic components with an Attachment-Building connotation. When he chose the sensory shaker, he called the balls "puppies" and would corral them with him inside an enclosure he created. This play expanded to include feeding them and letting them out to play in an enclosed space so they would not run away or get lost.

"Baby Doggy" and "Mommy Doggy"

One day, Andy began to play a "baby doggy," and he assigned Diana to play the "mommy doggy." He created a version of a toddler chase-me game by pretending to run away so that she could catch him. On one occasion, Andy stopped in his tracks, placed his finger to his head, and murmured, "Hmmm," as if enacting the sudden awareness of a new idea. He then pulled a thick yellow jump rope out of a drawer and wanted it tied around his waist. When he tried to run away, Diana was to pull him back, and keep him close and safe. Thus, he created the embodied dramatic play in which, with every tug of the rope around his waist, he had a felt sense of connection to his foster mom. Often, he asked at the end of a session to take a "puppy" home to take care of it, his way to link therapy games to home. In this play, Diana and I Fully Participated and Followed his lead. We were struck by the relevance of the stories he created to his life, past and present, and the solutions he created in this play.

Andy began creating houses as he became more organized and intentional. When he was using big gym mats, he needed our help and told us what to do to help create the house. Much time was spent figuring out how to create walls, a doorway, and a roof that would all stand up. Often, my job was to stand outside and hold up the walls. I encouraged him to invite his foster mom in, and offered to support or fix the structure so they would be safe. Over time, he began to incorporate signs of comfort—a small rug, a blanket, the big soft pillow, a stuffed animal. Most importantly, when he wanted the company of Diana, the house became more of a home.

The Big Bad Wolf

Now that Andy could symbolize his problems in embodied dramatic play, he created an important game in which he addressed his aloneness with his traumatic fears and building a mother into his experience. First, he wanted someone to play the Big Bad Wolf. Diana was loath to play a threatening creature, and we agreed that I should play the frightening roles, to leave open the possibility that he would see her as a secure base, a protector, or an ally. If I had not taken on this role, his inner drive to explore and master his fear would have been thwarted. Over and over, I had to crawl on all fours, slapping my hands loudly on the floor as I approached the house with him in it, and with a faux roar, threaten to blow it down. At first, it felt like a reenactment of a frightening moment in his life, and I worried that I might truly scare him. However, he insisted I do this, and in fact, one day, he asserted, "This is just play!" as if he needed me to understand that he was okay. Within a moment, Andy rushed out and chased me off into a corner. He then demanded that we play this game again, and I Followed his wishes.

For a number of months, Andy wanted to play this game over and over. But there was a metamorphosis in his methods for dealing with the Wolf. He tried to scare the Wolf back, he chased the Wolf away, and then he trapped the Wolf by throwing multiple blankets over me. Later, he asked Diana to be in the house with him, and he told her to attack me alongside him. Then, for a while, he watched her frighten away the Wolf, and finally, she was to watch him as he vanquished the Big Bad Wolf. We Followed his lead as Andy directed us through these variations. These embodied actions showed a range of self-protective responses that were impossible when he was an infant and a young toddler, because of his dependence and developmental stage. But now, as a young child, he was creating a repertoire of ways to move out of helplessness and defend himself.

Children who have been traumatized in the context of caregiving relationships do *not* automatically run to caregivers for protection. They feel isolated and alone when afraid. So when Andy brought Diana into his house to protect and help him, I knew that an attachment was forming. In this embodied dramatic play, he was exploring how he might trust a caregiver to support and help him, a lesson to which we have returned many times in different forms.

The Big Bad Wolf approaches a frightened child

The child charges the Wolf and masters his fear

Trapping the Wolf, protecting Mom, and vanquishing his fear

The child and Wolf become friends, creating a sense of safety

The Big Bad Wolf game emerged within the first four months of treatment and was the earliest form of Trauma Processing in Andy's therapy. While he played this game in therapy, at home he began to verbalize his fears to Diana. He told her, for example, that going over a big bridge, seeing shadows on the ceiling, and watching movies were scary. When asked if he would be scared if he watched the movie with her, he said, "No. I used to be alone, you know. I'm not alone anymore." This was a moving, yet startling statement from a three-year-old boy. This embodied dramatic play that he created in therapy, in which his foster parents and I participated, helped him evolve from a boy suffering from chronic fear, isolation, and loneliness to a boy who had parents to help him neutralize the threat so he could feel strong and connected to another human being.

A "Long, Lazy Courtship": Attachment as a Two-Way Process

In the SMART room, Andy allowed his foster mother to play with his toes, sing songs, and give names to his toes—a game that increased body awareness, but also brought him closer to her. He explored physical contact through sensory motor play, including crawling and squeezing between her back and a wall, or being with her inside a body sock. As time went on, the sensory shaker balls became baby doggies who had two mothers, which helped him address this fact of his life. He created enclosures to keep them from wandering off, and so that they would be taken care of.

Overcoming Andy's rejection of Diana's touch was very important to their mutual bond. As Diana came to understand Andy's high need for sensory Tactile Input, and experienced his efforts to connect himself to her in the SMART room through body socks and doggy leashes, she overcame her feelings when he rejected her, and she created home rituals of "snuggle time" on the couch. This brought him physical connection and warmth that he latched onto and learned to ask for when he needed soothing and comfort.

The SMART room became a therapeutic space to explore how to feel connected to and protected by a caregiver, but also what to do about having one mother who was nearby and one who was far away. When Andy's play showed representations of both his birth mother and his foster mother, his foster mother realized she needed to come to terms with her family's wishes regarding adoption. She and Bill sought independent consultation to sort out their thoughts and feelings in regards to permanency planning for Andy.

Another adoptive mother at the clinic said a "long, lazy courtship" had helped her family come together successfully. For Andy and Diana, a therapy that accessed the senses, afforded the opportunity for physical play, and Followed the child's process was important to this courtship. It allowed both the mother and the child time and space to develop their unique rhythms of engagement, increase their understanding of each other, and explore their feelings together. I believe Andy's invitation to his foster mother to participate in his embodied dramatic play enhanced the attachment from both sides, helping both to feel connected in the meaning-making of their relationship.

Trauma Processing

The "Dust Storm" Settles: Intrusive Memories Bubble Up

As the dust storm of hyperarousal settled and the parents, child, and therapist knew when and how to use his regulation toolbox, Andy's profile changed. His pervasive high levels of hyperarousal diminished, and lower levels of anxiety were reflected in attention problems in school and fearfulness; for example, of going upstairs at home by himself. At the same time, the intrusive memories that plagued him became clearer to us. When reflecting on Andy's therapy over time, a recurring theme of fires stood out. His adoptive mother had told me of his panicked reaction to fire alarms, and she worried that his dollhouse play of fires in preschool would scare others. In early SMART room play, he pretended that a bike inner tube was a fireman's hose and put out a fire in the toy bench. Later, as his motor and cognitive control improved, Andy drew many pictures of houses on fire with and without rescue vehicles nearby.

The House Fire and a Rescue

While Andy's birth mother slept, a smoldering cigarette had set an accidental fire in their house. The locked door of his bedroom—by which his mother intended to keep him safe—meant firemen had to break into Andy's room to rescue him from his crib. Although this was a known fact, how to address this traumatic memory was a therapeutic challenge.

It had become clear that Andy's preoccupation with fires was a somatically embedded memory and was triggered by sounds of sirens and percepts of flashing lights in the community as well as on the busy street outside the clinic. As Andy became more regulated, his embodied dramatic play of being a fireman showed an effort to get control over the experience, and later, his drawings depicted some form of visual memory. I began to wonder if the Big Bad Wolf game also had to do with the terror he experienced during the house fire. But the embodied dramatic play with a fireman's hose that had a brief narrative, and his many drawings, could not have been plainer: he had a vivid memory of a house on fire, fire trucks, police cars, and ambulances with bright lights coming to the rescue.

Andy, now six years old, used language to express himself. His verbal expression showed a rich vocabulary, complex thoughts, and occasional verbal insights into his life story, some of which were quite painful. Also, his drawings expressed internal concerns through complex images that helped me understand an inner life of fears, memories, and experiences. Diana and I decided to plan a session in which we introduced a narrative of the house fire from which he had been rescued.

A house fire and rescue vehicles, age six

With my support, his mother explained to him what had happened in a few sentences. Alert, he listened but said little. However, rescue play and drawings of house fires stopped. Nonetheless, he remained vigilant to passing police cars, suggesting the possibility that other intrusive memories remained to be processed.

Many Memories, Many Opportunities: Complex Trauma Is Different from PTSD

Trauma Processing became a regular part of Andy's therapy for a period of time. For children with so many frightening experiences, it is not possible to identify one event for processing and expect that treatment will conclude.

Andy's embodied dramatic play often alternated with regulation play over the course of a session—a dance of the two. His self-initiated play seemed to help him overcome and master fears rather than to avoid what scared him. When the content related to historical events, he often invited his adoptive mother to witness or participate in this play, as if it was important that she know about his life before he came to live with her. In other instances, he processed triggers from his current life.

The Cannonball and the Boy in the Tunnel: "I Coulda Choked!"

In one session, the need for collaboration of the child, parent, and therapist to process an event and solve the problem that came up between the parent and child became apparent. At school pickup time, Andy had reacted angrily to Diana and pushed her away. Diana arrived to therapy feeling hurt and confused; however, Andy proffered a drawing that he had worked on throughout the long drive to therapy. He described in detail the elements of the drawing, including "all those cannonballs that were supposed to get just two people" and a cannon, camera, gun, and toolboxes. This drawing was elaborate, but I did not understand the message. Then, while his mother described to me her memory of the events at pickup time and her feelings of confusion about what caused the problem, Andy self-regulated by crawling under the big pillows on the other side of the room.

When it was Andy's turn, I went over to be nearer to him on the floor. His mother checked in with him, just as we would do when using the sensory motor tools: "Did I get the story right?" He angrily said, "Nope. I'm not telling." His mother expressed her frustration: "When he doesn't want to hear something, he just blocks his ears." I slowed the pace and with my Verbal Scaffolding, he began to report on his experience. He said he was eating, and was annoyed by a friend's noise. Suddenly, he yelled, "I coulda choked. One time I choked on a meatball because my parents didn't cut it up. I just choked on it … and I never want to eat a meatball again." His mother confirmed that this occurred and that he did avoid meatballs, and again he shouted with fear and anger in his voice, "Don't talk about it. It's too scary to talk about it!"

While he got up from the pillows to pull out the tunnel, his mother had an "aha" moment. "I think he is telling me the missing piece!" she said. "He put three Oreos in his mouth, and I said, 'Be careful … you have too much food in your mouth and you could *choke* on that.'" Andy shouted again, "Don't talk about the meatball!!! Too scary!" His strong affect told us she was right about the trigger moment, and he had identified the scary memory.

In her relief at figuring it out, Diana's thoughts tumbled out: that very day he told her that every time he goes over the bridge [on the way to therapy], he is afraid. "I never knew that." I said to his mother, but also to Andy, "That is a good thing. He is helping you understand what scares him so you can help him."

Andy's subsequent play showed that a complete reworking required both sensory motor regulation and embodied action to complete the work. Andy was setting up one of his familiar regulating activities, rolling in the tunnel, and recruited us to help him set it up and roll him in it. "Do you still like this?" I asked. "Are you kidding? I love it!!" he answered emphatically as he rolled. He also wanted to see if he could do it by himself, and self-regulated after this difficult conversation.

While we rolled him, I had my own "aha" moment: a boy in a tunnel looks something like a meatball in the esophagus. I said, "I think cannonballs look a lot like meatballs," smiling and thinking to myself, "and so does a small boy in a tunnel." When I showed him how the body has a way to get rid of something stuck in the throat by coughing it up, he said, "You know what's cool? Mine didn't cough. The meatball slided up. Then I just spit it out." Within a minute, he said, "I'm getting tired," and then crawled out, showing us his work was done. He then put his index finger to his head before purposefully going to get the sensory shaker—another familiar tool from his personal regulation toolbox.

The child, parent, and therapist collaborated to figure out the trigger and the nature of the traumatic material. However, Andy led us to the tools that he needed to self-regulate, to work through the traumatic event, and to show us his own capacity for healing. He chose a familiar tool—rolling in the tunnel—and, coupled with the Verbal Scaffolding of the therapist to the child (remember how your body worked for you), there was an embodied reworking of a meatball stuck in his throat. In this way, the memory, stuck at the point of intense fear (choking), was completed, and Andy could move on. With this present resolution, his psychological state, his mood, and his organization changed, as if the problem had been solved. The body had to "do it" in a new way in order to recover from the present moment fear and the scary memory, and to create a new body memory.

In his early life, Andy had witnessed one adult choking another. We also knew that he tried to choke another child in preschool—a possible reenactment. We cannot know with certainty whether his severe activation when reminded of choking had anything to do with this fact. However, the important outcome in this therapy session is that he learned, at the sensory motor, emotional, and cognitive level, his own body's capacity for recovery and resilience.

At this stage in treatment, the verbal narrative was added to embodied dramatic play because he could process the event with language as well as the body. With the narrative, his mother could better understand the problem. With this knowledge, she was better equipped to help him overcome his fears, and thus to strengthen his experience of himself. In this way, the verbal narrative helped the upset caregiver and frightened child to work through and move forward from this difficult moment in their day and to recover from the rift in their growing attachment bond.

Ongoing Regulation, Attachment-Building, and Trauma Processing

Andy's early treatment centered on helping him downregulate his chronic hyper-arousal and organize his haphazard sensory seeking by finding and using sensory motor interventions that provided Proprioceptive, Vestibular, and Tactile Inputs at the intensity and duration that he was seeking. If we watched what he was trying to do, we could often help shape his efforts into a more organized, playful form. When we hit upon the right sensory motor tools, the regulation activity became a playful game, reminding us of typical play with young children. His caregivers felt more effective as he sought their help to continue these co-created games. This was the groundwork for attachment to develop.

In school, Andy was able to sustain himself in the regular classroom life of a public school with an individualized educational plan and access to a school counselor who provided psychological support as needed in his school day. He also attended his church, was in a Cub Scout troop, and participated in carefully chosen after-school activities. Andy had not looked autistic since his regulation improved in the first year of treatment. His circle of friends was small. At times, he felt "different" from other kids, but, in fact, he was like "one of the kids" in all ways except the nature of his particular life journey.

Very quickly in the therapy, attachment play emerged from the regulation play. Andy created families and houses and homes with the equipment in the room. The SMART room became a therapeutic space to explore how to feel physically connected to and safe with a caregiver, especially when frightened by perceived threats.

Once he and his foster mother developed a more secure psychological attachment, and permanency was established through adoption, regulation and attachment play became the ground out of which trauma memories, both past and present, emerged for processing together. It was as if the safety and strength he felt through connection to his adoptive family allowed the more frightening memories to bubble up. Andy wanted his mother to be there to witness this play. She was often deeply saddened by what he showed us, but with therapist support, she stayed with him through it, and found ways to soothe him, to remind him that he was not alone, and that she would always be there for him.

Andy's relationships with his adoptive parents and with the older siblings continued to deepen, even while having periodic visits with his birth mother. He participated in all family events, including camping trips, weekends with many people and activities by a lake, and travels by plane to new places. Andy called his adoptive parents Mom and Dad, and explicitly understood that he needed them to raise him so he could grow up safely and with hope for the future.

Andy's treatment spanned the years from two years and nine months to ten years old. The treatment plan changed over time, and should remain flexible to include options for hiatuses, terminations, and new therapists. He continues to require opportunities for sensory motor regulation. One session toward the end of treatment, he wanted to play chess. While waiting for me to take my turn—a long time by his standards—he self-regulated by rolling on a physioball. He had become a more patient person. We completed a game over forty minutes, and then he sought out deep pressure for relaxation—the first time he allowed me to apply the pressure, and the first time I ever heard him say he felt "relaxed."

It is possible that having a therapeutic relationship will be valuable to him throughout his life as new developmental and life challenges present themselves. At this point, he sees a non-SMART therapist individually, and a parent joins to process particular questions or problems. He also is able to use other supports and strategies. The school guidance counselors have always played a vital supportive role for him in addressing classroom needs for support, social development, and his need for individual support in the educational setting. Now he can use biofeedback such as Heart Rate Variability (HRV) training, or cognitive behavioral strategies such as learning to "turn off" or distract himself from worries.

The neglected child's default experience of despair, isolation, and loneliness in the world continues to crop up at times of intense fear or sadness, and he needs reminders that he has people to whom he can turn for solace and help. However, with a family and a therapist he can call when needed, Andy has hope for a future full of possibility.

8

THE JOURNEY FROM "IMPOSSIBLE" TO "POSSIBLE"

Emilio's Treatment from
Seven to Thirteen Years Old

HEATHER FINN

The following case describes a SMART therapy with a latency-aged boy, Emilio, and his adoptive parents when he was between the ages of seven and thirteen years old. This chapter will explore how addressing Somatic Regulation on a sensory motor level led to more adaptive Trauma Processing through embodied action, and ultimately increased Emilio's capacity for building a more secure attachment with his adoptive parents.

After experiencing chronic neglect and instances of physical abuse by his biological parents between birth and age three, Emilio began to regard any caregiving adults as a potential threat, and regularly reacted to his adoptive parents with physical aggression when they attempted to meet his basic needs. Emilio's parents expressed feeling completely overwhelmed and frustrated when they could not find effective ways to soothe their son, which negatively impacted the entire family's sense of connection.

As Emilio utilized SMART tools to discover more effective forms of Somatic Regulation, themes from his trauma history began to spontaneously emerge in his play and were immediately available for Trauma Processing during therapy sessions. Emilio created action-oriented games that supported his discovery of a range of effective defensive and protective responses to promote feelings of safety and agency (Finn et al. 2018). He also requested that his parents join and Fully Participate in this play. It appeared important to Emilio that both parents bear witness as he reworked past traumatic experiences, and join him as he learned new ways of protecting himself. He also began to experiment with allowing his parents to help and protect him, allowing for greater Attachment-Building.

You will see examples of Emilio and his parents integrating embodied dramatic play and Regulation Tools to safely explore building trust, reaching out for support, accepting help, and communicating his needs, ultimately strengthening Emilio's feelings of security within his primary attachment relationships and increasing his self-confidence.

Case Study

Emilio was seven years old when his adoptive parents, Nancy and Lee, contacted a trauma specialty outpatient clinic seeking treatment. At the time of referral, they described Emilio as a highly anxious child who experienced regular nightmares, who struggled to verbalize his needs, and who exhibited "rage" states that would last for "hours at a time" and were accompanied by hitting, scratching, and biting. His parents regularly sustained bruises and bite marks on their bodies, and reported feeling completely overwhelmed and frightened by these outbursts. Though precursors to aggression were not always clear, Emilio's parents noted that he often appeared to be triggered when experiencing the sensation of hunger or having to make a bowel movement, when receiving any physical touch to his head or face, or when making any form of eye contact. In fact, Emilio's reactivity to eye contact was reportedly so severe that his parents had decided to remove all portraits from the walls of their home to decrease his level of distress.

History of Developmental Trauma

Emilio's first three years of life were described as chaotic and significant for repeated attachment disruptions, chronic neglect, exposure to violence, and experiences of physical and emotional abuse when in the care of his biological parents. State child protective services had been involved with Emilio's family prior to his birth due to reports of ongoing domestic violence occurring within the home. Emilio's birth records noted the presence of "thick meconium" and facial bruising that suggested fetal stress at the time of delivery. He experienced his first attachment disruption at three months of age when he was placed in foster care following supported reports of neglect and exposure to domestic violence. Emilio briefly reunified with his biological mother at eighteen months, but was permanently removed from her care at age two when she failed to seek medical attention for a second-degree burn on his hand. From ages two to three, Emilio resided in his father's custody, where he allegedly experienced physical abuse that included caretakers rubbing soiled diapers in Emilio's face during toilet training and hitting him in the face while out in a public setting.

Emilio was placed in his adoptive family's home on an emergency basis when he was three years old, and they reported that he had observable scratches on his forearms and cheeks when he arrived. Nancy and Lee described him as initially "quiet," with little language, and noted that he was vigilant to his surroundings. Nancy specifically recalled Emilio looking fearfully at a television cord and stating, "You not going to hit me with that, are you?" He was not yet toilet trained and exhibited angry, "attacking" behaviors during diaper changes. Emilio also became highly distressed and "inconsolable" when Lee was leaving for work.

The family responded to this range of concerns by immediately seeking therapeutic services for Emilio within their community. They followed treatment recommendations that integrated weekly play therapy with at-home behavioral interventions, including time-out techniques to decrease aggressive behaviors, and holding techniques to increase connection and attachment with caregivers. When Nancy and Lee attempted to implement recommended holding techniques at home, Emilio would close his eyes and speak in a "different voice," his vocalizations shifting from sounding "angry" to "terrified." Over time, Emilio started to hide in the closet if he anticipated that his parents were going to hold him. Behavioral time-outs also led to increased running away and hiding behaviors, with Emilio stating, "Just hit me" when placed in time-out. After consistently utilizing these techniques for six months, without positive effect, Nancy and Lee decided to stop using time-out and holding techniques at home. They did note that Emilio was able to enjoy time *together* when they engaged in physical and fantasy play, and that Emilio particularly enjoyed when his parents launched him into couch cushions while playing the "Superman" game. They described feeling most connected to Emilio during these playful moments.

When Emilio transitioned to school, Nancy and Lee observed that he seemed anxious around his peers and tended to "stand back from others a lot." His parents described him as highly sensitive to physical or competitive play with other children, such that he avoided activities where he might be unexpectedly jostled or bumped within the course of play. Emilio also was easily fatigued during play, and expressed the fear of getting angry when around his peers. As a result, his parents noted that, despite being an athletic child, he often would not fully engage with his peers on the playground and struggled to develop friendships. At home, Emilio's level of aggression was continuing to escalate, and both Nancy and Lee expressed feeling fearful for his safety, as well as their own.

Beginning Trauma-Informed Treatment

Emilio's parents, Nancy and Lee, sought out trauma-informed treatment following Emilio's seventh birthday, with the hope that addressing his early traumatic exposures would decrease aggression at home and improve family life. Treatment occurred on a weekly basis and integrated a combination of individual and family sessions along with parent consultation. For the first two and a half months, I met with Emilio in a traditional child therapy office within the clinic, and he frequently used displaced, symbolic play with a dollhouse and stuffed animals in session. During this time, Emilio engaged in repetitive play narratives with stuffed animals that would become physically or emotionally hurt, seek affection (e.g., hugs), and react to affection with aggression.

When engaged in this play, Emilio's ability to express himself became noticeably regressed, and he often used a high-pitched voice with many squeals, grunts, and physical gestures to communicate. The quality of his interactions felt chaotic and disconnected, and his behaviors were observably dysregulated, as he repeatedly made the animals fight and bite one another, and then threw them around the room. I found it difficult to connect with Emilio when he was in this state, and noted that using words or introducing helper animals to provide validation, safety, or support within the play were ineffective means of reaching or regulating him.

During family sessions held in the same child therapy office, I focused on teaching Emilio and his parents' more cognitively based regulation strategies, such as identifying feelings using body mapping and feelings thermometers. They also practiced Somatic Regulation skills such as breathwork through using bubbles and progressive muscle relaxation techniques to help Emilio modulate his arousal in moments of distress. At home, however, Emilio continued to respond to basic limits and routines with aggressive behaviors that often resulted in Nancy and Lee being injured while attempting to provide safety and containment. It was clear that these aggressive incidents had a strong negative impact on Emilio's sense of self, as he began drawing pictures of himself crying, with captions such as "Stay away from me, I hurt my [parents]!" and writing "I want to die" on pieces of paper that he attached to his door. After nine weeks of utilizing symbolic play and cognitively led interventions as the primary treatment method, I began to recognize that the family required an alternate approach and introduced SMART.

SMART Treatment
Somatic Regulation

Upon introduction to SMART, Emilio immediately sought a combination of sensory tools that provided him with intense, multisensory experiences emphasizing Tactile, Proprioceptive, and Vestibular Inputs. Specifically, he explored stacking piles of Cloud Nine cushions on the floor, jumping from a trampoline or bench in the room, and landing on the pillows. In the first month of SMART treatment, Emilio typically spent the majority of a fifty-minute session engaged in variations of this jumping and crashing action, steadily increasing the challenge by adding rolls or flips as part of the landing. Lee noticed that this play of jumping and falling into pillows felt reminiscent of the "Superman" game that they played as a family when Emilio first arrived at their home.

Having opportunities to engage his body in sensory motor movement during session helped Emilio stay more regulated and connected to his parents when they wanted to check in with him verbally. Notably, however, in this early stage of SMART treatment, Emilio often used the sensory tools with such intensity and vigor that he did not notice when his body became overheated or fatigued. Nancy reported that, after session, he frequently complained of muscle soreness and appeared exhausted. This suggested a lack of body awareness and general disconnection from his physiological experience. In order for Emilio to learn to effectively regulate his internal arousal states, he needed to become more aware of and attuned to his body in the present moment.

The SMART room provided ample opportunities to help Emilio practice slowing down and listening to his body while engaging in fully embodied play. I focused on Tracking Emilio's physiological experience during play, and encouraged pauses in the action by introducing a "time-in and time-out" component to the game. If "time-out" was called by Emilio or one of his parents, everyone in the room paused to notice the temperature of their bodies and pace of their breathing. The family was encouraged to take a few deep breaths or notice if they needed a water break to "refuel" for more play. By Leading in this way, I hoped to playfully support Emilio to reflect on his experience and take in care from his parents within the context of a game.

Finding a Safe Space

Each time Emilio was invited to slow down and notice his body, he became angry and reacted by yelling, swearing, and hiding behind a large gym mat in the room. Slowing down and being seen appeared overwhelming to him, whereas staying in constant motion seemed to be how he attempted to regulate. Tracking that Emilio repeatedly hid behind mats when upset, I wondered if Safe Space could also be a helpful regulatory tool. Choosing to Follow Emilio's lead, we began to create Safe Spaces in session, using gym mats, blankets, and pop-up tents, for use when he needed a break. Having access to a Safe Space in session allowed Emilio to experiment with modulating physical closeness and eye contact, and to discover the level of contact that felt tolerable for him in that moment. As he learned a new way to regulate in session, Emilio's capacity to self-reflect and communicate his experience increased. Now, when he was asked to pause and notice how his body was feeling in session, Emilio would enter his Safe Space, think for a moment, and give a thumbs-up or thumbs-down to communicate how he was doing.

Emilio and his parents also discussed ways that they could create Safe Spaces together at home. The family created a blanket fort in his room that included bubbles to practice breathing, pillows to squeeze for needed Tactile Input, and drawing material to support alternate forms of communication when Emilio was upset and needed a break. Having the frame that Emilio was using these spaces as a Regulation Tool, rather than showing avoidant or disrespectful behavior, helped Nancy and Lee support him to access this space when he felt overwhelmed. The result was less physical aggression at home, and his parents reported that the Safe Space helped Emilio calm down and reintegrate into family life more quickly after a period of distress.

Needing "Much More"

As treatment progressed, Emilio continued to add complexity and challenge to his play in session. Tracking Out, I observed Emilio jump into the Cloud Nine pillows, roll sideways, and pull another pillow on top of his body. Curious that Emilio could be seeking more intense Tactile Input, I chose to contact his action verbally: "Sometimes kids like the feeling of piling lots of pillows onto their bodies when they land. Would you like to try it?" Emilio enthusiastically agreed and indicated that he wanted me to stack all of the pillows and mats in the room on top of his body. I continued to Follow his lead and slowly stacked one object at a time, pausing in between each to check if he wanted me to continue. If Emilio had ignored or declined this verbal invitation, I would have continued Following and Tracking his physical movements, staying open to learning about his regulatory needs. Might Emilio be pulling pillows on top of his body to decrease external visual stimulation, or to create a boundary, rather than needing deep touch pressure?

After all of the available pillows and mats were stacked on top of his body, Emilio verbalized that he wanted "much more" pressure. I considered how to meet this need and offered to push against the mats by using my arms. Tending to Safety, I paused to share my idea with Emilio and offer him choices. Emilio and I collaborated closely to ensure that he received an amount of pressure that felt just right, and that he was fully engaged and present. When Emilio's need for deep touch pressure was satiated, he spontaneously announced, "I'm gonna try to break out," and asked me to continue to provide resistance through pushing on the pillows while he crawled out from underneath. After experiencing this intense Tactile and Proprioceptive Input, Emilio released a deep sigh, indicating Sensory Satiation had been reached. He presented as more relaxed, oriented to his surroundings, and socially engaged. Emilio continued to request this activity throughout treatment, and began seeking this form of co-regulation from his parents both in and outside of session.

When Emilio received enough sensory input to regulate his somatic experience, he began to communicate his ideas with less frustration. For example, Emilio initiated rhythmic ball tossing games in session that often accompanied competency-based discussions about his strengths or future-oriented goals. In one session, while rhythmically attempting to toss a ball at an intended target, Emilio described his developing skills as a baseball player and his hopes to be a "mother's helper" for his younger cousin. In another session, he engaged in a sustained discussion about themes of "trust" and "honesty" while receiving intense Proprioceptive Input by hanging "like Spider-Man" on a trampoline leaning against the wall. These self-regulating activities appeared to support further verbal exploration of Emilio's developing sense of self.

Trauma Processing

As Emilio's capacity for Somatic Regulation increased, trauma themes that had been emerging in his symbolic play became more available for reworking in a fully embodied way. Emilio continued to bring stuffed animals to session and engaged in dysregulated, looping play where the animals hit and bit each other. He ignored my verbal or symbolic interventions focused on validating angry feelings, creating safety, or introducing a "helper" character. In fact, Emilio seemed disconnected when engaged in this play, as if he and I were not in the same room. After observing this shift into a Hyperaroused Traumatic State occur several times, both in and out of the SMART room, I Chose to use an embodied form of Leading by standing up and suggesting that Emilio could "do something to help the animals with their hurt feelings." This embodied intervention immediately piqued Emilio's curiosity, causing a brief pause in the looping play. I pulled pillows out of the way to create space, and we uncovered a trampoline under the pillows. Emilio saw the trampoline and spontaneously started to make his stuffed animals bounce and dance in a manner that he himself had used in prior sessions for self-regulation. This small postural and movement-focused intervention suddenly opened up a whole range of possibilities that had not been previously available.

As Emilio made the animals dance together on the trampoline, he began singing, laughing, and moving his body along in rhythm. Observing this state shift, I wondered if the animal dance might be indicative of what Emilio also needed to regulate. I asked Emilio if he might like to join his animals in the dance. Emilio immediately responded by climbing onto the trampoline and jumping vigorously for a few minutes before crashing into pillows on the floor and pulling the pillows on top of his body. With the goal of increasing Somatic Regulation, I made a Choice to Follow Emilio's action and his request to stack more cushions on top and apply resistance so he could "break out." This additional Tactile and Proprioceptive Input seemed to provide the intensity of sensory input he needed to satiate.

"Throw It at My Face"

Once in a more regulated state, Emilio lay down on the floor and attempted to repeatedly hit a large physioball into the air with his hands. On one occasion, I offered him the ball, and Emilio spontaneously looked at me and stated, "Throw it [the ball] at my face." I paused, knowing that his face was a particularly sensitive area, and asked, "Do you mean a head-butt?" When Emilio answered affirmatively and physically demonstrated a plan to sit up and head-butt the ball away, I decided to Follow his lead.

After releasing the ball, I observed Emilio lift his head slightly, but primarily allow the ball to hit him squarely on the face. Somewhat shocked, I asked Emilio if he was okay, to which he responded with laughter, exclaiming, "That was fun!" He promptly lay back down and asked me to repeat the action. Although hesitant, I assessed that Emilio was in an Integrated State, as he was smiling, was making good eye contact, and appeared fully engaged with me in the present moment. I also felt confident that Emilio and I could access sensory tools as needed to support his return to regulation if he shut down, reacted aggressively, or withdrew from me.

At this Choice Point, I continued to Follow his lead, and tossed the ball a second time while simultaneously Tracking his affect and body for any signs of dysregulation. Emilio allowed the ball to hit him in the face a second time, caught the ball, and immediately tossed it back. This time, he presented as even more focused, and looked directly at me when he requested, "Throw it again." Tracking Out, I assessed that Emilio continued to present as regulated and socially engaged. Tracking In, I felt a strong sense that Emilio needed me to continue to Follow his lead, and that together, we were actively working on an issue that represented an ongoing challenge in his life (contact to his face). I decided to Follow his lead one additional time. However, I had also made the internal decision to stop the action if he did not make an attempt to protect his face upon the next toss. I was particularly aware that we were working in the High Intensity Fluid Zone, and that I needed to ensure that he did not dissociate or enter into a traumatic reenactment or reexperience some aspect of his early trauma. The goal of my intervention at this time was to support effective reworking of the experience from a place of felt safety in the present moment.

On the third toss, Emilio used his hands to successfully push the ball away from his face, hitting it in the air several times and laughing. He asked me to repeat this action several more times, and with great focus, experimented with different protective and defensive responses to each ball toss: catching the ball, punching the ball away, kicking the ball away, rolling on the ground in several different directions to dodge the ball, and finally standing up and hitting the ball back using both hands and the full strength of his entire body. As this embodied action unfolded, it became clear that Emilio was exploring, through his actions and posture, a variety of defensive and self-protective responses that had not been possible when he experienced trauma to his face as an infant and toddler.

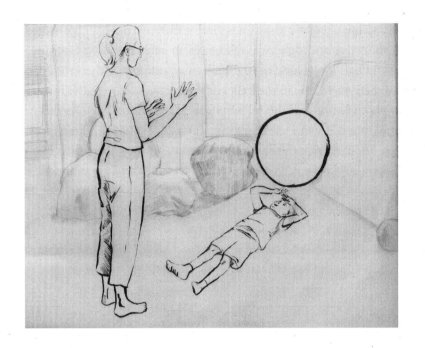

As he engaged in a process of reworking this traumatic experience from the safety of the present moment, Emilio experimented with postural shifts and protective stances that required full-body engagement and exhibited a forward developmental progression. For example, Emilio initially hit the ball back while lying down on his back, in a relatively vulnerable, infant-like manner. Slowly, he began exploring options for movement through rolling or crawling, and finally stood up on his feet in a solid, well-integrated, and agentic posture. The nature of his interactions also progressed from more rigid and repetitive actions, and developed into a more playful, flexible, and exploratory game in which he could experience a sense of mastery.

Showing a well-regulated and capable sense of himself within the context of this embodied game, Emilio verbalized a wish for his parents to join the session and demonstrated to them his ability to successfully protect his face by hitting

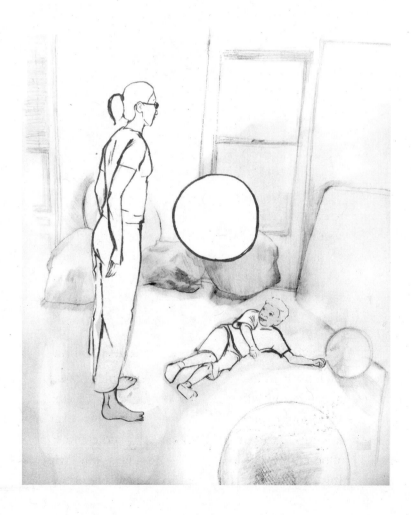

the ball away with various parts of his body. Nancy and Lee each expressed shock and surprise that Emilio was able to tolerate potential contact to his face without entering into a state of terror or rage. Through this embodied game, the family discovered a safe method that enabled Emilio to explore the strength and power of his body, in a playful manner, and that helped him effectively regulate his physiological arousal when encountering a perceived threat or potential stressor. It seemed to be important that Emilio share his discovery with his parents, and that they bear witness to his underlying vulnerability and experience his developing strength alongside them.

As Nancy and Lee demonstrated their capacity to witness and support his full range of experience, the focus of Emilio's actions evolved beyond primary survival response patterns. His attention shifted to relational engagement and his connection with his parents. For example, Emilio focused on establishing a pattern of "turn-taking" with both parents by creating a rhythmic, cooperative, three-way game of catch as a family. Emilio expressed a desire to continue the game with them outside of therapy, reporting that it helped him feel more "calm." In response to his request, we joined together to discuss ways the family could safely implement this game at home and within their community.

Following this session, I scheduled a parent consultation session with both parents to review the progression of the session, to provide psychoeducation regarding the nature of the Trauma Processing that had occurred, and to gain additional insight into each parent's experience of participating in that session. Both Nancy and Lee intuited the significance of Emilio being able to successfully protect his face from the ball, and expressed deeper empathy and understanding regarding his physically aggressive responses to certain forms of caregiving; e.g., wiping his face or brushing his hair. From this point forward, Emilio requested that both parents join him for all subsequent sessions, and treatment goals shifted from working primarily on finding Tools of Regulation, to using his regulatory skills to support further Trauma Processing and Attachment-Building work.

"We Have Plenty of Diapers and Plenty of Time"

During family sessions, Emilio's use of sensory equipment expanded, helping him to maintain regulation while also reworking early trauma and attachment experiences through embodied dramatic play. For example, Emilio frequently used a body sock, receiving regulatory Tactile and Proprioceptive Inputs, as he embodied the role of "Baby," a "homeless boy" who was frightened and rejecting of adults who attempted to help or soothe him. In one notable session, Emilio, as "Baby," spent several minutes crawling around the room in a chaotic manner, screaming out inconsolably, and then proceeded to throw a large ball against the wall so that it rebounded and hit him squarely in the face. Upon impact, Emilio collapsed to the floor and lay there until one of his parents tried to provide care. As Nancy approached, he suddenly crawled away, exhibited a frightened affect, and resumed screaming. When both parents sat still and offered him their open arms, Emilio cocked his head, looked at them with a confused expression, and used baby talk to communicate that he had soiled his diaper.

Seeing this as an opportunity for trauma reworking, I encouraged both parents to Follow Emilio's lead, and they responded by expressing their desire to change Baby's diaper in dramatic play. Emilio immediately consented, which was particularly significant to his parents in light of his ongoing pattern of rejecting both Nancy's and Lee's attempts to provide caregiving at home. After a successful "diaper change" in dramatic play, Emilio used the same baby voice to announce that he had soiled himself once again. Nancy, beautifully attuned, responded in an unconditional manner that suggested accidents were okay: "Baby, we have plenty of diapers and plenty of time." Emilio responded to this verbal reassurance by crawling to a ball, punching it several times with his fists, and then collapsing to the ground as if he had been knocked out.

Perceiving that Emilio was communicating something to his parents about his experience of having accidents as a toddler, I encouraged both Nancy and Lee to care for "Baby," who appeared to be hurt. Emilio pretended to be unresponsive to his parents' attempts to revive him, and his parents, Fully Participating in this embodied dramatic play, decided to call "911 for more help." Responding to this invitation, I took an active participant role by embodying a doctor who could bring medicine to "Baby's" parents. Emilio slowly accepted the "medicine" from his parents, and allowed them to help him recover. After a period of time, Emilio, using the voice of a toddler, repeated the word "home" and affirmed that healing had occurred.

In the context of this embodied dramatic play, Emilio explored receiving care and nurturance from his parents in a manner that had been neglected when he was an infant and a toddler. Upon completion of this play, Emilio spontaneously announced that he was ready to take off the baby PJs and asked to "check in." He spent the remainder of the session, fully engaged at an eight-year-old developmental level, talking with his parents about a frightening peer interaction that had occurred at school, and receiving support and guidance from his parents around his concerns.

Throughout the course of his treatment, Emilio continued to engage in various iterations of reworking early traumatic experiences through action-oriented games that focused on establishing defensive and protective responses, and in embodied dramatic play that worked on themes of basic care and safety within a caregiving relationship. By the end of his first year in treatment, Emilio stopped aggressive behaviors toward his parents at home, was less triggered by direct eye contact (his family could hang portraits back on the walls), and was more able to tolerate contact to his face and head within the context of caregiving. Both Nancy and Lee could brush his hair and help him wash his face, a small but meaningful change in the daily life of this child and his parents.

Attachment-Building

As Emilio engaged in the process of reworking early developmental traumatic experiences in treatment with the support of his parents, he appeared to feel safer in their relationship and showed a decrease in "fight" survival responses at home. As this protective strategy was less needed, Nancy and Lee noticed an increase in his expressions of vulnerability and negative beliefs about himself ("I am stupid"). He also presented with more anxiety about the security of his attachment with them, often saying to them, "You don't care," or articulating fears that his parents would die or get hurt. As Emilio's ability to tolerate experiencing and verbally expressing his feelings to his parents increased, the focus of treatment began to shift toward strengthening attachment within the family system.

When Emilio was between the ages of eight and ten, Nancy and Lee noted that he struggled with basic trust, and that he often was unable to identify his needs or ask them for help when he was in distress. In a state of frustration, Emilio frequently would yell at his parents to "figure it out" in a manner reminiscent of a screaming infant who requires parental trial and error to discover what is soothing. When they could not "figure it out," he would angrily reject their attempts to problem-solve or soothe him, by yelling, "You don't care! You hate me!" In the context of parent consultation, Nancy and Lee often expressed feeling tired, overwhelmed, and frustrated by this "I need you, go away" pattern of interacting. They paid attention to the manner in which their own stress levels compounded Emilio's feelings of distress. Specifically, Emilio presented as hyper-attuned to subtle shifts in each parent's mood or facial expression, often interpreting parental stress or confusion as evidence that they felt angry or "hated" him.

During this time period, regular parent consultation sessions proved essential to help both parents better understand the survival responses of children who have experienced trauma in the context of primary caregiving relationships. Specifically, they learned how it is more protective for a traumatized child to react immediately to potential cues of anger in caregivers in order to stay safe, rather than take the time to assess for nuanced emotion and risk being physically harmed. With this information, Nancy and Lee were better able to understand and attune to Emilio's needs and noticed themselves feeling less reactive to his outward behaviors. They were also able to utilize ongoing parent consultation sessions to find ways that they could support one another and effectively regulate themselves when they felt overwhelmed by and reactive to Emilio's behaviors.

At this point in treatment, the primary therapeutic goal focused on finding ways to help Emilio experience a greater sense of trust, felt safety, and capacity for co-regulation with his parents, to build a more secure attachment pattern within their relationship. Weekly family therapy sessions in SMART focused on Tending to Safety (physical, emotional, and relational) through using equipment in the room (mats/pillows), and Embodied Attuning by experimenting with proximity to, or closeness and distance in relationship with, his parents. For example, Emilio often used mats and pillows to create two "houses" where he could experiment with inviting his parents into his home to visit or help him with a project, and then communicate when he would like them to return to their home so he could have some time and space to himself.

I focused on supporting communication and attunement within the family system, paying particular attention to helping Emilio notice any internal or external cues that signaled the level of connection he was seeking, and practice verbalizing these needs to his parents in session. Nancy and Lee reported that this work slowly translated to life at home. For example, Emilio learned to notice when he was feeling "annoyed" by his parents, and could independently decide to take a break in his room as a way to calm down. The family work in the SMART room helped Nancy and Lee understand Emilio's retreat to his room as an attempt at self-regulation, rather than a sign of disrespect.

Reworking Disorganized Attachment Patterns: "I Need You, Go Away!"

As Emilio's work in the SMART room became more attachment-focused, Nancy and Lee noticed that he began to express fears that "something bad could happen" to one of them. Emilio also exhibited increased anxiety about being alone and went through a period of sleeping in his parents' room. During this time period, Emilio began talking in session about memories he had that were related to the fact that Lee required surgery shortly after he arrived at his adoptive home. Emilio described his recollections of the long recovery period and feeling frightened by the extensive scarring on Lee's body as a result of the operation.

When engaging with equipment in the SMART room, Emilio also began to show greater awareness of the possibility that his own body could become hurt. This greater sensitivity coincided with a preadolescent growth spurt, as a result of which he began having more difficulty navigating his growing body through space without bumping into things. When Emilio's body was unexpectedly jostled in session, he would collapse to the floor, disengage, and indicate that he experienced physical pain. In session, he typically demonstrated ambivalence about what appeared to be his growing desire to accept support and nurturance from his parents, and equally strong feelings of mistrust and fear that their interventions would hurt him.

At age eleven, this pattern was demonstrated in a session when Emilio began hitting a ball back and forth with his parents while checking in about his week. In this check-in, Emilio expressed memories of his mother's, Lee's, surgery. While engaged in this activity, Emilio hit the ball toward me and the ball accidentally hit me in the face. After witnessing this occurrence, Emilio immediately collapsed to the floor and reported that he had hurt his arm when he hit the ball. It seemed Emilio felt frightened by seeing me get hit in the face, and started to move into a state of hypoarousal. Tending to physical, relational, and emotional Safety, I focused on helping Emilio notice what was hurting him, communicate what he noticed to his parents, and explore whether he could accept their support.

Emilio responded to my Verbal Scaffolding by saying that he had banged his elbow after he collapsed onto the floor. With encouragement, Emilio tentatively experimented with seeking support by reaching for his mother, Nancy, and saying, "Help." However, as she gently examined his arm, Emilio hit her leg and yelled, "Go away!" in a manner that started out playfully, but became increasingly aggressive. Because we had been working on clear boundaries, Nancy responded to Emilio's behavior by moving back to give him space. In response to her withdrawal, Emilio reacted and immediately grabbed for her arm, stating, "No! You didn't check it." Both parents were able to briefly name this pattern in session and said they were feeling "confused" about how to help Emilio when he felt hurt, as it was either "too much [or] not enough."

After this pattern was named in session, Emilio showed increased curiosity about the possibility of accepting more support from his parents, and placed his arm in his mother's, Nancy's, hands. While Emilio was being supported by his mother, I spent a few moments helping him Track his body's response and focus on noticing whether the touch "hurt" or "felt good." After a few seconds of noticing, Emilio stated, "I don't know, I think it feels good." When I asked Emilio if he could describe what felt good about the touch, he stated, "It feels like it's helping." Treatment continued to focus on activities to widen Emilio's Window of Tolerance for trust with his parents by exploring ways that Emilio could experiment with asking for and accepting "help" from them when he needed it.

Healing Old Wounds and Finding Security in Attachment

After an additional six months of focused work, Emilio began to demonstrate greater capacity to slow down, attune to, and name the sensations and emotions he felt while engaging with the Regulation Tools and interacting with his parents in the SMART room. As a result of that work, Nancy and Lee reported that he began to ask for help at home when he felt distressed, rather than require that they "figure it out." During one parent consultation session, Lee shared, with tears in her eyes, "He let me hug him" after he expressed his fears about a hurricane reported on the news. It was the first time she felt able to soothe her son effectively when he felt frightened.

As Emilio's sense of trust and security in his attachment relationships increased, I noted that there were more opportunities for weaving the threads of Somatic Regulation, Trauma Processing, and Attachment-Building into family therapy sessions. In one important session, shortly after his twelfth birthday, Emilio created a game where he repeatedly leaped over a large Dolphin air pillow toward his mother's, Nancy's, outstretched arms. Without hesitation, Emilio explored how he could grasp her hands in a manner that allowed him to land securely on the large inflated rocking cushion. His mother, Lee, provided additional support and security by holding the Dolphin pillow steady for a soft landing.

This embodied action seemed to support Emilio's self-regulation by Tending to Safety and actively providing a combination of intense Vestibular (rocking), Proprioceptive (jumping, pulling with his arms), and Tactile (clasping hands, crashing on his stomach) Inputs within the context of a supportive co-regulatory attachment relationship. He trusted his parents to catch him and stabilize the cushion each time he jumped.

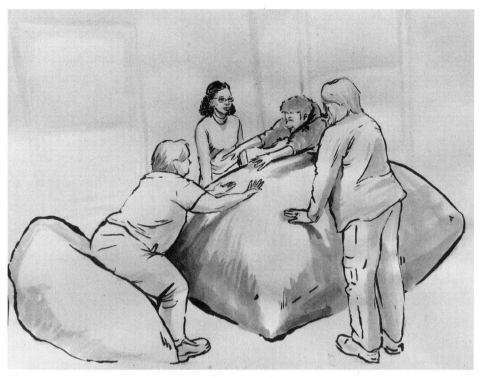

The child on large Dolphin air pillow: Attachment-Building with parents

While engaged in this attachment-oriented regulation game, the entire family was relaxed, playful, and able to laugh together. When I commented on this, Emilio and his parents identified feeling an increased sense of trust in each other. Emilio's parents reported particularly feeling more secure "knowing that he'll let us help him when he's hurt." The family then shared their experience of a "scary" event that they successfully navigated together over the course of that week. Specifically, Emilio reported getting burned by a hot cup of tea and feeling "scared" by the burning sensation. Instead of fighting his parents, he allowed them to help him care for the burn by applying cool water to the impacted area, and recognized that their intervention felt "good." Emilio had been permanently removed from his birth mother after she neglected to treat a second-degree burn on his hand, and so this experience was of particular importance for Emilio and his adoptive parents in reworking an early traumatic experience of neglect. Over the course of this session, Emilio noticed that he felt more open to accepting his parents' help and more able to trust that their actions represented an effort to help him, rather than harm him.

Finding Increased Security and Discovering Himself

As Emilio entered early adolescence at age thirteen, his need for more intense gross motor sensory input seemed to decrease, and he and his parents spent more time relaxing on Cloud Nine cushions and talking. This gentle regulatory support appeared to help Emilio sustain engagement in more complex cognitive functions requiring self-reflection and perspective-taking. Emilio also began to show an increased capacity for mindfulness and for noticing his internal experiences in a more nuanced way. Specifically, he could reflect for longer periods of time, and study his responses to feeling triggered by interactions with his parents.

For example, Emilio identified that a big trigger for him was being told "no" or that he had to do something he didn't want to do. Using Verbal Scaffolding to help Emilio to Track his internal experience, I asked him to notice what happened in his body when he expected to hear the word "no." Rather than stating "I don't know," Emilio was now able to observe and describe physiological sensations he noticed (tightness in his chest, hot face, burning stomach, an impulse to argue), and identified that he associated these sensations with feeling angry. This increased awareness of his body, as well as increased tolerance for noticing his internal experiences, represented a significant shift for Emilio and his ability to communicate his feelings and needs in more effective ways.

Emilio and his family were now able to spend time talking together in family sessions. I focused on normalizing his feelings and exploring ways that his parents could be most helpful to Emilio when his body told him he was getting angry. Emilio specifically noted a desire to "argue" or "get away," accompanied by a fear of "disappointing" his parents, when angry. This exploration helped the family as a whole to make a plan that responded to both his trauma triggers and attachment needs. Specifically, Emilio and his parents agreed to take space from one another when they noticed the impulse to argue or get away, with reassurance that they would check back in once calm. The goal of this response was first, to support regulation by decreasing verbal/auditory input, which often felt triggering for Emilio when he felt overwhelmed. Second, the goal was to support attachment by checking back in and attending to Emilio's anxiety that his feelings of anger would "disappoint" his parents and could result in his losing them.

Outside of session, Emilio was becoming more involved in his community and enrolled in his town's football and soccer teams. He particularly loved football, and responded positively to the intense combination of sensory inputs he received from the weight of the protective padding in the uniform and the action of tackling. Emilio's confidence and self-esteem improved, and he identified having several close friends at school and on his sports teams. In one session, Nancy and Lee proudly shared that Emilio's school counselor described him as a positive role model for his peers after Emilio encouraged a classmate to talk about his problems with his parents, rather than attempt to hide them.

The Journey from "Impossible" to "Possible"

Emilio and his parents had engaged in trauma-informed treatment for five years. Emilio made significant progress in his capacity to self-regulate and engage successfully in relationship. At thirteen years of age, Emilio's social and athletic activities began to take priority in his life, and he regularly expressed frustration prior to attending scheduled therapy sessions. Although there continued to be identified concerns that might have been addressed in treatment (Emilio expressing more awareness of having "sad" or "empty" feelings when thinking about his biological family, or feeling triggered when the football coach would yell), his parents and I agreed that his connection with his parents was secure enough to allow him to take in their support and to cope effectively with these experiences. Emilio and his parents discussed feeling open to returning to therapy in the future if he or his family felt they needed additional support.

In the final treatment session, Emilio and his parents decided to create a collaborative family drawing to depict their journey in treatment, and to look ahead to the future. They labeled their journey "Impossible to Possible," noting that, at the beginning of treatment, it felt as if they would "never be able to communicate together as a family, because everyone felt angry all of the time, and really sad." At the time of discharge, Emilio and his parents agreed that communication no longer felt impossible, and they now had a sense of trust and faith in their ability to work through challenges as a family. In their family drawing, Emilio and his parents depicted a circular pathway that began with a rocky entry, labeled "impossible," that spiraled out, becoming more smooth and dotted with growing flowers over time as it opened up to the future, labeled "possible." The path ended with a future-oriented family portrait depicting Emilio as a college-aged student studying architecture with his parents smiling proudly by his side.

Five months after the end of treatment, Emilio's mother Nancy joyfully called and left me a message to share that Emilio was doing well and that "as a family we are better than we ever have been." She described having an "amazing" interaction with Emilio in which he allowed her to help him care for a blister on his toe, in spite of a moment of "freaking out," and then "went back to skimboarding with his friends in no time." One and a half years post-treatment, she reached out again to share that Emilio was now a freshman in high school and that he "has had the most amazing six months or so." She said that there continued to be "tough moments," but rather than exhibit aggression, he typically expressed frustration through "outbursts of grumbling followed by a quick resolution and true apologies." Emilio's parents also described being more reflective of their own process while interacting with him during those "tough moments" and shared that "we are also more conscious of our own triggers and are careful to use less words when he is upset. Instead we give him time and space and trust."

9

FINDING MYSELF

Alexis's Treatment from
Ten to Eighteen Years Old

ANNE WESTCOTT

Through this case study we explore how one young woman utilized SMART treatment to address physiological, attentional, behavioral, self-, and relational dysregulation. Furthermore, the case study reveals how the therapist in a private practice setting with SMART tools available combined the SMART Therapist Skills, Regulation Map, and Regulation Tools to address the sequelae of the client's developmental trauma. The case reveals some of the unique challenges in working with Alexis as she navigated the coming of age process, a time of tremendous change physiologically, psychologically, and socially. This is a time when one seeks to define "who I am," "what I like and don't like," "what I want and don't want," and "where I want to go." This is a powerful time of shifting attachments and bonds from family to peers.

For Alexis, adolescence was hampered by early events and their ongoing sequelae. Her self-location, "experiencing herself as located within her body borders and knowing where she is in space, relative to others and to her surrounding environment," was compromised by sexual abuse under the age of three combined with ongoing medical interventions related to early physical trauma. Her ability to sense the world from an integrated first-person perspective—"I am looking out at the world from me"—was shattered by dissociation, traumatic flashbacks, and the many intersectionalities of her life. Her felt sense of agency—"I am the author of my own actions and thoughts"—was precarious. When the longing for attachment and closeness would become unbearable, she would lose all connection to her sense of self as author of her life and take on a traumatogenic attachment schema from her past, one of protecting, rescuing, caretaking, or sexually pleasing the other. These actions, although useful in creating an intense, strong connection, repeatedly put her at risk as she bonded with troubled men who exploited her. The treatment process shared in this chapter narrates one part of Alexis's journey to find herself and locate her own voice in the world.

This treatment for Alexis began as she entered puberty. She presented with swings in mood, disorganized thinking, and impulsivity, some of which was expected during this time period of neurobiological restructuring. For Alexis, we first needed to address Somatic Regulation. Her huge swings in arousal and affective states, characteristic of complex trauma, led to intense conflicts with her adoptive parents as well as highly concerning sexual behavior. Alexis's caregivers were vicariously traumatized by her intense reactivity. Thus, it proved essential to address all of the family members' hyperarousal as part of Alexis's spiraling journey.

In this case, I attempted to Track the arousal states of each family member as best I could within each session. By considering where they each were on the SMART Regulation Map, I had a quick reference guide for when to consider addressing Somatic Regulation and when to continue with talking or Trauma Processing. Choice Points like these arise frequently when working with children and their caregivers impacted by developmental trauma. When Somatic Regulation was attended to first and foremost, a sense of trust and confidence began to grow between myself and all of the family members. In this case, Tending to emotional Safety and prioritizing Somatic Regulation created trust within the therapy and built capacity within the client, the family as individuals, and the family as a system. Over time and with a growing sense of safety, Alexis was able to move more quickly into addressing the current issues, as well as the underlying early traumatic connections. As Alexis became more regulated, she was able to engage in meaningful Trauma Processing with me separately, due to her need for some privacy as a budding teenager. Once Alexis and I synthesized the trauma content, Attachment-Building and co-regulation could occur with the mother. These sessions helped Alexis's parents gain a better understanding of how Alexis's trauma history was impacting her present experience and daily behaviors. With repeated loops through the SMART Spiral, Alexis gained a greater capacity to manage her dysregulation and a broader understanding of her own life story while improving her connection with her family. As adulthood approached, Alexis turned her attention outward, away from her adoptive parents and their support. She initiated contact with her biological father's family, even moving in with them for a short while. She also made connections with wayward drug-using men who "needed her help" and began to use substances herself. This case reflects the realities of long-term impacts of developmental trauma.

Early History

Alexis's early beginnings revealed exposure to chronic maltreatment and compromised caregiving systems. She was born to a young Irish American woman in her early twenties, already mother to a two-year-old girl, Julianna, by the same father, a young South American man. Both parents were drug involved, and their home was often filled with unfamiliar individuals. Around seven months of age, little Alexis was rushed to the emergency room after she had fallen from her father's arms and hit her head on the floor at home. She was treated for a traumatic brain injury. Records indicated that neighbors reported seeing Alexis and her sister wandering in the neighborhood unsupervised. At age one and a half, Alexis was placed in kinship care with her maternal grandmother. Unfortunately, the grandmother's home was also chaotic, and she frequently took in Alexis's mother as well as other young adult relatives when they needed help.

When Alexis was three years old, her world turned upside down in minutes. While at daycare, her sister Julianna disclosed sexual abuse by a family member; both girls were removed immediately. During a therapy session years later, Alexis recalled being in the back of the police car next to her sister with "some lady." It was a big, long seat, and she described that both she and her sister were crying, and she did not know what was happening or where the car was going. She recounted walking into a house with lots of children and a big staircase. She never returned to her home and only had supervised visits with her birth mother after that day. Investigations eventually substantiated child sexual abuse as well as serious neglect, including lack of supervision, protection, health care, and proper nutrition. In addition, the children witnessed drug use and domestic violence.

Alexis and Julianna were placed together in a single foster home for two years, while criminal proceedings convicted the perpetrator, and the parents eventually surrendered their parental rights. A pre-adoptive home was identified, and the sisters were placed with and later adopted by the couple. Her adoptive parents described Alexis as a "little spitfire," both fearless and vocal, to the point of defiance. Moreover, she was the mouthpiece for her older sister, which became a problem as they entered school. Alexis's impulsive oversharing of information left Julianna feeling exposed and violated. Over the years, Alexis has shown extreme sensitivity to the distress of others, responding by caretaking in a manner detrimental to her own well-being, a symptom characteristic of Developmental Trauma Disorder (DTD).

Previous Treatment

Alexis received outpatient play therapy with her sister, as well as family support, in a community clinic from ages four to seven. Treatment with this outpatient provider was a constant in her very tumultuous life. The parents recalled the therapy as supportive to the family, as it provided a stable and consistent place to address many stressors, in addition to the children's symptoms. This treatment approach utilized traditional play therapy toys, manipulatives, dolls, and art, as well as significant parent education for the adoptive parents.

After the adoption at age five, the family's life became more settled and secure. Alexis's parents began to feel the therapy was not addressing her "trauma." They struggled at home with her emotional mood swings, destructive rages, impulsivity, head banging, poor self-care, erratic school performance, lying, and sneaking. Furthermore, her sexually inappropriate behaviors persisted.

Upon intake, caregivers shared their frustration with the previous therapists who they felt were not direct enough and did not get their child to "talk about the trauma." They shared their impression that their daughter could be very "surfacey and chatty" but avoided the real problems and symptoms they saw at home. They wanted a therapist who would be explicit. They saw Alexis's behaviors as negative and destructive to people, property, and herself. At times, they had even taken her bedroom door off, tired of repairing it from the damage she did slamming it.

Treatment

The SMART Spiral in Action: Age Eleven

The challenge of Alexis's disorganized attachment and sexual trauma emerged in the first months of this therapy, when parents discovered, via a cable bill, that Alexis had ordered hundreds of dollars of pornography. Initially, her mother's hurt and worry lay buried under her rage and incredulousness at her daughter's gall to lie when confronted. At this early stage, attending to Alexis's regulation was paramount. Work started with learning to rapidly identify the bodily signs she was heading toward a Traumatic State and with exploring what tools would help her return.

The mother and daughter entered the therapy office tense and virtually radiating sparks of energy. It reminded me of watching two mammals meeting, circling, and watching each other, while carefully keeping distance between them. The mother's jaw was set as if clamping down on her anger—her eyes were alert and her gaze was piercing. Mom's tone was harsh, her arms firmly crossed, and she appeared annoyed. Her daughter receded into the large purple chair across the room. The mother's eyes roved back and forth from her daughter to me, and she launched into reporting her discovery of the secretly purchased pornography. She was clearly angry and frustrated, yet also felt powerless and frightened. Tracking the daughter, I could see her body and face slip from shame and collapse to rage, defiance, and dismissiveness; her arms were crossed, her jaw was set, and her chest was puffed out.

As her mother's report continued with no sign of letting up, Alexis seemed to disappear into her chair, looking away and tuning out. With both members clearly out of their Windows of Tolerance, the mother in a Hyperaroused Traumatic State and Alexis in a Hypoaroused Traumatic State, I took the Lead. Tending to Safety, I asked Mom to step out of the room so I could meet alone with her daughter.

Attachment rupture

Alexis frequently sought the purple chair in early sessions. It is a big chair with high arms in the corner of the office. The family had christened it "The Throne," and curiously, the parents never sat there. In SMART, we focus on inputs that support increased Somatic Regulation. Safe Spaces provide embodied regulation, frequently with more powerful results than a metaphoric or visualized Safe Space exercise. Like many adolescents in SMART, she did not build a Safe Space as overtly as the younger children we see. Instead, like many teens, she created a Safe Space utilizing the oversized chair in my outpatient office, which proved to be a core Regulation Tool for Alexis over time when she was in a Traumatic State.

Trauma Processing

Once her mother left the room, I offered a weighted blanket or cozy throw, wondering if this Tactile Input might further support regulation. Alexis spurned the offer; however, she did pull a pillow from nearby, placing it right in her lap, as if generating more protection and coverage. I noted to myself her attempt to regulate herself, in part by not taking co-regulation offered by me. She made a classic teenage eye roll toward the door where her mother had just left, and let out an annoyed sigh.

Seeking relational and emotional safety in a Safe Space

I Tracked this increasing sign of engagement and affect, and it appeared she might be returning to her Integrated State with the exit of her mother. With this Choice Point in mind, I chose to ask in a matter-of-fact tone about her curiosity to watch TV shows with naked bodies and people having sex. As she curled up in her big purple throne, a rich conversation unfolded about how she wanted to know what had happened to her. She knew she was sexually abused as a little girl but had no memories. She shared how she wanted to see what sex was and try to figure things out. She felt glued to the images and was unable to stop herself from watching. She shared how some of it was scary, and what the adults did looked weird. I verbally labeled her curiosity, and normalized her healthy drive to make sense of being sexually molested as a two-year-old. She told me in an animated way about her various thoughts, fantasies, anger, and fear. She also shared her frustration at not having any "memories" and not "knowing" what had happened to her. This blank space clearly left her somehow incomplete, unfinished, and struggling to make sense of her history. I told her I thought it best if she had an adult help her get the information she wanted, instead of watching movies with actors having staged sex. I said I would be willing to help her get all the information she wanted.

Attachment-Building

With Alexis's agreement, we invited her mother back in. Tracking the mother in the hall, I could see her posture had softened some and her voice was less angry. Alexis remained in the purple chair, and her mother sat on the couch. Alexis decided I would take the lead to explain her actions as we had made sense of them. I explained to her mom how Alexis was very curious and was trying to figure out what happened to her when she was sexually abused as a baby. I told her mother that Alexis found it frustrating not to have any memories and having to rely on what others tell her. Alexis wanted to see what sex is, as if that would make memories come back. I said it is really normal that she wanted to make sense of her past. This was a form of Verbal Scaffolding for Alexis and her mother that could provide for them a shared understanding. Alexis piped up, tearfully blurting out in distress that she could not stop watching once she started.

The attachment rupture, a result of her bald-faced denial to Mom and her sneakiness, was now safe to address, because Mom was back in the Integrated State and Alexis was hovering in the Fluid Zone. I shifted gears to address the Attachment-Building thread. I verbally reflected to both that I could see her mom loves and worries about her. I wondered out loud if it worried Mom to find out Alexis had watched this porn all alone with no adult to help. Alexis became more tearful, and her mother visibly softened. I made a Choice to Lead by encouraging Alexis to move over to the couch next to her mom. Her mother reached toward Alexis with open arms inviting her in. Her mother held her, and Alexis cried. As Alexis took in her mother's soothing, the tension and constriction in her body gave way, and her feelings welled up and poured out. Her mother held her closely, talking in soothing tones with reassurance and understanding as the powerful emotions peaked.

Sitting with Alexis and her mother in this moment brought up memories in me of holding my own small daughter as tears arose inside and her body would heave with sobs. Tracking In, my internal experience provided an embodied understanding of the intensity of this moment for Alexis and her mother. There are few words that capture such raw primal emotion. Tracking In led me to provide steady verbal reassurance, using my tone and prosody as much as my words to convey a sense that this moment was just as it should be. I encouraged the mother to stay right with her daughter: "This is just what Alexis needs right now from you, just being here with her." I explained that emotions rise, peak, and quiet at their own pace. I encouraged the mother to continue reassuring her daughter with her words, but more importantly with her tone and her soothing gestures. By Tracking In, I also became aware of my profound respect for this mother, her daughter, and their courage to get close and to be vulnerable with each other in this moment. I was fully aware that more injuries, meltdowns, and hurts would come, making their courage and the power of their drive to attach deeply touching.

Bearing embodied witness to children's intense sorrow and emotional pain can trigger many of us out of our Window of Tolerance and into states of emotional flooding, dissociation, numbing, and problem-solving. This hijacking renders caregivers less able to be attuned in a manner Francis Weller describes as "a particular kind of paying attention, wedded with affection, offered by someone we love and trust." He goes on to say, "This deep attention is what enables us [children] to make painful experiences tolerable" (Weller 2017, 6). SMART incorporates the concept of Sensory Satiation, the theory that our nervous systems have innate intelligence and will spontaneously move on when allowed to obtain the input as long as desired. This concept helped guide me to Follow Alexis's emotional pace. Encouraging Alexis and her mother to take the time for this natural process to unfold, it was also important to reassure her mother that this was a healthy healing process given the intense triggering it can bring on for caregivers.

Alexis mumbled apologies as she cried, the shame and remorse emerging as she became more regulated from the increased security conveyed in the closeness, tactile pressure, and warmth from her mother, combined with the expression of intense feeling. More mutual apologies followed, as the mother continued to hold her daughter closely and stroke her hair, and as the attachment repair unfolded. Looking up at her mother with a tear-streaked face and sniffly nose, Alexis shared how hard it is "to know and yet not to know what happened to me." With hopes of promoting Attachment-Building, I shared how Alexis, now, has a mother who can help her with such hard things. When she was two, there were no adults to help; now her mother is here to protect and love her. Alexis then shared how tired she was as she snuggled up next to her mom and looked at me. This Verbal Scaffolding helped Alexis stay with her feelings and expand the moment.

Co-regulation and Attachment-Building through Tactile Input with a weighted blanket and touch from the caregiver

She yawned and asked if it was time to go home. This parasympathetic calming revealed the satiation in her body. Following her Lead, we wrapped up the session. Her mother shared later that Alexis slept soundly on the car ride home and had a calm evening.

As we consider the SMART Spiral, we can see how the child and her mother each began the session in Traumatic States and estranged from each other. By attending to Somatic Regulation first, Trauma Processing spontaneously emerged, followed by the opportunity for Attachment-Building and repair. This Spiral was observable over and over again in Alexis's treatment, as well as in that of many other children in SMART. However, there is no single correct order for the work to unfold in a session or across treatment. Each child and each relationship weaves its own unique pattern in the spiraling process.

Bits and Pieces of Alexis's Story: Age Twelve

About two years into treatment, Alexis was meeting individually with me, and her sister, Julianna, joined us. Alexis was upset and distressed, having witnessed an argument between her older sister and their mother over a stolen cell phone. Alexis recalled feeling frozen and stuck in the middle as she watched them yelling at each other. By this point in therapy, Alexis and I had built a strong therapeutic relationship, and she often was able to bring up current distressing events. Together we explored the fight at home, and Alexis described feeling anxious and upset. She knew and trusted her adoptive parents, but she felt panicked and had this voice telling her she had to protect her sister from their mom.

Assessing that Alexis was in the High Intensity Fluid Zone and that her reactivity to Julianna was out of proportion to the current situation, I Chose to head toward their traumatic attachment. I Led by sharing a piece of Alexis's story: "I know they called you a 'little spitfire' and that you often spoke for your big sister when you first came into care." A poignant early memory of neglect emerged. She recalled being very little and hungry. She remembered sitting at the kitchen table next to Julianna. There were no adults around, and her sister was crying quietly from hunger yet too scared to go to the refrigerator for food. In a curious tone, I asked where the adults were. This Verbal Scaffolding supported Alexis and Julianna to knit their own connections in order to create a coherent story. They both reflected and then shared that it was early morning, and the adults were likely "asleep" in the living room, as they often were. Again, in a curious and puzzled tone, I reflected that it was odd they were all asleep while she and her sister were awake. The girls spontaneously guessed that the adults must have been passed out from doing drugs the night before.

Alexis went on to share how she dragged a chair over to the refrigerator, climbed up, got a milk carton down, and poured a glass for both of them. Scaffolding the story one more step, I pointed out that her sister was bigger, and I thought it curious that she, not the bigger sister, was getting the milk. She shared that Julianna was too scared they would get upset with her. "Plus," she said, "I was such a tiny, spunky, cute thing, I did not get in as much trouble as Julianna. Everyone thought my sassiness was hysterical." Then she added, "I don't care what people do to me. I am going to take care of those I love." This fierce loyalty and spunk with seemingly no concern for the risks her actions may pose to herself were evident at two and a half and continued over her childhood and into adulthood to place her in unsafe situations where she is harmed.

The Emptiness Left Over: Age Thirteen
Regulation

After the Thanksgiving holiday, when Alexis was in seventh grade, her mother called prior to session and shared that Alexis was thinking a lot about her birth mother and seemed more down and apathetic. She was not showering, and her hygiene was poor. Her mother hoped maybe I could get her daughter to talk about whatever was coming up for her. In session, Alexis did appear more subdued, depressed, lethargic, and hypoaroused. While she was in the Low Intensity Fluid Zone, I tried some connecting conversation and a new tool. As we chatted about school and the holiday weekend, I invited her to sit on the physioball to get some gentle Proprioceptive and Vestibular Input.

She acquiesced, trying it limply. She sat and rolled around a bit on her sit bones, keeping herself upright. Within a minute, she left the ball for her big purple throne. She curled in, reminding me of a cat as she tucked her feet up under her. Then she reached for her big pillow, hugging it in her lap. I had

Introduced physioball for gentle Vestibular Input

Chosen to Lead by offering a new experience, the physioball, to see if it would provide another Regulation Tool for her; however, I resumed Following Alexis's lead when she returned to using her Safe Space. This does not mean the Choice to Lead was "wrong," but rather it provided me with more information about what Alexis was looking for in her current state.

I shared what her mom had told me: "It had been a tough few days at school, and you seemed unhappy." She agreed, and I asked when she began to notice this down feeling. She described spacing out in class, not being able to concentrate, and worrying about her birth mother. I Tracked her as she became visibly sad and tearful, and her body became more collapsed again, an indicator of hypoarousal. I was curious what class she was in when she noticed her thoughts going to her birth mom. She began to talk about her health class, where they were doing a substance abuse education unit. She said it was strange, because the teacher was showing the students drug paraphernalia, and she recognized the objects. She thought that was weird. The other kids did not seem to know what the objects were. She figured it was because her birth parents used drugs in the house when she was little. She recalled feeling as if she was going to cry and asking the teacher if she could go to the bathroom. She reported feeling out of it for the rest of the day.

Trauma Processing

Alexis appeared tearful, sad, and vulnerable, curled up in the big chair. She began to lament her birth mom, sharing the memory of when she last saw her at a visit when she was little. Her thoughts and questions poured out to me. She kept wondering and worrying about her birth mom, not her dad much, just her mom. She knew her mother had been drug involved but didn't know if she still was. She wondered what it would be like to see her again; she wondered a lot about her but was not sure she wanted to be in contact. In Tracking Alexis, her language was organized and coherent, she was engaged and making intermittent eye contact, and her emotions matched the content of her words. In this session, Alexis was able very quickly to use her therapy with me to address what had distressed her that day. She and I knew what was regulating for her, and once calmer, she could raise all the thoughts and feelings that lay underneath.

Coming of Age with Embodied Trauma: Age Seventeen

Alexis came into a session venting about her current boyfriend and debating with herself about whether to break up or not. I asked what she liked and did not like about him as she considered what to do. Having sex came up as one thing they did a lot. I was curious how that was for her. She said it was really good, and then her voice trailed off as she mumbled, "most of the time." Tracking this profound shift in her tone, her look away, and the flush of affect that crossed her face, I used Verbal Scaffolding, reflecting her words back to her, and matching her tone: "Most of the time, huh?" She shared that sometimes she "freaks out" and "it is weird"; she can't help it and it is embarrassing. She was self-conscious as she shared this, looking up and away, but also appeared confused by it. Tracking both her confusion and her embarrassment, I was able to sympathize with the embarrassment; however, I quickly Followed by amplifying her puzzlement: "Sounds confusing. And I bet that is really awkward and embarrassing when it happens with your boyfriend." She agreed. We went on to gently explore the body sensations, emotions, and any other sensory elements she noticed at these times when her body became "freaky" during sex.

She gave a classic description of hyperarousal. Her breath would get short, she would shake and tremble, her heart would race, and she would feel highly keyed up. I explained how our bodies often hold memories of early experiences as sensations, feelings, and muscle tension. She began to talk about her fear and panic that would come with the upset. It did not make sense, because she knew her boyfriend would respect her and stop when this happened. As she started to make sense of her body's experience, it no longer felt so confusing, weird, and embarrassing. She began to make connections between the early sexual abuse and how sex now seemed to trigger her body at times.

Speaking Up, Speaking Out: Age Eighteen

Alexis entered the session agitated, amped up, and emotional. She headed to the suspension hammock, seeking the Safe Space and containment. To explain, this session took place several years into SMART development. By then I had moved to a larger office with soundproofing to fully incorporate the Regulation Tools into my private practice. The purple throne had been replaced by an aerial silk swing. The suspension silk swing allows the client to feel enveloped, held, and protected physically while simultaneously providing gentle Vestibular Input and tactile holding. As Alexis's feet dangled and she swayed gently from side to side, she mentioned she'd had "a bad night last night." I waited, just reflecting in tone her words: "A bad night, huh?" She haltingly began to unpack the afternoon and evening she spent with a new guy she was seeing. She conveyed her anger; however, the deeper emotions did not emerge until she unloaded about their sex that night. He did not listen when she said to stop, and he seemed not to care or attend to her at all. "He should have seen that I was upset and crying," she said. She was distraught, incredulous, confused, and angry as she talked. She described how her body turned off, and she just went along when he did not respect her request to stop. I commented on her telling him to stop and said it seemed as if she knew from how she felt that she did not want sex at that moment, and she spoke up for herself.

She began to describe how intoxicated he was and connected his substance use to how "out of it" he was. I Tracked how her voice became stronger and filled with anger. Her posture lengthened, and she put her feet on the floor, leaning forward and becoming more agitated and increasingly angry. She looked stronger

Swing made of aerial silk for Vestibular and Proprioceptive Input, tactile deep touch pressure, body boundary, emotional and relational safety via containment, and visual barrier

and appeared older than she had moments before. I pointed out how she could speak up now to say stop. I contrasted that to when she was two years old and unable to have a voice.

She became more animated and shared how now she is an adult and can speak up for herself. When she was a small child, there was no one to help and no one to tell. She began to draw her own connections, seeing how her body went numb when her boyfriend did not listen to her words. Again, I offered that this is often the way small children's bodies respond to sexual abuse when there is no way to get away. My description of the normal human motionless defenses as strengths that live in our bodies proved extremely helpful to Alexis (Westcott and Hu 2017). Clearly, this session built upon the many years of earlier SMART work in which she developed her capacity to identify and describe her own bodily experiences and label her emotions.

Alexis decided to confront her boyfriend about his behavior. As we role played the conversation in the office, she realized she was susceptible to collapsing, and a voice inside would tell her, "It's okay. He was drunk; he didn't mean it." As she spoke, she raised her hands to her temples, creating blinders on either side. I was reminded of young children who think if they can't see it, it is not there. She shared how her mind comes up with excuses for him: "It's like it snows me into forgetting." We practiced the posture of an erect and elongated spine, and the strength of voice, that went along with her decision to confront him, helping her feel and stay in touch with her anger at his actions. In the end, she decided to take a friend with her and have the friend wait outside while she talked to her boyfriend.

At the next session, Alexis shared how well their conversation went. She was strong and straight with him. She told him what had happened and that he had nodded off after intercourse, leading her to realize he was likely "using" that day. When I asked if she went with anyone, she said no, but she had had her friend in her ear. This young client displayed her characteristic ingenuity. She called her friend before the confrontation began. By placing one earbud in, she entered her boyfriend's house with a friend in her ear and the support she needed to stand tall. Alexis's ability to creatively use co-regulation in this situation to help her feel stronger was markedly different from when she chose to reject my offer of co-regulation earlier in our treatment and rely solely on herself. Alexis's pattern of seeking romantic connections with unsavory characters continues to worry all of us who care about her and remains her biggest challenge. However, her reaching out to a girlfriend for active support reflected her growing capacity to make meaningful attachments as a result of the work with her mother, which bodes well for more progress.

Reflections

Talk was a key component of SMART for Alexis. Like many adolescents, she wanted to talk about her world, her friends, boyfriends, frustrations, and successes and vent her annoyance with school, her parents, and her sibling. This self-reflection and sorting through are core to a teen's developing sense of self. However, Alexis's Regulation Tools were always available. I intentionally employed Tending to Safety, Tracking In and Tracking Out, Embodied Attuning, Following, Leading, and Verbal Scaffolding in order to help Alexis attend to her somatic and inner body experiences and build language to describe her sensations. Over time, she built the capacity to identify and describe her bodily and emotional experiences. This kind of reflective process was key to helping her recognize indicators of distress and arousal. She also became conscious of what kinds of things shifted her distress and arousal. Only then could she proactively use the tools she had developed to self-regulate. Slowly, co-regulation came to be more available, as seen in her creative use of the earbud in her ear, connecting her to a friend while confronting a boyfriend.

Multiple Windows of Tolerance

In the case of Alexis and her parents, two worrisome trauma themes overwhelmed family members' ability to regulate, frequently leaving them hyperaroused, unable to think effectively, and fighting. The first theme was Alexis's inability to use her adoptive parents for co-regulation when distressed, due to her early neglect and lack of protection by adults. She would lash out with indiscriminate fight responses toward her parents, leaving them startled. They felt helpless when they could not move toward her in her distress. Her high state of vigilance left her on edge. She was reactive to every parental misstep, judgmental tone, askance look, or seeming inconsistency. Alexis's intense and seemingly irrational behaviors could overwhelm her parents. All caregivers, when chronically faced with such intense intimate relationships, can become dysregulated. Frequently, in such challenging moments, we see parents reacting with intense emotion and frustration. Caregivers' responses can add to their child's distress, leading to chronic escalation. This troubling loop reinforced Alexis's distrust of her caregivers and could keep her from seeking their support when she badly needed it.

The second trauma theme was Alexis's repetitive attempts to master her preverbal sexual trauma. Alexis's sexual behaviors fueled her parents' deepest fear-filled thoughts that their daughter was permanently damaged by the early abuse and would follow in her birth mother's footsteps. This fear, combined with Alexis's explosiveness, stoked the parents' own hypervigilance around their daughter's sexuality. The mother and daughter would ignite in session when this topic arose, just as they would at home.

Combined, these two patterns interfered with Alexis's ability to take in the support, soothing, and protection she needed when traumatic material emerged in session. Focusing on Somatic Regulation with both parents and daughter became the most effective way to interrupt this escalation cycle. Tending to each member's emotional safety and to each member's Somatic Regulation remained the underlying essential skill throughout the treatment.

Sense of an Embodied Self

Alexis's case reveals the discontinuous sense of being embodied discussed in chapter 2. The fragmentation and state-shifting evident in her treatment manifested in her daily life as well, exposing her to greater risk of traumatization. Many factors contribute to this subjective sense of a fragmented self, including domestic violence exposure and possible substance exposure in utero, early neglect, and head trauma, followed by sexual abuse and sudden disruptions in her attachments. Her time in therapy revealed her deep drive to locate and define herself in her body, her body in space, and her story across time. She seemed to intuit how essential it was to create a sense of continuity in her life story in order to engage fully in the world—a world where she would be reminded of her traumatic past in everyday adolescent and young adult activities.

The SMART framework focusing on core regulation and the Regulation Tools helped her to tolerate much more time in the Fluid Zone working to make sense of, sort through, and process trauma memories, so many of which were held in her somatosensory memory. This history, sadly, is all too common for children with developmental trauma, and challenges us as therapists to expand how we identify and process traumatic material.

SMART with Adolescents

SMART with a seventeen-year-old looks different from SMART with a seven-year-old. At seventeen, Alexis's bottom-up inputs were much more subtle and socially conforming. I continued to use the SMART Regulation Map even as the therapy looked more like classic talk therapy. During our conversations, I would Track Out for spontaneous use of Regulation Tools, as well as offer tools when it appeared she was in one of the Fluid Zones at the edge of her Window of Tolerance. For Alexis, these tools steadily included Safe Space and deep and moderate touch pressure from the pillows on her lap and later the aerial hammock for similar input. As her sense of self and agency grew, she was able to use grounding and "standing tall and strong."

SMART treatment aims to expand the child's ability to take in co-regulation from a supportive other, in Alexis's case, first the therapist and eventually her adoptive parents. For Alexis, as is true with most complexly traumatized children, this process was deeply disrupted. Over the course of treatment, Alexis's need for deep touch pressure, Safe Space, holding, and snuggling remained constant. In early adolescence, she often sought these inputs from her mother in the therapy room and at home at times of emotional distress.

As Alexis matured, these touch moments with parents tailed off and she began to seek them via contact with boys, eventually in sexual relationships. Her attractions to and connection-seeking with men revealed her deep need for connection combined with her struggle to recognize healthy and unhealthy relationships. Her hunger to be wanted and feel special made her especially susceptible to manipulation and exploitation. Her sexual trauma, regulation needs, and attachment wounding permeated the developmentally normal exploration of bonding and sexuality.

Closing

I would like to say that from our therapy Alexis has resolved her trauma and is able to form long-term secure attachments. I would like to say she no longer needs outpatient therapy and is doing well in her life. She *is* doing well in her life, meeting amazing challenges; yet, she still struggles with intimate relationships and regulation, and she still uses the safety of therapy to help her handle new challenges. She has long-term friendships with people who care deeply about her, she graduated high school, and she attempted residential college three hours from home.

Developmental trauma of this magnitude frequently has lifelong and multigenerational impacts. As a young adult, Alexis continues to see me, and she ebbs and flows in her investment in the therapy, coming more when facing challenges like transitioning to college or emergency neurosurgery due to her childhood head trauma. In the delicate process of navigating therapy with Alexis, the family came to see the SMART room and the therapeutic relationship as an expansion of Safe Space. As she has grown, the therapy shifted to individual sessions with occasional parental involvement. However, she and her parents continue to ask to meet with me when they need to address charged subjects. Steadily Tending to Safety turned therapy into a Safe Space. A constant across her journey when she was distressed, Alexis sought her Safe Space, whether it was the aerial hammock, a corner of the couch with her protective pillow in place, or therapy itself.

10

APPLICATIONS OF SMART

SMART was developed as a mental health therapy in the context of a specialty outpatient clinic for trauma treatment. However, almost immediately, therapists in other settings for children and teens with complex trauma were attracted to the model. Among the early adopters were residential treatment centers, community-based in-home teams, clinics for young children, and therapeutic schools for older children. Private practitioners have also adapted offices for use of SMART tools. In each case, the opportunity to view many video recordings and reflect on implementation was critical to adaptation and refinement of the application in the setting.

Our first opportunity to collaborate on applying SMART occurred within residential treatment centers, where we learned through trial and error the importance of clinician-driven SMART treatment plans created in collaboration with the youth; ongoing collaboration between clinical and milieu staff to support implementation; and establishing guidelines for the use of the SMART treatment space. Next, we collaborated with community-based in-home teams, again learning through shared experiences how the SMART model works in the complexity of the in-home setting. This mutual learning process also became the template for work in an eating disorder treatment center, a therapeutic school for the deaf, and treatment centers for developmentally disabled clients, each of which has served many children and teens with histories of adverse childhood experiences.

In addition to applying SMART across a number of treatment settings, we have also worked with providers and families from a variety of cultural and ethnic backgrounds. Adaptation of any model to address different cultural needs and presentations is fundamental to quality and ethical mental health treatment. Thus, we begin our chapter on applications with a review of our experience working with families and providers from a variety of different backgrounds and living circumstances. Next, we will examine applications for residential and community-based in-home treatment teams that emerged from our collaboration with program directors and clinical staff. Then we will focus on the natural compatibility of SMART in settings for young children. Finally, we will end with considerations for integrating SMART into private practice settings.

Application of SMART in Diverse Cultures

One must consider the cultural contexts of the community in which SMART is being utilized. Assessment and treatment should take into account "the contextual embeddedness of the child in his social environment" (Keller 2014, 2) and avoid holding a narrow dyadic attachment perspective reflective of prevailing "Western" attachment theory. Keller goes on to say, "cultural contexts differ widely in their models of autonomy and relatedness, socialization goals, and caregiving strategies" (Keller 2014, 12). Thus, attachment and attachment processes will present with variation in the SMART room. The authors encourage curiosity about and openness to a multitude of "healthy" attachment styles. For example, in America, due to systemic racism, the permissive style of white privilege parenting often contrasts sharply in the SMART room with that of African American parenting, where stern limits may be used to keep an adolescent son out of harm's way (Menakem 2017). In other cases, the decision of which "parent" to invite into the room may mean welcoming an older sibling, several family members, a grandparent, or even a neighbor helping as a surrogate parent. SMART therapists, like all therapists, are vulnerable to holding implicit expectations about what is healthy; however, Video Reflection with clinical teams of diverse staff members creates a rich resource to counteract implicit bias and to expand knowledge and inclusivity of difference.

In the early days of SMART, we were invited to train clinicians from diverse cultures, both within the United States and abroad. People found us through the National Child Traumatic Stress Network (NCTSN) (www.nctsn.org), internet searches, and connections with colleagues. Invitations have taken us to places we have never been, such as Hong Kong, Montana, and rural Tennessee, as well as cities and towns in our own backyards. Looking back, we see that our learning about SMART in different cultures has occurred on a case-by-case, rather than systematic, basis. We have been surprised by SMART's adaptability and seeming universality. The key to each new invitation is to approach the agency, the culture, and the people with respect, curiosity, and openness to collaborating and developing new ways of applying SMART.

In 2011, we were invited to train and consult at a therapeutic school in Elkton, Maryland, near the Chesapeake Bay. The second invitation came from Pittsburg, Kansas, a city with a proud coal mining and immigrant history, where the director of children's services of an early childhood program was looking for a treatment consistent with Bruce Perry's (2009) work. We welcomed these opportunities to examine SMART's generalizability to communities different from our Northeastern home. Thus began the first explorations of how SMART would fit in different contexts.

The word "culture" came to encompass many dimensions for us. As we traveled to train and consult around the country, our awareness grew of the vast differences in culture within the borders of the United States, based on socioeconomic status, historical context of the communities, rural versus urban settings, as well as self-identification of race, ethnicity, religious beliefs, sexual orientation, and disability. These visits around the country also gave us the opportunity to learn how SMART was received by therapists of different professional and cultural backgrounds, working in diverse treatment settings, with different age ranges and populations.

Families and children from across the globe have walked into SMART rooms, some with foster or adoptive parents, and some with biological family members. The cultural experiences of each person always impact the work of therapy. We have observed differences in the use of touch, in tolerance for our child-centered focus, and in comfort with "embodied play" that involves adults and children with intense action, affect, and language. We have consulted for therapists working with families from diverse Latino backgrounds, including Puerto Rico, Central America, and South America; from southeast Asian countries impacted by trauma such as Cambodia and Laos; with children born in Ethiopia, the Congo, Romania, Russia, and Ukraine; and with people of African American heritage, including the many Caribbean cultures.

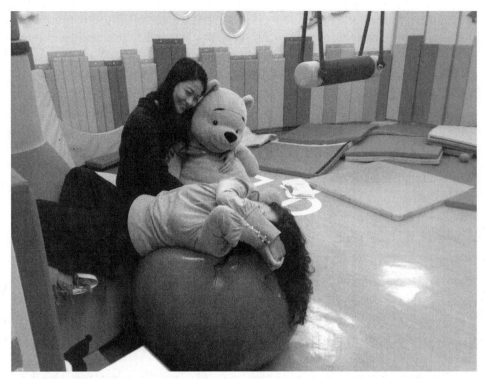

A Hong Kong SMART room

We have navigated this journey by remaining open and curious about what we could learn from our clients and the communities we serve, and about how our child-centered, body-based, sensory motor, playful therapeutic approach fits. With populations with which we had little experience—for example, youth with eating disorders or hearing impairment—we entered by saying we would collaborate with the expert professionals to figure out how SMART would work for them. For adolescent girls with an eating disorder, "befriending the body" had new meaning. For the hearing impaired, their vigorous use of Vestibular Inputs has awakened their therapists' and our interest in the special nature of this sensory seeking. For the developmentally disabled, the fact that SMART does not depend on language but prioritizes Somatic Regulation fits right in with their needs. This exploratory attitude has been at the core of our approach to different cultures.

During these years, the Trauma Center hosted numerous groups of Japanese professionals interested in approaches to treatment of trauma. Consistent among the groups of Japanese professionals who visited was a sense of playfulness, curiosity, and creativity in exploring Somatic Regulation through the use of the equipment in the SMART room. The nonverbal language and playfulness of SMART allowed us to communicate across the language barrier without words. We also learned that a child-centered approach is important in the raising of young children in Japan and may inform their professional openness to SMART. A colleague who is Japanese told us, "We Japanese are raised to read body language as a clue to feelings, not to speak about them."

An experienced art therapist from Hong Kong who wanted to start the first child trauma treatment service in her city came to an introductory SMART workshop. After returning home and consulting with her colleagues, she invited us to provide a SMART training to her team and other therapists from diverse settings in Hong Kong. She pointed out that they did not yet have any epidemiological information on the prevalence of child trauma. It was only in 2015, when we were invited again to train in Hong Kong, that a survey of PTSD in the adult population had recently been completed (Wu et al. 2019). Through a year of SMART consultation over the internet, we learned that children in Hong Kong, coming from culturally diverse Chinese backgrounds, responded to SMART's approach in similar ways as had the American children we had seen in video recordings. Although child-raising practices differed, the therapist-trainees found the Therapist Skills easy to learn and use—and felt they were consistent with their prior therapy style and training.

As we continue to train and teach, we anticipate that we will find cultures and peoples for whom SMART is not a good fit. We have learned that it has not been a good fit for certain caregivers; and it is likely that some cultures, perhaps those with good communally based approaches that know how to use indigenous rituals to heal trauma, may not need what we have to offer. Perhaps we will learn from them, just as we have learned from the many children, families, and therapists who have allowed us to view their work, and thus to develop the SMART model as we know it today. The future holds promise of continued learning and evolution through respectful collaboration.

Application of SMART in Residential Treatment

Upon learning about SMART as an outpatient treatment approach, providers in residential treatment settings expressed interest in bringing the SMART model to their programs. Local residential treatment programs in Massachusetts had been seeking ways to minimize the use of restraint and seclusion for youth in their care (Fleischner, Rucker, and Stefan 2007; see also a summary

table of seclusion and restraint policies by state/territory at https://tinyurl.com
/qlcsnfp, US Department of Education 2010). Residential treatment providers
in particular identified a strong need to develop new regulation tools that did
not rely on language to support youth who often engaged in aggressive, externalizing behaviors and required physical restraint (Champagne and Stromberg
2004). Thus, began the process of learning how to apply the SMART therapy
model to meet the needs of highly trauma-impacted youth residing in residential treatment settings.

We began this collaborative journey at Cohannet Academy, a Justice
Resource Institute (JRI) facility in southeastern Massachusetts. One of the
first issues occurred when milieu staff brought residents into the SMART
room, but did not have training in SMART, or understanding that Somatic
Regulation can lead to Trauma Processing. Some of the teens became more
dysregulated when in the SMART room with milieu staff, and later refused
to return for treatment. We also began working with Glenhaven Academy,
another JRI program, where the room designated for SMART was a large
multipurpose room that was located near the classrooms. In this situation,
the SMART model became diluted because it wasn't intentionally separated
from the educational setting or from general use. Learning from the experiences above, our next two residential schools—Walden School and Pelham
Academy—each held separate SMART trainings for their residential staff,
and created smaller but separate SMART rooms that were designated for
clinical use only. From there, we began training at residential programs across
the country, including ones with other specialties, such as developmental
disabilities.

Each of these programs was crucial to helping us understand how to integrate SMART into residential settings. Our first adaptation was to develop a
training specifically for milieu staff that focused on Somatic Regulation Tools
and acknowledged the likelihood of Trauma Processing as teens became more
regulated with suggestions on how to redirect that material back to the therapy.
One of the strengths each of these organizations had in common was that
someone in the program became a SMART champion, and took on the role of
helping support SMART across programming. In some programs it was a clinician, and in others an administrator, and we found that identifying individuals
to fulfill this role in each program was an essential component of success. Many
residential programs have a problem with staff turnover at all levels. However,
with a series of champions, SMART became woven into the culture of the
agency, so that it did not feel like starting over with a new round of turnover.

Adolescent residential treatment SMART room

Several key issues specific to residential treatment emerged as we implemented SMART in various residential treatment programs. Because Somatic Regulation often leads to Trauma Processing, SMART is not a contained, independent form of treatment. Thus, in a residential program it is important to be thoughtful about how SMART treatment is understood by the youth, the milieu staff, the administration, and the clinical team. First of all, communication among the youth, the clinician, the milieu and educational staff, and the administration proved to be critical, particularly in generalizing the tools from session. Second, Attachment-Building in a residential program is broader than it is in outpatient treatment in that we are oftentimes facilitating connection to the staff as much as to the family. Third, we emphasize the importance of preserving the SMART room as a separate treatment space, so that it does not become diluted or confusing for the residents. Lastly, we found it useful to include administration, educational and milieu staff, in addition to clinical staff, in the consultation and Video Reflection process to facilitate communication and conceptualization of the youth's needs across all aspects of their day.

Communication and Collaboration to Support Somatic Regulation

The most effective therapeutic process for translating Regulation Tools from the SMART room to the milieu and educational settings proved to be maintaining an active feedback loop between the youth, the therapist, and residential staff. This process is held and driven by the therapist, and first takes place in the SMART room with the therapist and resident working together to identify what tools help the youth. Next, therapists and residential staff work in tandem to make these tools available on the milieu and in class, thus implementing regulation plans across settings. Finally, staff and the youth practice utilizing identified tools and share their observations with the therapist.

Collaboration between the Youth and the Therapist

SMART treatment within residential care begins as a collaborative process between the youth and the therapist, and is grounded in the same therapeutic principles as SMART outpatient treatment. When SMART is applied in the residential treatment setting, emphasis is placed on increasing felt safety, building regulatory capacities, and supporting healthy relationships. As a resident learns what Regulation Tools in the SMART room are calming or energizing, the therapist and youth work together to create an individualized regulation plan to be used on the milieu and at school. The goal of this plan is to support the youth to utilize these tools as needed during the other twenty-three hours of their day.

The regulation plan helps staff meet the needs of individual residents by identifying specific tools and equipment that support regulation throughout the day and during moments of crisis. Rather than taking a quick, one-size-fits-all approach, the therapist collaborates with youth to design a specific "regulation prescription." For example, one regulation plan prescribed that staff offer Proprioceptive Input to a thirteen-year-old resident who enjoyed playing vigorous ball tossing games in SMART therapy, and showed he was "about to lose it" when he clenched his fists and paced. While developing the plan with his therapist, the teen suggested specific equipment he could use at different times of the day, including pulling a resistance band in class, tossing a weighted ball on the unit, or shooting hoops at the gym. By including youth in this process, they often are more willing to use the tools in the plan when dysregulated on the milieu.

Collaboration between Milieu Staff and the Therapist

When SMART was implemented within residential treatment programs, the powerful role that milieu and educational staff serve in supporting the youth to engage in Regulation Tools was abundantly clear. Communication between team members worked best when clinicians could demonstrate tools and explain the resident's regulation plan to staff working with a particular youth. Residential teams also benefited immensely when milieu and educational team members joined clinicians in Video Reflection. During this process, therapists help staff learn to recognize when state shifts occur for a particular resident, and what specific tool they can offer to provide regulation. Staff began to see how talking and problem-solving when residents were dysregulated often increased activation. With more effective ways to help residents when dysregulated, staff could replace talking and problem-solving with Regulation Tools.

In one SMART consultation, a milieu staff member described how a resident would hide behind his bed every day during quiet time, despite repeated redirection and limit-setting. When considering the hiding behavior from a SMART regulation perspective, staff and therapists wondered whether the resident was seeking a Safe Space to regulate distress felt at quiet time. With this perspective, the team's interventions shifted from behavioral limit-setting to focusing on regulation. Specifically, they discussed ways to work with the youth to access identified Safe Spaces within the program that could enhance felt safety.

Milieu staff generally spend the most time with residents in leisure or recreational activities. Exploring how youth seek sensory inputs while engaged in daily life can also provide useful information to the treatment team about preferred and helpful inputs. As staff began to understand the role of inputs, they were able to identify and share with clinicians how a particular resident seemed more alert when listening to music or tapping his pencil while working on his homework. This same resident learned that dribbling a basketball helped calm his agitation when talking about difficult topics, something he did frequently with milieu staff support. By collaborating with milieu staff, the SMART therapist was able to learn more about the resident, and chose to further explore Rhythmicity as a potential Regulation Tool the next time he was in the SMART room for therapy.

Generalizing Regulation Tools

Early in our development of SMART applications to residential treatment, we discovered that the equipment quickly migrated to the bedrooms of the youth. As youth learned that, for example, a weighted blanket felt good and was calming, they would want to use it outside of their therapy session. Clinicians found it became important to make sure the equipment in the SMART room remained consistent so that residents could access their favorite tools during therapy sessions. To address these needs, many program directors have included Regulation Tools as part of their program budget when youth benefit from using a particular piece of equipment to regulate. Clinicians and staff also discover creative ways to support youth to generalize what they are learning in SMART therapy to other parts of the day. Staff have been found swinging on a park swing next to a student who liked Vestibular Input, or jumping rope with a resident who frequently used a trampoline in session. Additionally, accessing community resources such as a local trampoline park or YMCA can also support youth regulation throughout the day.

During this ongoing collaboration, we decided to evaluate the impact of SMART within the residential treatment population. A matched-control quasi-experimental pilot study was completed that demonstrated significant reductions in internalizing symptoms—in particular, somatic complaints and anxiety/depression—and a trend approaching significance of reductions in overarousal (Warner, Spinazzola et al. 2014), all areas targeted by SMART. There was also evidence to suggest that the combination of an emphasis on Somatic Regulation in therapy, and the generalization of Regulation Tools to the youth's whole day, contributed to these findings.

A Case Example: SMART Collaboration Supporting Somatic Regulation in a Residential Treatment Setting

Stacia, age fifteen years, had been living in a residential treatment program for three years. She was adopted from an eastern European orphanage at two years old after experiencing chronic neglect and abuse. She experienced significant expressive and receptive language processing delays, and exhibited severe aggression toward herself and others that required numerous restraints in her first year at this program. Stacia's therapist introduced SMART a few months into treatment to address these significant regulation challenges.

When in the SMART room, Stacia enjoyed burrowing her body deep into a beanbag chair and used weighted blankets to help her settle. Milieu staff reported that she also enjoyed using ankle and wrist weights available in the gym. The team created a milieu regulation plan that incorporated hourly sensory breaks with weights to provide needed deep touch pressure and proprioception. After a year of individual SMART treatment with a coinciding milieu regulation plan, Stacia's level of aggression decreased, and she went almost a year without restraint. In the SMART room, Stacia's ability to notice how her body was feeling consistently increased. With this growing awareness, Stacia told staff that she would like to use her weights on community outings, as they helped her manage frustration better and made her feel less stressed. This collaborative process between Stacia, her SMART therapist, and milieu staff resulted in Stacia feeling safer and able to successfully engage in program and community activities.

Trauma Content and the Milieu

A significant area of struggle for traumatized youth is the way in which traumatic activations can take over their day, and disrupt their ability to be present for school and community life. In residential treatment, this can pose a particular challenge for milieu staff, who often are the recipients of disclosures or reenactments. A primary goal is to help youth learn how to bring traumatic content to therapy, where closer attention can be given to effectively process the material so that daily life can be lived to the fullest.

When developing milieu regulation plans, clinicians can prepare staff for the possibility that as youth become more regulated, unprocessed trauma content is likely to emerge in their day, and that the emergence of traumatic content is activating. The role of milieu staff is to support youth to contain the traumatic content, to effectively regulate distress in the moment, and to bring the traumatic content to their therapist.

In trauma-informed residential programming, it is essential that youth feel adequately supported and contained by staff when traumatic material is expressed. Supportive staff responses acknowledge the importance of what the youth is sharing, without exploring the content of the disclosure or communicating to the youth that the disclosure is not appropriate to share. After acknowledging the youth's experience, the milieu staff's primary goal is to stay present with the youth, and return focus to regulating any somatic activation that accompanies the disclosure. Staff can engage specific sensory tools recommended by the clinician to support youth regulation and grounding. Once the resident is in a regulated state, staff can develop a plan for the youth to communicate with the therapist and support a return to the structure of the milieu.

Attachment-Building

Youth who require treatment at a residential level of care often struggle to build safety and trust within family relationships and with others. Although factors such as distance, lack of contact, and discord within the family can impact necessary family Attachment-Building work in residential care, clinicians can provide psychoeducation to caregivers about their child's particular regulation needs and make recommendations regarding how to integrate sensory tools into life at home in preparation for visits and discharge. Clinicians also may choose to hold family sessions within the SMART room, when possible and clinically indicated, to help parents learn the youth's Regulation Tools and find ways to regulate more effectively as a family when addressing difficult topics. Parents will often more readily incorporate tools at home when they witness those tools being used in a SMART room session. This work, in itself, is Attachment-Building and is a productive way to do family therapy.

The work of Attachment-Building can also be addressed in the relationships that youth form with therapists, milieu staff, or peers within the milieu treatment environment. Many youth in residential care struggle with managing the intensity of relationships, and can become dysregulated by interactions that are perceived as "too relational." Youth who have been impacted by interpersonal trauma often learn to simultaneously pull in and push away relational connection to manage relational intensity. Milieu staff can experience this dynamic as confusing, particularly following incidents of being assaulted by a resident with whom they had been laughing and having fun earlier that day. One therapist invited a residential supervisor to join a session with a youth after a difficult interaction the prior evening. The therapy session was used to support relational repair and problem-solving when the youth could self-regulate by swinging in a suspended swing while his therapist scaffolded the conversation between the supervisor and the youth. The supervisor exclaimed that such a session completely changed his understanding of and rapport with the youth, with whom he previously had a contentious relationship.

Protecting the SMART Treatment Space

Over the years, SMART teams have come to recognize the importance of preserving the SMART room as a safe, therapeutic space for the youth and therapist to explore trauma treatment themes related to Somatic Regulation, Trauma Processing, and Attachment-Building. Several times, clinicians reported that a youth would suddenly no longer want to go into the SMART room, or would go in and begin using the tools in ways the therapist was not accustomed to. With a little exploration, the therapist often found that the resident was using the room with milieu staff outside of therapy. These non-SMART experiences seemed to puncture the safety of the therapeutic space, derailing treatment. Now, the SMART model emphasizes the importance of maintaining the SMART room as protected therapy space within the residential setting, and strongly discourages using the space as a multipurpose sensory room.

In a training designed for milieu staff, they learn about the relationship of Somatic Regulation and Trauma Processing and how there is a greater chance that trauma content from therapy may emerge when they bring residents into the SMART room. Such experiences can be dysregulating to the resident and overwhelming to staff. This can undermine the effort to contain traumatic material to therapy and, thus, blur therapeutic spaces, resulting in decreased feelings of safety and containment for the youth in both settings.

SMART Consultation

A key factor contributing to successful integration of SMART within residential treatment programs is consistent and ongoing video consultation with the treatment team. Ideally, the residential SMART consultation team will include at least one milieu or educational supervisor. These staff members bring expertise regarding residents' functioning outside of treatment that further informs treatment planning.

SMART video consultation has been described as the residential program's most effective tool for building a therapist's clinical skills. According to Program Director Michelle Vaughan, "Being able to see a therapy session, and have the whole team see it, helps the team develop more intentionality and awareness" (pers. comm. 2017). For therapists who are newer to clinical work, watching clinical video with colleagues helps them learn the Tracking and observation skills essential for supporting regulation. Experienced therapists continue to benefit from watching video recordings, further refining their skills and their understanding of the treatment process.

In one consultation with a team, a residential supervisor made connections between a youth's tendency to sit at the edge of the room during group activities and her preference for talking with her therapist while sitting behind a mat as shown in the video. The treatment team discussed supporting the youth's need for physical distance and Safe Space during group activities. By participating in the Video Reflection, milieu and educational staff gain a deeper understanding of how to support youth regulation across the programming, thus creating a more integrated approach. The team involvement in SMART video consultation helps teams refine their responses to the youth's evolving regulation and attachment needs over the course of treatment in support of common goals.

Application of SMART in Community-Based In-Home Therapy

In Boston, Tiffany Naste, a social worker trained in SMART, recognized the potential value of SMART for the kids who were being referred to her new community-based program within a large agency. "The kids' inability to regulate and a modality that didn't rely on language and talking about things [made it seem] like a natural model given the kids that we were seeing" (pers. comm. 2017). At first, she and a young colleague tossed around the idea of a "SMART-mobile" van that they could drive around the community to families. They laughed and agreed that finding parking in Boston's dense urban neighborhoods would be impossible. But their real challenges inspired them to ask if we could work with them to bring SMART into the homes of their clients.

Reasons for referrals for community-based in-home services included externalizing behaviors, extreme emotional dysregulation, self-harm, and other major safety concerns within the family and in the community. Some of the families had members with addictions and substance abuse, mental illness, medical illness, or other problems, and few support resources. For many, intergenerational trauma impacts the caregivers responsible for the referred children. Beginning in 2009, in-home teams became frontline responders for children up to twenty years old whose behavioral problems were so challenging that placements outside the home in hospitals, acute care stabilization programs, foster care, and residential treatment had previously been considered the only options.

Thus began a process similar to the original SMART development process: train in-home therapists in the SMART model, send them into homes with some SMART equipment and a video recording system, and study their flexible and creative use of the SMART principles with their clients and families. The viability and effectiveness were clinically demonstrated over the course of three years of collaborative efforts in implementation and consultation. Since then, we have been invited to train in parts of the United States, particularly in rural areas, where families live great distances from clinics, and where in-home therapists must travel to families to ensure that children receive mental health services.

> In-home therapy is organized differently across the country in terms of levels of resources and support (Centers for Medicare and Medicaid Services 2014). We are frequently asked how it is structured in Massachusetts. Precipitated by the failure of the Commonwealth of Massachusetts to provide "medically necessary, intensive home-based services" to nine individual plaintiffs and thousands of other Medicaid-eligible persons under the age of twenty-one with "intensive mental health needs" as mandated by federal law under the 1967 Early and Periodic Screening, Diagnostic and Treatment (EPSDT) Medicaid benefit, the Rosie D. class-action lawsuit was filed in US District Court, District of Massachusetts, in 2001 (*Rosie D. ex rel. John D. v. Swift,* 310 F.3d [1st Cir. 2002]). By 2006, the Commonwealth of Massachusetts was ordered to develop a remedial plan for provision of mental health services for children (*Rosie D. et al. v. Romney et al.,* 410 F. Supp.2d 18 [D. Mass. 2006]). The suit resulted in a remedial plan to ensure the provision of comprehensive home-based services that included in-home behavioral and therapy services, family training and support, mobile crisis intervention and stabilization, and intensive care coordination via teams (*Rosie D. et al. v. Patrick et al.,* 497 F. Supp.2d 76 [D. Mass. 2007]). Consequently, community-based, interdisciplinary in-home teams of clinicians and paraprofessionals are providing these needed services throughout the state.

Adaptation to a Variety of Home Settings

The context of community-based services and in-home treatment is complex. The wide range of circumstances for in-home cases demands high levels of flexibility and resourcefulness. Homes vary from small apartments in dense neighborhoods to single-family homes with backyards or basement rooms. Families range from those with few economic resources to those with comfortable incomes. Caregivers include biological parents, grandparents, aunts and uncles, adoptive parents, and long-term foster parents for children who have experienced high levels of neglect, abuse, and multiple attachment disruptions. Therapists often encounter siblings and extended family members who reside in the home or who come and go.

Given the contextual complexity and the active nature of SMART, and the use of equipment, the application in homes required a specific kind of creativity. Therapists learned to introduce the modality to caregivers by first explaining the purpose of sensory motor play with this equipment for the child's behavioral and emotional dysregulation. They chose equipment they could carry up apartment stairs, and tried out hockey bags and small shopping carts to transport it; they collaborated with parents to determine how and where it would work. Therapists rapidly learned to use what was acceptable to caregivers or already available in the home. Couch cushions instead of weighted blankets, Bosu ball jumping instead of a trampoline, and a desk chair instead of a spinning board were equally effective. Blankets and pillows from a child's bed served well to create a home Safe Space that could be used anytime the child needed time to calm her body. A quarterback pass of a Nerf football to a boy, who dove onto his bed, satisfied his need for a vestibular challenge and deep pressure.

Once therapists and team members could engage in Video Reflection and see what sensory inputs attracted the child, they became adept at creating opportunities. Often, children or youth found their own solutions in their homes once they learned to tend to their own safety and could feel their parents' acceptance of their need for new ways of regulating themselves.

When in-home settings were unsafe or too chaotic, therapists searched for nearby local playgrounds, church basements, community center rooms, and parks with trees to climb as settings to find sensory motor inputs that would be regulating for their clients. The SMART tools—the sensory motor inputs— remained the same, as long as a therapist could translate them to varied contexts.

In-Home Treatment Planning

SMART in-home treatment plans prioritize Tending to Safety, Somatic Regulation, Attachment-Building, and co-regulation with caregivers. We learned through experience that when Trauma Processing arises, the therapist confronts a Choice Point about whether to continue this work in the home or to transfer the therapy to an outpatient setting.

Tending to Safety

Community-based teams prioritize safety. First of all, challenges to child and family safety are a foremost reason for referral to the in-home teams. Children are at risk because of their own dysregulation, and their caregivers struggle with how to tend to child and family safety. Moreover, emotional and behavioral dysregulation is accompanied by lack of body awareness, inattention to physical safety, accidents, reactive flight-or-fight responses, or destructiveness in the home.

As occurs in outpatient SMART, the use of sensory motor tools downregulates the behavioral and emotional dysregulation that is most challenging, and the Full Participation of therapists for co-regulation supports this process. The therapist models the process for the child and the caregiver in vivo, where and when the problems occur. This approach mitigates the safety issues relatively quickly when caregivers learn to implement the tools.

One parent described his incorporation of what he learned about safety through regulation:

> *Our family has gotten so much out of SMART tools. The foremost thing is being in tune with our kiddos' energy and the warning signs of when upsets are coming on. We're more aware of potential triggers and feel more prepared for the reactions they elicit. Sometimes we've even adapted SMART tools on the fly at home. For instance, there was a stretch of several months when our youngest daughter would totally erupt, and somehow we figured out one way out of the upset for her would be jumping on one of us as we were holding a couch cushion or a large pillow. She'd start out aggressively—really trying to dish out some pain—and we'd sell our reaction almost like a pro wrestler taking a hit, even though it didn't hurt at all. After a couple of minutes, it would start being fun for her. She'd really get into it and pour her energy into jumping on us. We'd be all smiles by the end.*

This parent was able to match the vitality of his child's energy but not her angry affect while allowing her to jump on a cushion; this approach resulted in a shift to playfulness and safety for all. In SMART terms, this therapist had succinctly explained to the caregiver and the child simultaneously how to Tend to Safety by Verbally Scaffolding the "yes, you may try this, and let's together make it safe …" approach. The same principle applies to developing relational and emotional safety of children and caregivers while showing Regulation Tools that help downregulate the child's anger.

Regulation for the Child

The majority of clients referred for these services have experienced interpersonal trauma, making family life frequently the most triggering domain, and therefore the most in need of intervention. The greatest value SMART adds to in-home treatments is developing Regulation Tools for the child or youth to use with caregivers in the context of family life.

> One young child, Omar, who had been abused and neglected by his birth parents, lived with his custodial grandparents in the same apartment where the trauma occurred. Due to the grandparents' physical limitations, therapy had to occur in the home. This increased the effectiveness, as daily life needs were addressed more immediately than in an outpatient setting. Omar startled frequently, and shifted states quickly, going back and forth from the High Intensity to the Low Intensity Fluid Zones throughout a session. Initially, he could not accept co-regulation from his grandmother, but did accept the therapist's help with spinning or arcing on the spinning board while he lay on his back or side. Once calmer, Omar then sought higher-energy play, for example, being pulled across the floor with latex bands, or learning to jump over a rope. Eventually, his grandmother held the band, and his grandfather helped him to jump rope in the living room after the in-home therapist and the Therapeutic Training and Support (TTS) person modeled how to do it. The grandparents witnessed the team's effectiveness and then modeled themselves on this approach.

For parents of adolescents in crisis, the pull to "talk about" problems may be met with slammed doors, broken furniture, or angry arguments. Adolescents can learn to use their room as a Safe Space for "chilling out" and downregulating when overwhelmed or reactive. The therapist provides caregiver psychoeducation, using the SMART Regulation Map, so that caregivers learn to wait until the child is more regulated before trying to problem-solve. This intervention is particularly effective when provided in the home where the conflict occurs.

Attachment-Building

The child's relationships with caregivers are often the most challenging, stemming from the amount of attachment disruption and neglect or abuse that has occurred. The use of Regulation Tools by caregivers is one way of building attachment. As the caregivers feel more effective in co-regulating their child, they will feel more connected and able to be the parent they want to be. The more the child allows this to occur, the more secure she feels with her caregiver. In the case of Omar living with his grandparents, experiencing safety and regulation in the same house in which he had earlier in his life been abused and neglected built a sense of security in the attachment bonds.

Finally, working in the home allows the team to look for additional sources of support for the child in their immediate social context. For example, an aunt or uncle who stops by the home regularly may have a gift for sensory motor play that offers a grandmother respite and meets the needs of the child.

Co-regulation for the Caregiver

Caregivers in need of in-home support are generally highly stressed by the experience of raising the child. In order to help their children, caregivers need support and co-regulation from the therapist. When a therapist places a cushion to support the back of a caregiver seated on the floor during therapy, the caregiver experiences a felt sense of support that says, "This therapist understands what I need."

> *Omar needed a great deal of sensory motor input on a daily basis. His grandmother suffered from a chronic respiratory illness and was sometimes overwhelmed by this need. When the therapist observed the grandmother arcing the spinning board by gently pushing it with her foot, she realized that she could help the caregiver and child replicate this in their small yard so he could play while his grandmother watched from a chair. As the grandmother learned to co-regulate in a way she could physically manage, her grandson felt more connected and did not run off. This reduced the grandmother's anxiety, and thus her stress in caring for her grandson.*

The in-home therapist experiences the challenges alongside the caregiver; and her ability to share observations and scaffold new experiences, taking limitations and opportunities into account, all in the life context of the home, is a powerful form of support for caregivers.

Trauma Processing: Special Considerations

As in SMART outpatient therapy, when kids become regulated, they often begin to process traumatic experiences and fears. Because caregivers are present at all times during in-home therapy, the question of the caregiver's Window of Tolerance for Trauma Processing arises. Of particular note are cases in which a child has been placed in a kinship family because of neglect or abuse by a birth parent. The caregiver's feelings, thoughts, and judgments about the birth parent's personal problems, parenting limitations, and treatment of the child arise at different moments in time. In some cases, the birth parent is more or less present in the home, which may trigger the child's fears and worries, and challenge caregiving further. In-home therapists may be privy to this information in a way that outpatient therapists often are not.

Nonetheless, children of all ages have a drive to metabolize and process their current and past experiences. An accepting response by the caregiver to a child's disclosure of abuse is an important positive prognostic indicator (Ullman 2007). Similarly, the acceptance of a child's drive to process her traumatic experience is important to progress in therapy. Whether the caregiver can tolerate witnessing the child's experience, when expressed in embodied dramatic play, in games, or via symbolic means such as drawing or talking, is important for the therapist to Track. Does the caregiver's nonverbal communication express openness and curiosity, or does it express anxiety, withdrawal, or rejection, thus impeding the child's process?

We have arrived at the understanding, through clinical practice, that the in-home therapist must address this as a Choice Point. Can the Trauma Processing—so necessary to the child's healing and growth—be done in the home, or would it be better to transfer therapy to an outpatient setting where presence of the caregiver can be more intentionally determined? Or can the caregiver, with sufficient support and consultation from the therapist, accept and witness the child's experience? Or will it be necessary for the child to travel this part of the journey with a therapist, without caregivers present? Although many adult survivors have had to follow this latter path, when a child is in treatment, therapists must explicitly address this question and make a choice. In-home therapists may determine it will be best for the child's therapy to transfer therapy to an outpatient setting.

Use of Video Recordings

Consent to video record therapy sessions has been given by the majority of families, to the surprise of some program directors who doubted parents would allow video recording inside the privacy of their homes. This was particularly true when the caregivers could see the therapist's curiosity to learn what would help their child and their family. And some parents, when they saw the Regulation Tools in action, and independently tried them out, consented to the use of video recording for training and education, wishing to help other families like themselves. However, we note that children involved in pending legal cases have not been video recorded, and the Massachusetts Department of Children and Families has generally not permitted video recording for any child in their legal custody.

The use of video recording in the home requires experimentation with a good wide-angle lens, small and large tripods, and proper camera placement to get the best view. The in-home setting has many added levels of consideration not found in outpatient settings, such as the presence of siblings and pets. During Video Reflection this adds complexity and richness to the therapist's understanding and to his supervision. In SMART consultation, therapists report they learn not only from the expertise and guidance of the SMART consultant but from the questions, observations, and reflections of their fellow in-home team members. Finally, using Video Reflection, the SMART development team was able to assess the application's face validity for use in the homes, to formulate the best way to implement SMART in collaboration with the early adopters, and to reflect on the interface with school and other social contexts with which in-home teams must coordinate care.

SMART as an Application for Young Children

The application of SMART for young children with complex trauma has shown that this therapy approach is a natural fit, both for the children and for the therapists who choose to work with this population. The fit was evident during the Foundations Training when trainees crawled through tunnels and played in body socks in the experiential exercises. At two early adopting sites—in a community mental health center in Kansas and a preschool outreach program in Massachusetts—the therapists easily moved into Full Participation in this playful sensory motor approach. We surmised that therapists of young children were used to getting down on the floor with children and quickly recognized that many of their young clients would positively respond to this fully embodied approach that did not depend on language. In addition, many therapists of young children consult to preschools regarding mental health and trauma, in part to prevent expulsions of dysregulated children (Loomis 2019). They reported that the SMART tools for addressing dysregulation in children were transferable to the schools and strengthened their recommendations to teachers.

The good match of SMART with this population was based on a number of factors. For preschool-aged children, navigation of the world occurs at a sensory motor level, and communication is often at a nonverbal symbolic level. The language skills of three- to six-year-olds are in early stages of development. Furthermore, at these ages, the early phases of behavioral and emotional regulation are part of the normal development challenges. And finally, young children naturally and happily gravitate toward sensory motor play with adults and peers.

The SMART Room

The simple design of SMART rooms aims to minimize visual and auditory distractions and to maximize sensory motor play for young children. Small objects and toys are kept outside the room. One site had a very large space used by occupational therapists that was richly equipped. However, in practice, they found it too large for the more intimate Trauma Processing and Attachment-Building work of SMART therapy, and the many options were overwhelming to young children. A space in the range of fourteen by fourteen feet, with gym mats on the floor for protection for all the rolling and tumbling of young children with sufficient—but not too much—equipment to access all the Tools of Regulation, is ideal.

A Boston clinic specializing in young children and with a large client population found their SMART room was in high demand and estimated that up to 75 percent of their clients benefited from SMART (pers. comm. 2019). They eventually added on two more SMART rooms, each with its own ball pit. Curiously, the addition of ball pits eliminated the need some children had to dump the balls all over the room, and afforded more opportunity to access the sensory experience for regulation and body awareness and to create embodied dramatic play. Given the overall demand for the space, directors of this program determined that it was important to increase accessibility, particularly when learning that the young clients found it disruptive and dysregulating to alternate weeks with another therapist/client due to space limitations.

SMART room in a clinic for young children

The SMART Spiral Applied

Young children with complex trauma present with behavioral and emotional dysregulation, excessive fears, separation anxiety, insecure attachments, somatic complaints, and delayed development in different domains. In SMART therapies with young children, all three threads of the Spiral—the processes of Somatic Regulation, Trauma Processing, and Attachment-Building—show up almost immediately. Through watching many video recordings, it appears that this modality is a trauma treatment made for young children.

Somatic Regulation. The readiness with which the young children engage with the equipment makes finding Regulation Tools easy. Many children gravitate quickly to the big pillows for jumping into and deep pressure. But they also use them to create hide-and-seek games with caregivers, make Safe Spaces, and work on mastering fears of the dark or of monsters. Similarly, the tunnels are used for crawling, rolling, and hiding, as well as games of self-protection and safety; the body socks are used for deep pressure and proprioception, hiding, and bonding games with caregivers; and the ball pits are used for increased body sensation and Somatic Regulation and Trauma Processing play of all kinds.

Trauma Processing. The readiness with which young children create embodied dramatic play in SMART is striking. In this symbolic form, their current fears and implicit traumatic memories are turned into stories and reworked via embodied play in a way that is easily understood by adults. When caregivers can go along with and join the play without a need to control, their children will invite them to participate. For the curious parent, this frequently opens up new understandings of their child. And with scaffolding from the therapist, the story's relevance to the child's past and present life is often easily discerned.

Attachment-Building. Rhythms of engagement, which have been either compromised by abuse or never developed in the context of neglect, are easily created in SMART through the young child's drive to repeat fun games many times. The addition of Rhythmicity to any game or form of play adds predictability, which helps caregivers better respond to the child, thus supporting the building of more secure attachment patterns. Creating a serve-and-return activity, even if in a simple ball toss, or taking turns in a hide-and-seek game, assists this process. It also builds in, at a sensory motor level, the bodily procedures needed to maintain the connection. Inevitably, therapists and caregivers report feeling more "connected" when there is some predictability to the child's actions. Only then can surprise and novelty feel fun and truly playful.

Parent Consultation Time

The younger the child, the more readily a good collaboration of the parent and therapist translates into progress. Every therapy requires parent consultation time for the therapist to hear about home life, to develop a collaborative working relationship, and to explain the trauma treatment process as it progresses. The more traumatized the parents, either from events within the relationship with their child or due to their personal history, the more parent consultation is required. However, no parent is truly prepared for the journey of healing and growth emanating from traumatic experience. Thus the parent consultation time, which supports the caregiver work in sessions, is essential and ensures better navigation of the child's journey of healing and growth.

Application of SMART in the Private Practice Setting

SMART works effectively in private practice settings where children are seen. Some practitioners set up a completely separate SMART room, similar to that shown throughout this book, whereas others utilize a hybrid office combining the elements of a SMART space with more traditional seating. There are several considerations for adding SMART treatment to your practice. These include the size of the room, furnishings, soundproofing, video and film storage, educating your officemates, and safety.

After attending a SMART training, a therapist may be tempted to gather some key SMART equipment, add it to an existing practice space, and call it SMART. We encourage you to avoid this temptation. The space conveys messages both about what kinds of actions are welcome as well as what kinds are not. One clinician found it possible to work effectively and safely with more constricted children in her private practice utilizing the framework and some equipment. However, when the internalizing symptoms lessened, the children joyfully sought out more robust full-body play, and the office could not safely accommodate this healthy sensory motor seeking, nor help the families fully explore the Tools of Regulation needed.

As the case studies have revealed, traumatic material and dysregulation emerge without warning, requiring the therapeutic space to provide a solid and consistent sense of physical safety. A rupture in physical safety inevitably leads to a lack of emotional and relational safety for the child. Furthermore, when the space and equipment are limited, the child may not discover what regulates him, or he may be unable to obtain the intensity needed for Sensory Satiation. Frequently, the child seeks actions much younger than his current age and size; thus the room and tools must accommodate the embodied play and Trauma Processing of a larger child engaged in full-body activities.

Setting Up a Hybrid SMART Office

A relatively large room is needed to combine seating, multisensory equipment, and a center space in which to use the equipment. One practitioner's office that effectively offers this combination is twenty by fifteen feet. It is important to select decor and furniture that are simple, unbreakable, and sturdy with no hard edges. Therapists should not be surprised if the child uses furniture as part of the play and sensory seeking actions. For instance, couch cushions can become crash pads, Safe Spaces, or sources of compression for Tactile Input. This can be helpful when it is time to generalize regulation inputs to the home, demonstrating the creative use of everyday objects into Regulation Tools. In a hybrid office, caregivers seem more compelled to correct their child's behavior to fit the "office" setting and often are unsure what you mean by letting the child explore, test, and play. Caregivers will need an explicit explanation that these kinds of behavior are welcome in the SMART space.

A SMART room in a private practice setting

SMART can be loud, with bouncing and banging. Physioballs may be thrown against the wall. Soundproof the room well, or select an office that shares as few walls as possible with neighbors. Adding a sound machine outside the door will mask voices but not rough-and-tumble play. Educate your officemates about SMART, what the tools provide, and why robust play is an essential element of the treatment. Frequently, other clients will be very curious about your room and how different it looks. Children poke their heads in when the door is open and look longingly. Frequently, they may ask, "Can we meet there?" Perhaps, as more colleagues become interested, a designated SMART space can be shared.

Video Reflection is a core element of SMART treatment. This means having a camera available in your office to film, obtaining informed consent from care-givers, and developing a locked storage system for videos. One therapist made the loading and unloading of the video part of her client's clinical rituals. At the end of each session, the youngster would carefully lock her SD card, containing the material from the session, in the lock box. Wisely, the therapist engaged the client in building physical, emotional, and relational safety together (see the appendix).

Integration with Other Child Trauma Models

One of the strengths of the SMART model has been how well it integrates with other child trauma models that agencies may already be using. For exam-ple, the Neurosequential Model of Therapeutics (NMT) developed by Bruce Perry (2009; Perry and Dobson 2013) and his team is a neurobiologically informed, developmentally sensitive method for assessment of at-risk children of all ages. Therapists trained in NMT report that SMART, as an interven-tion method, addresses some of NMT-identified targets such as regulation and rhythm. The Attachment, Regulation and Competency (ARC) Framework model, developed by Margaret Blaustein and Kristine Kinniburgh (2019), is an excellent framework for therapists interested in trauma treatment and care of traumatized children of all ages in homes and in larger systems; and SMART with young children—as well as older children and adolescents—nests well in this framework. Another model for work with young children and parents and caregivers that integrates well with SMART is Child-Parent Psychotherapy (CPP) developed by Alicia Lieberman (Lieberman, Ippen, and Dimmler 2019) of the Child Trauma Research Program.

11

CONCLUSION

Core Elements of SMART

We began this SMART journey to find ways to be helpful to traumatized children. With the assistance of Jane Koomar and her lens of Sensory Integration, we discovered basic sensory motor tools appropriate for a psychotherapy environment to calm, to energize, and to settle. After developing some regulatory capacity, the children began to express what needed to be healed from their traumatic pasts. The form of expression ranged from physical actions and postures, to embodied dramatic play, to more symbolic manifestations, such as artwork or narratives. The next question was how to integrate the caregivers into this powerful work. Thus was born the SMART Spiral: the interweaving of Somatic Regulation, Trauma Processing, and Attachment-Building. This model is the overarching guide for SMART treatment.

If the Spiral is the guide, then the SMART Regulation Map shows where to begin. The Regulation Map depicts the arousal spectrum so that therapists can track children's presenting arousal level, their response to interventions, and their response to traumatic triggers. The Integrated State reflects a moderate level of arousal in which a child can think, plan, feel, and connect with others. When children have become totally overaroused and lost connection with the therapist and the environment, they are in a Hyperaroused Traumatic State; whereas if their arousal level plummets and they lose connection with the therapist and environment, they are in a Hypoaroused Traumatic State. In these Traumatic States, the child is unreachable and lost in her own world, often caught in a traumatic memory or reenactment. The Fluid Zones are on the boundaries between the Traumatic States and the Integrated State, in which the child is on the edge of hyperarousal or hypoarousal but is still reachable; thus, these zones provide wonderful opportunities for psychological reworking and development of new skills.

Once the child's state is identified using the Regulation Map, the SMART therapist has three sets of tools (the three-legged stool referred to in Part 2) to draw from: SMART Tools of Regulation, Therapist Skills, and Video Reflection. Each of these mechanisms contributes to the ultimate goal of interweaving the threads of the Spiral in order to widen a child's Window of Tolerance. The sensory motor Regulation Tools are essential for facilitating Somatic Regulation, but also are conducive to Trauma Processing and Attachment-Building. The Therapist Skills are used to advance all three threads of the Spiral. Over the course of our journey, the crucial role of Video Reflection became apparent as a means to understanding all three strands of the Spiral, but particularly the aspects of our work that are unspoken and less obvious. Video Reflection essentially increases the therapist's prefrontal cortex activity and observing ego capacity. With the Spiral, the Regulation Map, the sensory motor Tools of Regulation, the Therapist Skills, and Video Reflection, the SMART therapist has everything needed; these are the core elements of SMART.

Adaptation of SMART

With the core elements of SMART, one can adapt to many different settings and types of disorders. Because trauma has such a widespread impact, there are many types of manifestations. For example, when we worked with an eating disorder residential facility, we were able to collaborate with the eating disorder experts to adapt SMART as a way to "befriend your body" and to use play, as opposed to working out, as a means of physical expression. Similarly, we have worked with an agency that serves the deaf. Again, using the core elements of SMART in collaboration with their expertise, we have been able to apply the model in a manner that feels useful and additive to the agency. The key concepts here are clarity about the core elements of SMART, and respectful collaboration with experts of other fields to generate new applications.

Future Directions

While we offer this book as a complete representation of our thinking to date about the SMART model, we are continuing the journey of exploration. We are interested in adapting the model for adults, as many of our parents, as well as providers in our trainings, have benefited from exploring the SMART Tools of Regulation. In addition, we are particularly interested in studying the neurobiological mechanisms of action that make SMART effective. By measuring physiological data correlated with sensory motor activity while children are in the SMART room, we hope to add to our understanding of the mechanisms of change. In cooperation with a neuroscience lab that studies adult Complex PTSD and brain circuitry relevant to SMART, such as the vestibular network, we will further explore the role of brain stem function and its impact on higher-level cortical functions such as emotional regulation and integration, language processing, and the executive functions for traumatized children.

> *Aidan enters the SMART room for the first time. He immediately starts rolling over a physioball to crash into some large pillows. His therapist asks what he would like her to do while he is crashing, and he invites her to take a turn crashing after he carefully explains to her exactly how to do it safely. He then amplifies the challenge by jumping off a trampoline, and then jumping off a wooden bench. Aidan finds this activity increasingly exciting to the point where his old presentation pops through. He leaps off the bench and then reports that he landed on some "bitches" and he "fucked them up." Even with his intense traumatic activation, he stays in connection with his therapist via a cooperative game of catch with a large physioball. After exploring deep touch pressure through getting "squished" and spinning on a board with cushions piled on top for long intervals, Aidan says to his therapist, "Thank you for going with what I said, instead of just going with what you said. Thank you." His therapist replies, "I have noticed that you are saying please and thank you lots today. What do you think is making that happen?" Aidan responds, "I am so surprised my manners are going up and up and up today."*

In the *first* session in the SMART room, Aidan was able to use Tactile, Vestibular, and Proprioceptive Input, Rhythmicity, and Sensory Satiation to stay regulated throughout his therapy session even as he danced near the Hyperaroused Traumatic State. With his newfound Somatic Regulation, Aidan could form a positive relationship with his therapist that involved turn-taking, mutual respect, and even vulnerability, thus building an attachment that had seemed impossible in a regular child therapy room.

We are so grateful for the opportunity to have developed this model from the ground up by watching video recordings together and collaborating with other professionals. We look forward to continuing the journey!

APPENDIX

CREATING A SMART PROGRAM

When creating a SMART room, there are several factors to take into consideration. These include:

- Size of the room
- Matting options
- Maintaining privacy
- Selection of equipment
- Seating options for caregivers
- Purchase and placement of video equipment
- Storage of video-recorded clinical sessions

The size of the room is the first key consideration in creating a SMART room that affords children the space to engage in full-bodied play at the level of intensity needed to support Sensory Satiation and felt safety. The prototype SMART room measured fourteen by seventeen feet, allowing enough space for a child to complete a full cartwheel across the room or to engage in a vigorous ball tossing game. It is critical that the room be no smaller than twelve by twelve feet; however, a room of fourteen by fourteen feet or larger is ideal.

A second consideration to support Full Participation and Tending to Safety in SMART is matting. It is important to purchase mats designed to meet the density and impact requirements for the age and weight of children that you are treating. In some cases, programs have had professional, gym-quality matting installed permanently on the floor. These mats are durable and made to absorb the impact of a child flipping and landing on the mats with some force. Permanently installed mats are level with the floor and tend to minimize the chance of children tripping on an edge or of mats sliding unexpectedly while a child is engaged in play. This option may help clinicians and caregivers to feel more comfortable with children exploring fully embodied, gross motor movements such as cartwheels, and diving or crashing into cushions on the floor. One limitation of this option is that it does not support equipment with wheels, such as scooter boards. Other programs have elected to cover the floor with gym-quality, movable mats that attach together with Velcro. This option may be slightly more affordable and provides flexibility within the space. For example, the mats may be flipped back to allow children to use equipment with wheels, or have opportunities to bounce a ball with greater intensity than is possible on a matted surface. However, these mats are also more prone to slipping on the floor or having raised edges that could be tripped over.

In addition to floor mats, it is also important to have at least four smaller (three by five feet) movable mats that can be placed along the walls or against any corners that may exist in the room, to create further safety. These mats are particularly useful for preventing children from hitting walls with their arms or legs when engaging in actions such as jumping and crashing into cushions, or rolling on a large physioball. Additionally, these mats can be used intentionally as a tool to help children learn to tend to their own physical safety. For example, a therapist may engage a child in orienting to the room and thinking collaboratively about the best place to put these mats during a particular game or activity. Finally, children also regularly use these mats to create forts, or other small Safe Spaces, to regulate and regroup throughout therapy.

If there are windows, it is important to cover these with opaque plastic contact material to create privacy. In addition, with due consideration for fire laws, glass may be replaced or covered with a nonbreakable plastic. The room should be free from standing lamps or other lighting that might be damaged if hit by a thrown ball. Recessed overhead lighting options are recommended, and it can be helpful to have a dimmer switch that enables children to modulate light intensity as they wish. In some instances, cork panels have been added to the walls to provide a greater sense of safety, a place for art projects, and a sound buffer when children wish to throw the large physioballs against the wall. White noise machines are used outside the room to buffer the sound of enthusiastic or louder voices when children or parents are engaged in play.

SMART Equipment Considerations

When designing a SMART room, it is important to consider what equipment will best meet the developmental needs of the population being served, fit within the space, and meet the budgetary needs of the program. The space should be simple, and the affordance of the room should invite movement, play, and exploration. Additionally, the equipment chosen for the room must allow children and adolescents to fully explore all seven SMART Regulation Tools (see chapter 3). Some materials can be made by hand, such as crash cushions, weighted blankets, or spandex "Snoochies." Other equipment, such as used bicycle inner tubes, can be obtained for free from a local bike shop. The remaining equipment may be purchased from specialty sensory or occupational therapy shops, department stores, sporting goods shops, and online retailers.

The following chart lists SMART Equipment Basics, which represent the foundational equipment needed to develop a SMART room. The second chart, SMART Equipment Additions, lists additional pieces of equipment that can be added over time to provide a wider variety of sensory and regulation opportunities based on client needs, physical space, and program budget. The final list outlines specific equipment suggestions geared to the unique needs of preschool and adolescent populations in SMART. Notably, adolescent clients tend to feel more comfortable engaging with equipment purchased from a sporting goods store, and that is less brightly colored than traditional sensory integration equipment.

SMART Equipment Basics

For a list of possible purveyors and estimated costs, please visit www.smart movespartners.com.

Equipment	Number	SMART Tools
Floor Matting	Dependent on size of space	Supports full engagement with all tools
Movable Three-by-Five-Foot Mats	4	Tactile, Safe Space, Proprioception
Physioball	2–4	Tactile, Proprioception, Vestibular, Rhythmicity
Crash Pad / Cloud Nine Cushions	2–4	Tactile, Proprioception, Safe Space
Mini-Trampoline	1	Proprioception, Vestibular, Rhythmicity

Equipment	Number	SMART Tools
Weighted Blanket: Ten Pounds and Fifteen Pounds	1 of each weight	Deep Touch Pressure / Tactile, Proprioception
Body Socks: Sizes Small to Extra Large	2–4	Tactile, Proprioception, Safe Space
Spinning Board	1	Vestibular, Rhythmicity
Tunnel	1	Proprioception, Vestibular, Safe Space, Rhythmicity
Balance Beam	1	Vestibular, Proprioception
Weighted Ball	2	Proprioception, Deep Touch Pressure / Tactile, Rhythmic opportunities
Bike Inner Tubes / Resistance Bands	Unlimited	Proprioception, Tactile, Rhythmicity
Blankets	2–5	Tactile, Safe Space
Spandex	Approx. 14 yards	Tactile (Deep and Light Touch Pressure), Proprioception, Vestibular (swinging)
Electric Air Pump	1–2	To inflate equipment
First Aid Kit with Ice Packs	1	To support Tending to Safety

SMART Equipment Additions

For a list of possible purveyors and estimated costs, please visit www.smart movespartners.com.

Equipment	Number	SMART Tools
Air Pillow: Dolphin Pillow or Walrus Pillow	2–3	Vestibular, Tactile, Proprioception, Rhythmicity
Bosu Ball	1	Vestibular, Proprioception
Balance Board/Disc	1–2	Vestibular, Proprioception, Rhythmicity
Pop-up Tent	2	Safe Space
Sensory Shaker	1	Dynamic Tactile, Safe Space, Vestibular, Proprioception, Rhythmicity
Stepping Stones / River Stones	1 box of 6	Tactile, Proprioception, Vestibular
Suspended Swing	1	Vestibular, Rhythmicity, Proprioception, Tactile, Safe Space

Equipment	Number	SMART Tools
Yogibo Beanbag Seating	1–2	Tactile, Proprioception, Vestibular, and Safe Space
Spandex Snoochie (long piece of spandex with ends sewn together)	1	Proprioception, Tactile, Safe Space, Rhythmicity
Peanut Ball	1	Proprioception, Vestibular, Rhythmic, Tactile opportunities
Scooter Board	1	Vestibular, Proprioception, Rhythmic, Tactile
Wobble Cushion	1–2	Vestibular, Proprioception, Rhythmicity, Tactile
Duck Walker Balance Board	1	Vestibular, Proprioception, Rhythmicity, Tactile
Flashlight	1	To support Tending to Safety, modulating sensory input, mastery

Adolescent Equipment Options	Preschool Equipment Options
Yogibo Bean Bag Chairs	Sensory Shaker or Ball Pit
Large Crash Mats	Sit-n-Spin or IKEA Egg Swivel Chair
Large Physioballs	Hoppity Hop
Suspended Swing	Tunnel
Bosu Ball/Board	Weighted Blanket: 5 pounds
Mini-Trampoline	Body Sox: small and large
Resistance Bands	Small Physioballs
Balance Board	Stepping Stones
Weighted Blanket: 15 pounds and up	Cuddle Swing
Body Sox: large or XL	Scooter Board
Peanut Ball	Bilbo Seat
Spinning Board	Spandex Snoochie
Weighted Balls	Small Trampoline with Handles
Arm or Leg Weights	
Large Tunnel	

Providing caregivers with a variety of seating options that support comfort and opportunities for connection with their child is an important consideration. Some caregivers are comfortable sitting on the floor supported by a pillow or cushion, or on a BackJack floor chair. One particular piece of equipment that tends to appeal to adults and kids alike is a large body-conforming beanbag chair that supports the entire body, such as a Yogibo. Other caregivers prefer more traditional seating such as a chair or bench. With sufficient space, a small loveseat or foldable couch could also be provided to create a cozy space for connection between parent and child during a session. When seating options are being considered, it is necessary to ensure that the room continue to have enough space for free movement and play, the primary goals of SMART.

A well-organized room free from clutter is essential for inviting movement, supporting exploration, and Tending to Safety. To maintain the simplicity of the room, methods for storing equipment are also a consideration. In our prototype SMART room, large wooden storage benches were placed along one wall and served the dual purpose of storing smaller pieces of equipment (e.g., stepping stones, blankets, or resistance bands) and providing a seating area for caregivers. In another setting, a closet or cabinet may suffice as a place for storage. When larger pieces of furniture with edges, such as benches or cabinets, are placed in a SMART room, it is necessary to have movable three-by-five-foot mats available to cover edges that might be bumped into during full-bodied, gross motor play. Finally, we have found that posting a printed picture of an organized SMART room on the door or wall can help both children and clinicians during cleanup routines, and encourages taking care of the space.

Video Recording Equipment

As video recording is a core component of SMART treatment, emphasis must be placed on determining the appropriate video equipment for the space when designing the room. It is recommended that programs purchase a video camera with a wide-angle lens, and mount the camera approximately five feet off the ground. The placement of the camera should allow for a full panorama view of the room and account for interactions where the therapist and client(s) may be sitting or standing. To ensure consistent recording, it is paramount that the camera setup is easily accessible to clinicians and simple to use. Ideally, a clinician can walk into the room a few minutes before the beginning of a session, flip a switch to start recording, and invite their client into the space with the camera already running. We have found in SMART video consultation that it is often clinically useful to Track how a client enters a room, and that actions observed within the first minutes of session often have relevance as the session unfolds.

Video Storage

A video storage and archiving system that accounts for the confidential nature of clinical video recording must also be established. Any recording of clinical sessions is considered part of the clinical record and must be protected accordingly. Many programs use a flash drive or other removable storage device for a client, and identify the device with the client's initials. After each session, place the device in a client-specific storage container that can be double-locked. Other programs store video on an encrypted terabyte server managed by their IT department. Laws regarding HIPAA protected data and storage of clinical records vary by state, and programs are responsible for familiarizing themselves with the requirements of their state and accreditation boards as part of the SMART implementation process. In addition, appropriate consent forms that reflect the possible uses of the video should be developed by the clinic or practitioner and included as part of the usual intake packet.

Consent and Recording

As part of the consent process, it is helpful to explain to clients and caregivers the purpose of using video as part of SMART. The therapist communicates to caregivers that the sensory motor nature of the treatment makes video review necessary to fully assess the child's needs and assist in ongoing treatment planning. When communicating the purpose of video recording to children or adolescents, it is often beneficial to let them know that the goal of video is to help the therapist do a good job helping them. The therapist is also clear with the client about who is allowed to see the video and how privacy is maintained.

On occasion children and adolescents may be wary or reluctant to be video recorded for a variety of reasons, including self-consciousness, fear of being seen, or that video recording may trigger aspects of their trauma history. We have found that providing opportunities for taking time to understand and address client concerns by increasing opportunities for choice and addressing safety or privacy around video recording can provide clients with a developmentally appropriate sense of agency that supports reworking of fears and increases feelings of mastery. The following represents general suggestions that have been helpful in supporting children or adolescents who feel particularly anxious about video recording.

- Fully explain the purpose and process of video recording and video storage to the client.

- Highlight a range of options available to the client regarding choices for when and how video recordings can occur.

- Engage the client in setting up, finalizing, and locking up clinical recordings to reinforce felt safety, privacy, and agency around the process.

- Invite caregivers into the conversation as appropriate, to support felt safety, provide permission, and help answer their child's or adolescent's questions.

- Consider, with clinical consultation, whether it would be beneficial to watch any portion of a clinical session with a client.

Special Considerations: Video Recording When Treating Victims of Sexual Abuse Who Have Been Video Recorded or Photographed

The following case example illustrates the collaborative approach developed by an outpatient SMART therapist, Jennifer Moore, LMHC, to support a nine-year-old client, Dennis, who had a history of sexual exploitation and had expressed fear about having sessions recorded. To support Dennis's larger therapeutic goals of increasing feelings of self-empowerment and agency, his therapist took time to explain the purpose of video recording and ask if he was interested in learning how the video recorder worked. Dennis responded to this invitation with curiosity. His caregiver joined the process and allowed Dennis to record him in a manner that felt safe and playful. The therapist also showed Dennis how recordings were stored within the clinic and emphasized the importance placed on protecting privacy by locking up the video recordings.

Prior to each session, his therapist presented a range of options, including: not recording on a particular week, starting and stopping recording at any time, or recording the session and including Dennis in each step of the process. When Dennis agreed to video record a session, he fully participated in the process of setting up, finalizing, storing, and locking up the recording. Dennis was particularly engaged in the process of locking and then double-locking the recording device in the storage area. This routine was repeated in each session, and according to his therapist, "provided a clear, concrete, client-led opportunity" to successfully work through traumatic experiences and build "an authentic, coherent, and developmentally appropriate sense of agency within the context of the therapist–client relationship."

REFERENCES

Foreword by Margaret E. Blaustein, PhD

Beltran, Monica, Abena Brown-Elhillali, April Held, Patrice Ryce, Mirian E. Ofonedu, Daniel Hoover, Kaitlin Ensor, and Harolyn M. E. Belcher. 2016. "Yoga-Based Psychotherapy Groups for Boys Exposed to Trauma in Urban Settings." *Alternative Therapies in Health and Medicine* 22, no. 1 (January): 39–46.

Bremner, J. Douglas. 2002. "Neuroimaging Studies in Post-Traumatic Stress Disorder." *Current Psychiatry Reports,* no. 4 (August): 254–63.

D'Andrea, Wendy, Lou Bergholz, Andrea Fortunato, and Joseph Spinazzola. 2013. "Play to the Whistle: A Pilot Investigation of a Sports-Based Intervention for Traumatized Girls in Residential Treatment." *Journal of Family Violence* 28, no. 7: 739–49. doi:10.1007/s10896-013-9533-x.

D'Andrea, Wendy, Julian Ford, Bradley Stolbach, Joseph Spinazzola, and Bessel A. van der Kolk. 2012. "Understanding Interpersonal Trauma in Children: Why We Need a Developmentally Appropriate Trauma Diagnosis." *American Journal of Orthopsychiatry* 82, no. 2: 187–200. doi:10.1111/j.1939-0025.2012.01154.x.

De Bellis, Michael D., Matcheri S. Keshavan, Heather Shifflett, Satish Iyengar, Sue R. Beers, Julie Hall, and Grace Moritz. 2002. "Brain Structures in Pediatric Maltreatment-Related Posttraumatic Stress Disorder: A Sociodemographically Matched Study." *Society of Biological Psychiatry* 52, no. 11 (December): 1066–78. doi:10.1016/S0006-3223(02)01459-2.

De Bellis, Michael D., and Lisa A. Thomas. 2003. "Biological Findings of Post-Traumatic Stress Disorder and Child Maltreatment." *Current Psychiatry Reports* 5, no. 2: 108–17.

De Bellis, Michael D., and Abigail Zisk. 2014. "The Biological Effects of Childhood Trauma." *Child and Adolescent Psychiatric Clinics of North America* 23(2): 185–222. doi:10.1016/j.chc.2014.01.002.

Dvir, Yael, Julian D. Ford, Michael Hill, and Jean A. Frazier. 2014. "Childhood Maltreatment, Emotional Dysregulation, and Psychiatric Comorbidities." *Harvard Review of Psychiatry* 22, no. 3: 149–61. doi:10.1097/HRP.0000000000000014.

Ehud, Miron, Bar-Dov An, and Strulov Avshalom. 2010. "Here and Now: Yoga in Israeli Schools." *International Journal of Yoga* 3, no. 2 (July–December): 42–47. doi:10.4103/0973-6131.72629.

Ford, Julian D., Damion Grasso, Carolyn Greene, Joan Levine, Joseph Spinazzola, and Bessel van der Kolk. 2013. "Clinical Significance of a Proposed Developmental Trauma Disorder Diagnosis: Results of an International Survey of Clinicians." *Journal of Clinical Psychiatry* 74, no. 8: 841–49. doi:10.4088/JCP.12m08030.

Greeson, Johanna K. P., Ernestine C. Briggs, Cassandra L. Kisiel, Christopher M. Layne, George S. Ake, Susan J. Ko, Ellen T. Gerrity, et al. 2011. "Complex Trauma and Mental Health in Children and Adolescents Placed in Foster Care: Findings from the National Child Traumatic Stress Network." *Child Welfare* 90, no. 6: 91–108.

Ito, Yutaka, Martin H. Teicher, Carol A. Glod, and Erika Ackerman. 1998. "Preliminary Evidence for Aberrant Cortical Development in Abused Children: A Quantitative EEG Study." *Journal of Neuropsychiatry and Clinical Neurosciences* 10, no. 3 (Summer): 298–307. doi:10.1111/j.1749-6632.1997.tb48277.x.

Jennissen, Simone, Julia Holl, Hannah Mai, Sebastian Wolff, and Sven Barnow. 2016. "Emotion Dysregulation Mediates the Relationship between Child Maltreatment and Psychopathology: A Structural Equation Model." *Child Abuse and Neglect* 62 (December): 51–62. doi:10.1016/j.chiabu.2016.10.015.

Kisiel, Cassandra, Margaret Blaustein, Joseph Spinazzola, Caren Swift Schmidt, Marla Zucker, and Bessel van der Kolk. 2006. "Evaluation of a Theater-Based Youth Violence Prevention Program for Elementary School Children." *Journal of School Violence* 5, no. 2: 19–36. doi:10.1300/J202v05n02_03.

Kisiel, Cassandra, Tracy Fehrenbach, Larry Small, and John S. Lyons. 2009. "Assessment of Complex Trauma Exposure, Responses, and Service Needs among Children and Adolescents in Child Welfare." *Journal of Child and Adolescent Trauma* 2, no. 3: 143–60. doi:10.1080/19361520903120467.

Morey, Rajendra A., Courtney C. Haswell, Stephen R. Hooper, and Michael D. De Bellis. 2016. "Amygdala, Hippocampus, and Ventral Medial Prefrontal Cortex Volumes Differ in Maltreated Youth with and without Chronic Posttraumatic Stress Disorder." *Neuropsychopharmacology* 41, no. 3 (February): 791–801. doi:10.1038/npp.2015.205.

Palidofsky, Meade, and Bradley C. Stolbach. 2012. "Dramatic Healing: The Evolution of a Trauma-Informed Musical Theatre Program for Incarcerated Girls." *Journal of Child and Adolescent Trauma* 5, no. 3: 239–56. doi:10.1080/19361521.2012.697102.

Schore, Allan N. 2001. "The Effects of Early Relational Trauma on Right Brain Development, Affect Regulation, and Infant Mental Health." *Infant Mental Health Journal* 22, nos. 1–2: 201–69.

Stark, E. A., C. E. Parsons, T. J. Van Hartevelt, M. Charquero-Ballester, H. McManners, A. Ehlers, A. Stein, and M. L. Kringelbach. 2015. "Post-Traumatic Stress Influences the Brain Even in the Absence of Symptoms: A Systematic, Quantitative Meta-Analysis of Neuroimaging Studies." *Neuroscience and Biobehavioral Reviews* 56 (September): 207–21. doi:10.1016/j.neubiorev.2015.07.007.

Teicher, Martin H., Susan L. Andersen, Ann Polcari, Carl M. Anderson, Carryl P. Navalta, and Dennis M. Kim. 2003. "The Neurobiological Consequences of Early Stress and

Childhood Maltreatment." *Neuroscience and Biobehavioral Reviews* 27, nos. 1–2 (January 1): 33–44. doi:10.1016/S0149-7634(03)00007-1.

van der Kolk, Bessel A. 2005. "Developmental Trauma Disorder: Toward a Rational Diagnosis for Children with Complex Trauma Histories." *Psychiatric Annals* 35, no. 5 (May): 401–408.

Foreword by Ruth A. Lanius, MD, PhD, and Sherain Harricharan, PhD

Bechara, Antoine, and Nasir Naqvi. 2004. "Listening to Your Heart: Interoceptive Awareness as a Gateway to Feeling." *Nature Neuroscience* 7, no. 2: 102.

Bell, Andrew H., and Douglas P. Munoz. 2008. "Activity in the Superior Colliculus Reflects Dynamic Interactions between Voluntary and Involuntary Influences on Orienting Behaviour." *European Journal of Neuroscience* 28, no. 8: 1654–60.

Bisson, Jonathan I., Anke Ehlers, Rosa Matthews, Stephen Pilling, David Richards, and Stuart Turner. 2007. "Psychological Treatments for Chronic Post-Traumatic Stress Disorder: Systematic Review and Meta-analysis." *British Journal of Psychiatry* 190, no. 2: 97–104.

Blanke, Olaf, and Shahar Arzy. 2005. "The Out-of-Body Experience: Disturbed Self-Processing at the Temporoparietal Junction." *Neuroscientist* 11, no. 1: 16–24.

Champagne, Tina. 2011. "The Influence of Posttraumatic Stress Disorder, Depression, and Sensory Processing Patterns on Occupational Engagement: A Case Study." *Work* 38, no. 1: 67–75.

Cohen, Judith A., and Anthony P. Mannarino. 2008. "Trauma-Focused Cognitive Behavioral Therapy for Children and Parents." *Child and Adolescent Mental Health* 13, no. 4: 158–62.

Craig, A. D. 2003. "Interoception: The Sense of the Physiological Condition of the Body." *Current Opinion in Neurobiology* 13, no. 4: 500–505.

Day, Brian L., and Richard C. Fitzpatrick. 2005. "The Vestibular System." *Current Biology* 15, no. 15: R583–86.

De Ridder, Dirk, Koen Van Laere, Patrick Dupont, Tomas Menovsky, and Paul Van de Heyning. 2007. "Visualizing Out-of-Body Experience in the Brain." *New England Journal of Medicine* 357, no. 18: 1829–33.

De Waele, C., P. Baudonnière, J. Lepecq, P. Tran Ba Huy, and P. Vidal. 2001. "Vestibular Projections in the Human Cortex." *Experimental Brain Research* 141, no. 4: 541–51.

Deblinger, Esther, Anthony P. Mannarino, Judith A. Cohen, Melissa K. Runyon, and Robert A. Steer. 2011. "Trauma-Focused Cognitive Behavioral Therapy for Children: Impact of the Trauma Narrative and Treatment Length." *Depression and Anxiety* 28, no. 1: 67–75.

Dixon, Matthew L., Alejandro De La Vega, Caitlin Mills, Jessica Andrews-Hanna, R. Nathan Spreng, Michael W. Cole, and Kalina Christoff. 2018. "Heterogeneity within the Frontoparietal Control Network and Its Relationship to the Default and Dorsal Attention Networks." *Proceedings of the National Academy of Sciences* 115, no. 7: E1598–607.

Doubell, Timothy P., Irini Skaliora, Jérôme Baron, and Andrew J. King. 2003. "Functional Connectivity between the Superficial and Deeper Layers of the Superior Colliculus: An Anatomical Substrate for Sensorimotor Integration." *Journal of Neuroscience* 23, no. 16: 6596–607.

Ehlers, Anke, David M. Clark, Ann Hackmann, Freda McManus, and Melanie Fennell. 2005. "Cognitive Therapy for Post-Traumatic Stress Disorder: Development and Evaluation." *Behaviour Research and Therapy* 43, no. 4: 413–31.

Engel-Yeger, Batya, Dafna Palgy-Levin, and Rachel Lev-Wiesel. 2013. "The Sensory Profile of People with Post-Traumatic Stress Symptoms." *Occupational Therapy in Mental Health* 29, no. 3: 266–78.

Farrer, Chloe, Nicolas Franck, Nicolas Georgieff, Chris D. Frith, Jean Decety, and Marc Jeannerod. 2003. "Modulating the Experience of Agency: A Positron Emission Tomography Study." *Neuroimage* 18, no. 2: 324–33.

Faull, Olivia K., Hari H. Subramanian, Martyn Ezra, and Kyle T. S. Pattinson. 2019. "The Midbrain Periaqueductal Gray as an Integrative and Interoceptive Neural Structure for Breathing." *Neuroscience & Biobehavioral Reviews* 98: 135–39.

Feeny, Norah C., Lori A. Zoellner, Lee A. Fitzgibbons, and Edna B. Foa. 2000. "Exploring the Roles of Emotional Numbing, Depression, and Dissociation in PTSD." *Journal of Traumatic Stress* 13, no. 3: 489–98.

Foa, Edna B., Gail Steketee, and Barbara Olasov Rothbaum. 1989. "Behavioral/Cognitive Conceptualizations of Post-Traumatic Stress Disorder." *Behavior Therapy* 20, no. 2: 155–76.

Ford, Julian D., Damion Grasso, Carolyn Greene, Joan Levine, Joseph Spinazzola, and Bessel van der Kolk. 2013. "Clinical Significance of a Proposed Developmental Trauma Disorder Diagnosis: Results of an International Survey of Clinicians." *Journal of Clinical Psychiatry* 74, no. 8: 841–49. doi:10.4088/JCP.12m08030.

Frewen, Paul A., and Ruth A. Lanius. 2006. "Toward a Psychobiology of Post-Traumatic Self Dysregulation: Reexperiencing, Hyperarousal, Dissociation, and Emotional Numbing." *Annals of the New York Academy of Sciences* 1071, no. 1: 110–24.

Geva, Ronny, Ayelet Dital, Dan Ramon, Jessica Yarmolovsky, Maor Gidron, and Jacob Kuint. 2017. "Brainstem as a Developmental Gateway to Social Attention." *Journal of Child Psychology and Psychiatry* 58, no. 12: 1351–59.

Harricharan, Sherain, Margaret C. McKinnon, Mischa Tursich, Maria Densmore, Paul Frewen, Jean Théberge, Bessel van der Kolk, and Ruth A. Lanius. 2019. "Overlapping Frontoparietal Networks in Response to Oculomotion and Traumatic Autobiographical Memory Retrieval: Implications for Eye Movement Desensitization and Reprocessing." *European Journal of Psychotraumatology* 10, no. 1: 1586265.

Harricharan, Sherain, Andrew A. Nicholson, Maria Densmore, Jean Théberge, Margaret C. McKinnon, Richard W. J. Neufeld, and Ruth A. Lanius. 2017. "Sensory Overload and Imbalance: Resting-State Vestibular Connectivity in PTSD and Its Dissociative Subtype." *Neuropsychologia* 106: 169–78.

Hitier, Martin, Stephane Besnard, and Paul F. Smith. 2014. "Vestibular Pathways Involved in Cognition." *Frontiers in Integrative Neuroscience* 8: 159.

King, Andrew J. 2004. "The Superior Colliculus." *Current Biology* 14, no. 9: R335–38.

Kohn, Nils, Simon B. Eickhoff, M. Scheller, Angela R. Laird, Peter T. Fox, and Ute Habel. 2014. "Neural Network of Cognitive Emotion Regulation—An ALE Meta-analysis and MACM Analysis." *Neuroimage* 87: 345–55.

Koomar, J. A. 2009. "Trauma- and Attachment-Informed Sensory Integration Assessment and Intervention." *Sensory Integration Special Interest Section Quarterly* 32, no. 4: 1–4.

Lanius, Ruth A., Peter C. Williamson, Maria Densmore, Kristine Boksman, R. W. Neufeld, Joseph S. Gati, and Ravi S. Menon. 2004. "The Nature of Traumatic Memories: A 4-T FMRI Functional Connectivity Analysis." *American Journal of Psychiatry* 161, no. 1: 36–44.

Lopez, Christophe, and Olaf Blanke. 2011. "The Thalamocortical Vestibular System in Animals and Humans." *Brain Research Reviews* 67, no. 1–2: 119–46.

Lopez, Christopher, Pär Halje, and Olaf Blanke. 2008. "Body Ownership and Embodiment: Vestibular and Multisensory Mechanisms." *Neurophysiologie Clinique/Clinical Neurophysiology* 38, no. 3: 149–61.

MacDonald, Angus W., Jonathan D. Cohen, V. Andrew Stenger, and Cameron S. Carter. 2000. "Dissociating the Role of the Dorsolateral Prefrontal and Anterior Cingulate Cortex in Cognitive Control." *Science* 288, no. 5472: 1835–38.

Meredith, M. Alex, and Barry E. Stein. 1985. "Descending Efferents from the Superior Colliculus Relay Integrated Multisensory Information." *Science* 227, no. 4687: 657–59.

Nicholson, Andrew A., Karl J. Friston, Peter Zeidman, Sherain Harricharan, Margaret C. McKinnon, Maria Densmore, Richard W. J. Neufeld, et al. 2017. "Dynamic Causal Modeling in PTSD and Its Dissociative Subtype: Bottom-up Versus Top-down Processing within Fear and Emotion Regulation Circuitry." *Human Brain Mapping* 38, no. 11: 5551–61.

Ogden, Pat, and Kekuni Minton. 2000. "Sensorimotor Psychotherapy: One Method for Processing Traumatic Memory." *Traumatology* 6, no. 3: 149–73.

Olivé, Isadora, Maria Densmore, Sherain Harricharan, Jean Théberge, Margaret C. McKinnon, and Ruth Lanius. 2018. "Superior Colliculus Resting State Networks in Post-Traumatic Stress Disorder and Its Dissociative Subtype." *Human Brain Mapping* 39, no. 1: 563–74.

Pollatos, Olga, Rainer Schandry, Dorothee P. Auer, and Christian Kaufmann. 2007. "Brain Structures Mediating Cardiovascular Arousal and Interoceptive Awareness." *Brain Research* 1141: 178–87.

Schimmenti, Adriano, and Vincenzo Caretti. 2016. "Linking the Overwhelming with the Unbearable: Developmental Trauma, Dissociation, and the Disconnected Self." *Psychoanalytic Psychology* 33, no. 1: 106.

Schore, Allan N. 2002. "Dysregulation of the Right Brain: A Fundamental Mechanism of Traumatic Attachment and the Psychopathogenesis of Post-Traumatic Stress Disorder." *Australian and New Zealand Journal of Psychiatry* 36, no. 1: 9–30.

Seth, Anil K. 2013. "Interoceptive Inference, Emotion, and the Embodied Self." *Trends in Cognitive Sciences* 17, no. 11: 565–73.

Shapiro, Francine. 2001. *Eye Movement Desensitization and Reprocessing (EMDR): Basic Principles, Protocols, and Procedures*. New York: Guilford Press.

Simmons, W. Kyle, Jason A. Avery, Joel C. Barcalow, Jerzy Bodurka, Wayne C. Drevets, and Patrick Bellgowan. 2013. "Keeping the Body in Mind: Insula Functional Organization and Functional Connectivity Integrate Interoceptive, Exteroceptive, and Emotional Awareness." *Human Brain Mapping* 34, no. 11: 2944–58.

Solomon, Eldra P., and Kathleen M. Heide. 2005. "The Biology of Trauma: Implications for Treatment." *Journal of Interpersonal Violence* 20, no. 1: 51–60.

Stein, Barry E. 1998. "Neural Mechanisms for Synthesizing Sensory Information and Producing Adaptive Behaviors." *Experimental Brain Research* 123, no. 1–2: 124–35.

Stewart, Lorraine P., and Patricia M. White. 2008. "Sensory Filtering Phenomenology in PTSD." *Depression and Anxiety* 25, no. 1: 38–45.

Taylor, Ann Gill, Lisa E. Goehler, Daniel I. Galper, Kim E. Innes, and Cheryl Bourguignon. 2010. "Top-down and Bottom-up Mechanisms in Mind-Body Medicine: Development of an Integrative Framework for Psychophysiological Research." *Explore* 6, no. 1: 29–41.

Terpou, Braeden A., Sherain Harricharan, Margaret C. McKinnon, Paul Frewen, Rakesh Jetly, and Ruth A. Lanius. 2019. "The Effects of Trauma on Brain and Body: A Unifying Role for the Midbrain Periaqueductal Gray." *Journal of Neuroscience Research* 97, no. 9: 1110–40.

van der Kolk, Bessel A. 1994. "The Body Keeps the Score: Memory and the Evolving Psychobiology of Post-Traumatic Stress." *Harvard Review of Psychiatry* 1, no. 5: 253–65.

Chapter 1

Ayres, A. Jean. 1972. *Sensory Integration and Learning Disorders*. Los Angeles: Western Psychological Services.

Gibson, James J. 1977. "The Theory of Affordances." In *The Ecological Approach to Visual Perception*, 126–37. Repr. 1986. Hillsdale, NJ: Lawrence Erlbaum.

Ogden, Pat, and Kekuni Minton. 2000. "Sensorimotor Psychotherapy: One Method for Processing Traumatic Memory." *Traumatology* 3, no. 3 (October): 149–73.

Siegel, Daniel J. 1999. *The Developing Mind: How Relationships and the Brain Interact to Shape Who We Are*. New York: Guilford Press.

Siegel, Daniel J. 2012. *The Developing Mind: How Relationships and the Brain Interact to Shape Who We Are*. 2nd ed. New York: Guilford Press.

Streeck-Fischer, Annette, and Bessel A. van der Kolk. 2000. "Down Will Come Baby, Cradle and All." *Australian and New Zealand Journal of Psychiatry* 34, no. 6 (January): 903–18.

Warner, Elizabeth, Alexandra Cook, Anne Westcott, and Jane Koomar. 2011. *Sensory Motor Arousal Regulation Treatment (SMART): A Manual for Therapists Working with Children and Adolescents: A "Bottom Up" Approach to the Treatment of Complex Trauma*. Brookline, MA: The Trauma Center at JRI.

Warner, Elizabeth, Alexandra Cook, Anne Westcott, and Jane Koomar. 2014. *Sensory Motor Arousal Regulation Treatment (SMART): A Manual for Therapists Working with Children and Adolescents: A "Bottom Up" Approach to the Treatment of Complex Trauma.* 2nd ed. Brookline, MA: The Trauma Center at JRI. First published 2011.

Chapter 2

Ainsworth, Mary D. Salter, Mary C. Blehar, Everett Waters, and Sally N. Wall. 1978. *Patterns of Attachment: A Psychological Study of the Strange Situation.* Hillsdale, NJ: Lawrence Erlbaum.

Anda, Robert F. 2002. "The Wide-Ranging Health Effects of Adverse Childhood Experiences." Paper presented at the 18th annual meeting of the International Society for Traumatic Stress Studies, Baltimore, MD, November 2002.

Arzy, Shahar, Istvan Molnar-Szakacs, and Olaf Blanke. 2008. "Self in Time: Imagined Self-Location Influences Neural Activity Related to Mental Time Travel." *Journal of Neuroscience* 28, no. 25 (June 18): 6502–507. doi:10.1523/jneurosci.5712-07.2008.

Assink, Mark, Anouk Spruit, Mendel Schuts, Ramón Lindauer, Claudia E. van der Put, and Geert-Jan J. M. Stam. 2018. "The Intergenerational Transmission of Child Maltreatment: A Three-Level Meta-Analysis." *Child Abuse and Neglect* 84 (October): 131–45. doi:10.1016/j.chiabu.2018.07.037.

Ayres, A. Jean, and Jeff Robbins. 2005. *Sensory Integration and the Child: Understanding Hidden Sensory Challenges.* Torrance, CA: Western Psychological Services. First published 1979.

Bagner, Daniel M., and Sheila M. Eyberg. 2007. "Parent–Child Interaction Therapy for Disruptive Behavior in Children with Mental Retardation: A Randomized Controlled Trial." *Journal of Clinical Child and Adolescent Psychology* 36, no. 3 (July): 418–29. doi:10.1080/15374410701448448.

Balaban, C. D. 2016. "Neurotransmitters in the Vestibular System." In *Handbook of Clinical Neurology: Neuro-Otology* 137 (3rd series), edited by J. M. Furman and T. Lempert, 41–55. Cambridge, MA: Elsevier. doi:10.1016/B978-0-444-63437-5.00003-0.

Bartlett, Jessica M., Chie Kotake, Rebecca Fauth, and M. Ann Easterbrooks. 2017. "The Intergenerational Transmission of Child Abuse and Neglect: Do Maltreatment Type, Perpetrator, and Substantiation Status Matter?" *Child Abuse and Neglect* 67 (January): 84–94. doi:10.1016/j.chiabu.2018.07.037.

Beebe, Beatrice. 2014. "My Journey in Infant Research and Psychoanalysis: Microanalysis, a Social Microscope." *Psychoanalytic Psychology* 31, no. 1: 4–25. doi:10.1037/a0035575.

Beebe, Beatrice, and Frank M. Lachmann. 2014. *The Origins of Attachment: Infant Research and Adult Treatment.* New York: Routledge.

Bergholz, Lou, Erin Stafford, and Wendy D'Andrea. 2016. "Creating Trauma-Informed Sports Programming for Traumatized Youth: Core Principles for an Adjunctive Therapeutic Approach." *Journal of Infant, Child, and Adolescent Psychotherapy* 15, no. 3: 244–53. doi:10.1080/15289168.2016.1211836.

Blanke, Olaf. 2012. "Multisensory Brain Mechanisms of Bodily Self-Consciousness." *Nature Reviews Neuroscience* 13, no. 8 (August): 556–71. doi:10.1038/nrn3292.

Blanke, Olaf, Mel Slater, and Andrea Serino. 2015. "Behavioral, Neural, and Computational Principles of Bodily Self-Consciousness." *Neuron* 88, no. 1 (October): 145–66. doi:10.1016/j.neuron.2015.09.029.

Blaustein, Margaret E., and Kristine M. Kinniburgh. 2019. *Treating Traumatic Stress in Children and Adolescents: How to Foster Resilience through Attachment, Self-Regulation, and Competency.* 2nd ed. New York: Guilford Press.

Bluhm, Robyn L., Peter C. Williamson, Elizabeth A. Osuch, Paul A. Frewen, Todd K. Stevens, Kristine Boksman, Richard W. J. Neufeld, Jean Théberge, and Ruth A. Lanius. 2009. "Alterations in Default Network Connectivity in Posttraumatic Stress Disorder Related to Early-Life Trauma." *Journal of Psychiatry and Neuroscience* 34, no. 3 (May): 187–94.

Blythe, Sally Goddard, Lawrence J. Beuret, and Peter Blythe. 2017. *Attention, Balance and Coordination: The A. B. C. of Learning Success.* 2nd ed. Chichester, UK: Wiley.

Booth, Phyllis B., and Ann M. Jernberg. 2010. *Theraplay: Helping Parents and Children Build Better Relationships through Attachment-Based Play.* 3rd ed. San Francisco: Wiley.

Bowlby, John. 1969. *Attachment and Loss: Attachment,* vol. 1. New York: Basic Books.

Bowlby, John. 1973. *Attachment and Loss: Separation Anxiety and Anger,* vol. 2. New York: Basic Books.

Bowlby, John. 1980. *Attachment and Loss: Sadness and Depression,* vol. 3. New York: Basic Books.

Bracha, H. Stefan, Tyler C. Ralston, Jennifer M. Matsukawa, Andrew E. Williams, and Adam S. Bracha. 2004. "Does 'Fight or Flight' Need Updating?" (letter to editor). *Psychosomatics* 45, no. 5 (September–October): 448–49.

Bradley, James. 2014. "Matters of Priority: Herbert Mayo, Charles Bell and Discoveries in the Nervous System." *Medical History* 59, no. 4: 564–84. doi:10.1017/mdh.2014.53.

Buckner, Randy. 2012. "The Serendipitous Discovery of the Brain's Default Network." *NeuroImage* 62, no. 2 (August): 1137–45. doi:10.1016/j.neuroimage.2011.10.035.

Bundy, Anita C., and Jane A. Koomar. 2002. "Orchestrating Intervention: The Art of Practice." In *Sensory Integration: Theory and Practice,* edited by Anita C. Bundy, Shelly J. Lane, and Elizabeth A. Murray, 241–60. Philadelphia: F. A. Davis.

Chaffin, Mark, Beverly Funderburk, David Bard, Linda Anne Valle, and Robin Gurwitch. 2011. "A Combined Motivation and Parent–Child Interaction Therapy Package Reduces Child Welfare Recidivism in a Randomized Dismantling Field Trial." *Journal of Consulting and Clinical Psychology* 79, no. 1: 84–95. doi:10.1037/a0021227.

Cloitre, Marylene, Chris Courtois, Julian Ford, Bonnie Green, Pamela Alexander, John Briere, Judith L. Herman, et al. 2012. "The ISTSS Expert Consensus Treatment Guidelines for Complex PTSD in Adults." Complex Trauma Task Force. https://tinyurl.com/ool38nf.

Cohen, Judith A., Anthony P. Mannarino, and Esther Deblinger, eds. 2012. *Trauma-Focused CBT for Children and Adolescents: Treatment Applications.* New York: Guilford Press.

Cook, Alexandra, Margaret Blaustein, Joseph Spinazzola, and Bessel van der Kolk. 2003. "Complex Trauma in Children and Adolescents: White Paper from the National Child Traumatic Stress Network Complex Trauma Task Force." Los Angeles: National Center for Child Traumatic Stress.

Cook, Alexandra, Joseph Spinazzola, Julian Ford, Cheryl Lanktree, Margaret Blaustein, Marylene Cloitre, Ruth DeRosa, Rebecca Hubbard, Richard Kagan, Joan Liautaud, et al. 2005. "Complex Trauma in Children and Adolescents." *Psychiatric Annals* 35, no. 5 (May): 390–98.

Craig, A. D. (Bud). 2015. *How Do You Feel? An Interoceptive Moment with Your Neurobiological Self.* Princeton, NJ: Princeton University Press.

Crittenden, Patricia M. 1985. "Maltreated Infants: Vulnerability and Resilience." *Journal of Child Psychology* 26, no. 1: 85–96.

Cuppini, Cristiano, Barry E. Stein, and Benjamin A. Rowland. 2018. "Development of the Mechanisms Governing Midbrain Multisensory Integration." *Journal of Neuroscience* 38, no. 14 (April 4): 3453–65. doi:10.1523/JNEUROSCI.2631-17.2018.

Damasio, Antonio. 2010. *Self Comes to Mind: Constructing the Conscious Brain.* New York: Vintage Books.

D'Andrea, Wendy, Lou Bergholz, Andrea Fortunato, and Joseph Spinazzola. 2013. "Play to the Whistle: A Pilot Investigation of a Sports-Based Intervention for Traumatized Girls in Residential Treatment." *Journal of Family Violence* 28, no. 7: 739–49. doi:10.1007/s10896-013-9533-x.

D'Andrea, Wendy, Nnamdi Pole, Jonathan DiPierro, Steven Freed, and D. Brian Wallace. 2013. "Heterogeneity of Defensive Responses after Exposure to Trauma: Blunted Autonomic Reactivity in Response to Startling Sounds." *International Journal of Psychophysiology* 90, no. 1 (October): 80–89. doi:10.1016/j.ijpsycho.2013.07.008.

Daniels, Judith K., Paul Frewen, Margaret C. McKinnon, and Ruth A. Lanius. 2011. "Default Mode Alterations in Posttraumatic Stress Disorder Related to Early-Life Trauma: A Developmental Perspective." *Journal of Psychiatry and Neuroscience* 36, no. 1: 56–59. doi:10.1503/jpn.100050.

De Bellis, Michael D., Stephen R. Hooper, and Jennifer L. Sapia. 2005. "Early Trauma Exposure and the Brain." In *Neuropsychology of PTSD: Biological, Cognitive, and Clinical Perspectives,* edited by Jennifer J. Vasterling and Chris R. Brewin, 153–77. New York: Guilford Press.

De Bellis, Michael D., Stephen R. Hooper, Eve G. Spratt, and Donald P. Woolley. 2009. "Neuropsychological Findings in Childhood Neglect and Their Relationships to Pediatric PTSD." *Journal of the International Psychological Society* 15, no. 6 (November): 868–78. doi:10.1017/S1355617709990464.

De Bellis, Michael D., Donald P. Woolley, and Stephen R. Hooper. 2013. "Neuropsychological Findings in Pediatric Maltreatment: Relationship of PTSD, Dissociative Symptoms, and Abuse/Neglect Indices to Neurocognitive Outcomes." *Child Maltreatment* 18, no. 3 (August): 171–83. doi:10.1177/1077559513497420.

Delafield-Butt, Jonathan T., and Colwyn Trevarthen. 2013. "Theories of the Development of Human Communication." In *Theories and Models of Communication*, edited by Paul Cobley and Peter J. Schulz, 199–222. Berlin/Boston: De Gruyter Mouton.

Egeland, Byron, and L. Alan Sroufe. 1981. "Attachment and Early Maltreatment." *Child Development* 52, no. 1 (March): 44–52. www.jstor.org/stable/1129213.

Elbers, Jorina, Cynthia R. Rovnaghi, Brenda Golianu, and Kanwaljeet J. S. Anand. 2017. "Clinical Profile Associated with Adverse Childhood Experiences: The Advent of Nervous System Dysregulation." *Children* 4, no. 98: 1–14. doi:10.3390/children4110098.

Emerson, David, and Elizabeth Hopper. 2011. *Overcoming Trauma through Yoga: Reclaiming Your Body*. Berkeley, CA: North Atlantic Books.

Ensink, Karin, Jessica L. Borelli, Lina Normandin, Mary Target, and Peter Fonagy. 2019. "Childhood Sexual Abuse and Attachment Insecurity: Associations with Child Psychological Difficulties." *American Journal of Orthopsychiatry*, March 4. doi:10.1037/ort0000407.

Felitti, Vincent J., and Robert F. Anda. 2010. "The Relationship of Adverse Childhood Experiences to Adult Medical Disease, Psychiatric Disorders, and Sexual Behavior: Implications for Health Care." In *The Impact of Early Life Trauma on Health and Disease: The Hidden Epidemic*, edited by Ruth A. Lanius, Eric Vermetten, and Clare M. Pain, 77–87. Cambridge: Cambridge University Press.

Felitti, Vincent J., Robert F. Anda, Dale Nordenberg, David F. Williamson, Alison M. Spitz, Valerie Edwards, Mary P. Koss, and James S. Marks. 1998. "Relationship of Childhood Abuse and Household Dysfunction to Many of the Leading Causes of Death in Adults: The Adverse Childhood Experiences (ACE) Study." *American Journal of Preventive Medicine* 14, no. 4: 245–58. doi:10.1016/S0749-3797(98)00017-8.

Felman, Shoshana, and Dori Laub. 1992. *Testimony: Crises of Witnessing in Literature, Psychoanalysis, and History*. New York: Routledge.

Fonagy, P., G. Gergely, and M. Target. 2007. "The Parent–Infant Dyad and the Construction of the Subjective Self." *Journal of Child Psychology and Psychiatry* 48, nos. 3–4 (March–April): 329–54.

Ford, Julian D., Joseph Spinazzola, Bessel van der Kolk, and Damian J. Grasso. 2018. "Toward an Empirically Based Developmental Trauma Disorder Diagnosis for Children: Factor Structure, Item Characteristics, Reliability, and Validity of the Developmental Trauma Disorder Semi-Structured Interview." *Journal of Clinical Psychiatry* 79, no. 5 (September/October): e1–e19. doi:10.4088/JCP.17m11675.

Gabowitz, Dawna, Marla Zucker, and Alexandra Cook. 2008. "Neuropsychological Assessment in Clinical Evaluation of Children and Adolescents with Complex Trauma." *Journal of Child and Adolescent Trauma* 1: 163–78. doi:10.1080/19361520802003822.

Gaensbauer, Theodore J. 2002. "Representations of Trauma in Infancy: Clinical and Theoretical Implications for the Understanding of Early Memory." *Infant Mental Health Journal* 23, no. 3: 259–77. doi:10.1002/imhj.10020.

Gaensbauer, Theodore J. 2016. "Moments of Meeting: The Relevance of Lou Sander's and Dan Stern's Conceptual Framework for Understanding the Development of Pathological

Social Relatedness." *Infant Mental Health Journal* 37, no. 2 (March/April): 172–88. doi:10.1002/imhj.21555.

Gallese, Vittorio, Luciano Fadiga, Leonardo Fogassi, and Giacomo Rizzolatti. 1996. "Action Recognition in the Premotor Cortex." *Brain* 119, no. 2 (April): 593–609.

Gendlin, Eugene T. 1982. *Focusing.* New York: Bantam.

Gendlin, Eugene T. 2012. *Focusing-Oriented Psychotherapy: A Manual of the Experiential Method.* New York: Guilford Press.

Gil, Eliana. 1991. *The Healing Power of Play: Working with Abused Children.* New York: Guilford Press.

Gil, Eliana. 2006. *Helping Abused and Traumatized Children: Integrating Directive and Nondirective Approaches.* New York: Guilford Press.

Gil, Eliana. 2017. *Posttraumatic Play in Children: What Clinicians Should Know.* New York: Guilford Press.

Gomez, Ana M. 2012. *EMDR Therapy and Adjunct Approaches with Children: Complex Trauma, Attachment, and Dissociation.* New York: Springer.

Goodill, Sharon W. 1987. "Dance/Movement Therapy with Abused Children." *The Arts in Psychotherapy* 14, no. 1 (Spring): 59–68. doi:10.1016/0197-4556(87)90035-9.

Greeson, Joanna K. P., Ernestine C. Briggs, Christopher M. Layne, Harolyn M. E. Belcher, Sarah A. Ostrowski, Soeun Kim, Robert C. Lee, Rebecca L. Vivrette, Robert S. Pynoos, and John A. Fairbank. 2014. "Traumatic Childhood Experiences in the 21st Century: Broadening and Building on the ACE Studies with Data from the National Child Traumatic Stress Network." *Journal of Interpersonal Violence* 29, no. 3: 536–56. doi:10.1177/0886260513505217.

Hara, Masayuki, Polona Pozeg, Giulio Rognini, Toshiro Higuchi, Kazunobu Fukuhara, Akio Yamamoto, Toshiro Higuchi, Olaf Blanke, and Roy Salomon. 2015. "Voluntary Self-Touch Increases Body Ownership." *Frontiers in Psychology* 6 (October): article 1509. doi:10.3389/fpsyg.2015.01509.

Harlow, Harry F., and Robert R. Zimmerman. 1959. "Affectional Responses in the Infant Monkey." *Science* 130, no. 3373 (August 21): 421–32.

Harricharan, Sherain, Andrew A. Nicholson, Maria Densmore, Jean Théberge, Margaret C. McKinnon, Richard W. J. Neufeld, and Ruth A. Lanius. 2017. "Sensory Overload and Imbalance: Resting-State Vestibular Connectivity in PTSD and Its Dissociative Subtype." *Neuropsychologia* 106 (November): 169–78. doi:10.1016/j.neuropsychologia.2017.09.010.

Harris, David Alan. 2007. "Dance/Movement Therapy Approaches to Fostering Resilience and Recovery among Adolescent African Torture Survivors." *Torture* 17, no. 2: 134–55. https://tinyurl.com/rvz2evr.

Herbert, Beate M., and Olga Pollatos. 2012. "The Body in the Mind: On the Relationship between Interoception and Embodiment." *Topics in Cognitive Science* 4, no. 4: 692–704. doi:10.1111/j.1756-8765.2012.01189.x.

Herman, Judith. 1992. *Trauma and Recovery.* New York: Basic Books.

Ho, Rainbow Tin Hung. 2015. "A Place and Space to Survive: A Dance/Movement Therapy Program for Child Sexual Abuse Survivors." *The Arts in Psychotherapy* 46: 9–16. doi:10.1016/j.tifp.2015.09.004.

Hoover, Adria E. N., and Laurence R. Harris. 2015. "Disrupting Vestibular Activity Disrupts Body Ownership." *Multisensory Research* 28, no. 5/6: 581–90. doi:10.1163/22134808-00002472.

Hughes, Daniel A. 2018. *Building the Bonds of Attachment: Awakening Love in Deeply Traumatized Children*. 3rd ed. Lanham, MD: Rowman & Littlefield.

Ionta, Silvio, Lukas Heydrich, Bigna Lenggenhager, Michael Mouton, Eleonara Fornari, Dominique Chapuis, Roger Gassert, and Olaf Blanke. 2011. "Multisensory Mechanisms in Temporo-Parietal Cortex Support Self-Location and First-Person Perspective." *Neuron* 70 (April): 363–74. doi:10.1016/j.neuron.2011.03.009.

Ionta, Silvio, Roberto Martuzzi, Roy Salomon, and Olaf Blanke. 2014. "The Brain Network Reflecting Bodily Self-Consciousness: A Functional Connectivity Study." *Social Cognitive and Affective Neuroscience* 9, no. 12: 1904–13. doi:10.1093/scan/nst185.

Kandel, Eric R., James H. Schwartz, Thomas M. Jessell, Steven A. Siegelbaum, and A. J. Hudspeth, eds. 2013. *Principles of Neural Science*. 5th ed. New York: McGraw-Hill Medical.

Kendall-Tackett, Kathleen A., Linda Meyer Williams, and David Finkelhor. 1993. "Impact of Sexual Abuse on Children: A Review and Synthesis of Recent Empirical Studies." *Psychological Bulletin* 113, no. 1: 164–80.

Koomar, Jane A., and Anita C. Bundy. 2002. "Creating Direct Intervention from Theory." In *Sensory Integration: Theory and Practice,* edited by Anita C. Bundy, Shelly J. Lane, and Elizabeth A. Murray, 261–302. Philadelphia: F. A. Davis.

Kornblum, Rena, and Robin Lending Halsten. 2006. "In-School Dance/Movement Therapy for Traumatized Children." In *Creative Arts Therapies Manual: A Guide to the History, Theoretical Approaches, Assessment, and Work with Special Populations of Art, Play, Music, Dance, Drama, and Poetry Therapies,* edited by Stephanie L. Brooke, 144–55. Springfield, IL: Charles C. Thomas.

Kozlowska, Kasia, Peter Walker, Loyola McLean, and Pascal Carrive. 2015. "Fear and the Defense Cascade: Clinical Implications and Management." *Harvard Review of Psychiatry* 23, no. 4 (July–August): 263–87. doi:10.1097/HRP.0000000000000065.

Kranowitz, Carol Stock. 2005. *The Out-of-Sync Child: Recognizing and Coping with Sensory Processing Disorder*. Rev. ed. New York: Penguin.

Lanius, Ruth A., Eric Vermetten, and Clare Pain. 2010. *The Impact of Early Life Trauma on Health and Disease: The Hidden Epidemic*. Cambridge: Cambridge University Press.

Laub, Dori, and Annette C. Auerhahn. 1993. "Knowing and Not Knowing Massive Psychic Trauma: Forms of Traumatic Memory." *International Journal of Psychoanalysis* 74: 287–302.

Layne, Christopher M., Joanna K. P. Greeson, Sarah A. Ostrowski, Soeun Kim, Stephanie Reading, Rebecca L. Vivrette, Ernestine C. Briggs, John A. Fairbank, and Robert S. Pynoos. 2014. "Cumulative Trauma Exposure and High Risk Behavior in Adolescence:

Findings from the National Child Traumatic Stress Network Core Data Set." *Psychological Trauma: Theory, Research, Practice, and Policy* 6 (S1): S40–S49. doi:10.1037/a0037799.

Lenggenhager, Bigna, and Christophe Lopez. 2015. "Vestibular Contributions to the Sense of Body, Self, and Others." In *Open MIND,* edited by Thomas Metzinger and Jennifer M. Windt. Frankfurt, Germany: MIND Group. doi:10.15502/9783958570023.

Lenggenhager, B., S. T. Smith, and O. Blanke. 2006. "Functional and Neural Mechanisms of Embodiment: Importance of the Vestibular System and the Temporal Parietal Junction." *Reviews in the Neurosciences* 17, no. 6: 643–57. doi:10.1515/REVNEURO.2006.17.6.643.

Levine, Peter A. 2010. *In an Unspoken Voice: How the Body Releases Trauma and Restores Goodness.* Berkeley, CA: North Atlantic Books.

Levine, Peter A. 2015. *Trauma and Memory: Brain and Body in a Search for the Living Past: A Practical Guide for Understanding and Working with Traumatic Memory.* Berkeley, CA: North Atlantic Books.

Levine, Peter A., and Ann Frederick. 1997. *Waking the Tiger: Healing Trauma: The Innate Capacity to Transform Overwhelming Experiences.* Berkeley, CA: North Atlantic Books.

Levine, Peter A., and Maggie Kline. 2006. *Trauma through a Child's Eyes: Awakening the Ordinary Miracle of Healing—Infancy through Adolescence.* Berkeley, CA: North Atlantic Books.

Lieberman, Alicia F., and Patricia van Horn. 2008. *Psychotherapy with Infants and Young Children: Repairing the Effects of Stress and Trauma on Early Attachment.* New York: Guilford Press.

Lyons-Ruth, Karlen. 2016. "The Interface between Attachment and Intersubjectivity: Perspective from the Longitudinal Study of Disorganized Attachment." *Psychoanalytic Inquiry* 26, no. 4 (June): 595–616. doi:10.1080/07351690701310656.

Lyons-Ruth, Karlen, Lyssa Dutra, Michelle R. Schuder, and Ilaria Bianchi. 2006. "From Infant Attachment Disorganization to Adult Dissociation: Relational Adaptations or Traumatic Experiences?" *Psychiatric Clinics of North America* 29, no. 1 (March): 63–86, viii. doi:10.1016/j.psc.2005.10.011.

Lyons-Ruth, K., P. Pechtel, S. A. Yoon, C. M. Anderson, and M. H. Teicher. 2016. "Disorganized Attachment in Infancy Predicts Greater Amygdala Volume in Adulthood." *Behavioral Brain Research* 308 (April): 83–93. doi:10.1016/j.bbr.2016.03.050.

Macfie, Jenny, Dante Cicchetti, and Sheree L. Toth. 2001. "The Development of Dissociation in Maltreated Preschool-Aged Children." *Development and Psychopathology* 13, no. 2: 233–54.

Madigan, Sheri, Chantal Cyr, Rachel Eirich, R. M. Pasco Fearon, Anh Ly, Christina Rash, Julia C. Poole, and Lenneke R. A. Alink. 2019. "Testing the Cycle of Maltreatment Hypothesis: Meta-Analytic Evidence of the Intergenerational Transmission of Child Maltreatment." *Development and Psychopathology* 31 (February): 23–51. doi:10.1017/S0954579418001700.

Main, Mary, and Judith Solomon. 1986. "Discovery of an Insecure-Disorganized/Disoriented Attachment Pattern." In *Affective Development in Infancy,* edited by T. Berry Brazelton and Michael W. Yogman, 95–124. Norwood, NJ: Ablex.

Namkung, Ho, Sun-Hong Kim, and Akira Sawa. 2017. "The Insula: An Underestimated Brain Area in Clinical Neuroscience, Psychiatry, and Neurology." *Trends in Neuroscience* 40, no. 4 (April): 200–207. doi:10.1016/j.tins.2017.02.002.

Naste, Tiffany M., Maggi Price, Jane Karol, Lia Martin, Kathryn Murphy, Jennifer Miguel, and Joseph Spinazzola. 2018. "Equine Facilitated Therapy for Complex Trauma (EFT-CT)." *Journal of Child and Adolescent Trauma* 11, no. 3 (September): 289–303. doi:10.1007/s40653-017-0187-3.

Ogden, Pat, and Janina Fisher. 2015. *Sensorimotor Psychotherapy: Interventions for Trauma and Attachment.* New York: W. W. Norton.

Ogden, Pat, and Kekuni Minton. 2000. "Sensorimotor Psychotherapy: One Model for Processing Traumatic Memory." *Traumatology* 3, no. 3 (October): 149–73.

Ogden, Pat, Kekuni Minton, and Clare Pain. 2006. *Trauma and the Body: A Sensorimotor Approach to Psychotherapy.* New York: W. W. Norton.

Patriat, Rémi, Rasmus M. Birn, Taylor J. Keding, and Ryan J. Herringa. 2016. "Default-Mode Network Abnormalities in Pediatric Posttraumatic Stress Disorder." *Journal of the American Academy of Child and Adolescent Psychiatry* 55, no. 4 (April): 319–27. doi:10.1016/j.jaac.2016.01.010.

Payne, Peter, Peter A. Levine, and Mardi A. Crane-Godreau. 2015. "Somatic Experiencing: Using Interoception and Proprioception as Core Elements of Trauma Therapy." *Frontiers in Psychology* 6 (February 4): 1–18. doi:10.3389/fpsyg.2015.00093.

Pfeiffer, Christian, Christophe Lopez, Valentin Schmutz, Julio Angel Duenas, and Roberto Martuzzi. 2013. "Multisensory Origin of the Subjective First-Person Perspective: Visual, Tactile, and Vestibular Mechanisms." *PLOS One* 8, no. 4 (April): e61751. doi:10.1371/journal.pone.0061751.

Pfeiffer, Christian, Andrea Serino, and Olaf Blanke. 2014. "The Vestibular System: A Spatial Reference for Bodily Self-Consciousness." *Frontiers in Integrative Neuroscience* 8 (April): article 31. doi:10.3389/fnint.2014.00031.

Piaget, Jean. 1952. *The Origins of Intelligence in Children.* Translated by Margaret Cook (1953). London: Routledge.

Porges, Stephen W. 2004. "Neuroception: A Subconscious System for Detecting Threats and Safety." *Zero to Three* 24, no. 5 (May): 19–24.

Porges, Stephen W. 2011. *The Polyvagal Theory: Neurophysiological Foundations of Emotions, Attachment, Communication, and Self-Regulation.* New York: W. W. Norton.

Porges, Stephen W. 2017. *The Pocket Guide to the Polyvagal Theory: The Transformative Power of Feeling Safe.* New York: W. W. Norton.

Proske, Uwe, and Simon Gandevia. 2012. "The Proprioceptive Senses: Their Roles in Signaling Body Shape, Body Position and Movement, and Muscle Force." *Physiological Review* 92 (October): 1651–97. doi:10.1152/physrev.00048.2011.

Putnam, W. Frank. 1997. *Dissociation in Children and Adolescents: A Developmental Perspective.* New York: Guilford Press.

Putnam, W. Frank. 2016. *The Way We Are: How States of Mind Influence Our Identities, Personality and Potential for Change.* New York: International Psychoanalytic Books.

Putnam, W. Frank, and Penelope K. Trickett. 1997. "Psychobiological Effects of Sexual Abuse: A Longitudinal Study." *Annals of the New York Academy of Sciences* 821, no. 1 (June): 150–59.

Qin, Pengmin, and Georg Northoff. 2011. "How Is Our Self Related to Midline Regions and the Default-Mode Network?" *NeuroImage* 57, no. 3 (August 1): 1221–33. doi:10.1016/j.neuroimage.2011.05.028.

Reed, Geoffrey M., Michael B. First, Cary S. Kogan, Steven E. Hyman, Oye Gureje, Wolfgang Gaebel, Mario Maj, et al. 2019. "Innovations and Changes in the ICD-11 Classification of Mental, Behavioral and Neurodevelopmental Disorders." *World Psychiatry* 18, no. 1 (February): 3–19. doi:10.1002/wps.20611.

Reynolds, Stacy, Samantha Costanza, Meghan Odom, Shelly Lane, Lauren Meeley, Ashely Owen, Gina Pepe, Miriam Chinn, Dawn Davis, and Lauren Wilson. 2015. "Effect of Engagement in Sensory-Based Tasks on Autonomic Nervous System Regulation." *American Journal of Occupational Therapy* 69, Supplement 1 (July): 6911520072p1. doi:10.5014/ajot.2015.69S1-RP101B.

Reynolds, Stacy, Shelly J. Lane, and Brian Mullen. 2015. "Effects of Deep Pressure Stimulation on Physiological Arousal." *American Journal of Occupational Therapy* 69, no. 3 (May/June): p6903350010p1-6903350010p5. doi:10.5014/ajot.2015.015560.

Sapolsky, Robert M. 2017. *Behave: The Biology of Humans at Our Best and Worst.* New York: Penguin.

Schneider-Rosen, Karen, Karen G. Braunwald, Vicki Carlson, and Dante Cicchetti. 1985. "Current Perspectives in Attachment Theory: Illustration from the Study of Maltreated Infants." *Monographs of the Society for Research in Child Development* 50, nos. 1–2: 194–201. doi:10.2307/3333833.

Schore, Allan N. 2003. *Affect Dysregulation and Disorders of the Self.* New York: W. W. Norton.

Schore, Allan N. 2012. *The Science of the Art of Psychotherapy.* New York: W. W. Norton.

Sherin, Jonathan E., and Charles B. Nemeroff. 2011. "Post-Traumatic Stress Disorder: The Neurobiological Impact of Psychological Trauma." *Dialogues in Clinical Neuroscience* 13, no. 3: 263. https://tinyurl.com/yxxp24g6.

Siegel, Daniel J. 2012. *The Developing Mind: How Relationships and the Brain Interact to Shape Who We Are.* 2nd ed. New York: Guilford Press.

Silberg, Joyanna. 2012. *The Child Survivor: Healing Developmental Trauma and Dissociation.* New York: Routledge.

Spinazzola, Joseph, Alison M. Rhodes, David Emerson, Ellen Earle, and Kathryn Monroe. 2011. "Application of Yoga in Residential Treatment of Traumatized Youth." *Journal of the American Psychiatric Nurses Association* 17, no. 6: 431–44. doi:10.1177/1078390311418359.

Stern, Daniel N. 2018. *The Interpersonal World of the Infant: A View from Psychoanalysis and Developmental Psychology.* London: Routledge. First published 1985.

Sylvestre, Audette, Ève-Line Bussières, and Caroline Bouchard. 2015. "Language Problems among Abused and Neglected Children: A Meta-Analytic Review." *Child Maltreatment* 21, no. 1: 47–58. doi:10.1177/1077559515616703.

Teicher, Martin H., Carl M. Anderson, Kyoko Ohashi, Alaptagin Khan, Cynthia E. McGreenery, Elizabeth A. Bolger, Michael L. Rohan, and Gordana D. Vitaliano. 2018. "Differential Effects of Childhood Neglect and Abuse during Sensitive Exposure Periods on Male and Female Hippocampus." *NeuroImage* 169 (April 1): 443–52. doi:10.1016/j.neuroimage.2017.12.055.

Teicher, Martin H., Susan L. Andersen, Ann Polcari, Carl M. Anderson, Carryl P. Navalta, and Dennis M. Kim. 2003. "The Neurobiological Consequences of Early Stress and Childhood Maltreatment." *Neuroscience and Biobehavioral Reviews* 27, nos. 1–2 (January 1): 33–44. doi:10.1016/S0149-7634(03)00007-1.

Teicher, Martin H., and Jacqueline A. Samson. 2016. "Annual Research Review: Enduring Neurobiological Effects of Childhood Abuse and Neglect." *Journal of Child Psychology and Psychiatry* 57, no. 3 (March): 241–66. doi:10.1111/jcpp.12507.

Teicher, Martin H., Jacqueline A. Samson, Carl M. Anderson, and Kyoko Ohashi. 2016. "The Effects of Childhood Maltreatment on Brain Structure, Function, and Connectivity." *Nature Reviews Neuroscience* 17, no. 10 (September): 652–66. doi:10.1038/nrn.2016.111.

Terr, Lenore. 1990. *Too Scared to Cry: How Trauma Affects Children … and Ultimately Affects Us All.* New York: HarperCollins.

Thornberry, Terence P., Kimberly L. Henry, Carolyn A. Smith, Timothy O. Ireland, Sarah J. Greenman, and Rosalyn D. Lee. 2013. "Breaking the Cycle of Maltreatment: The Role of Safe, Stable, and Nurturing Relationships." *Journal of Adolescent Health* 53, no. 4, Supplement (October): s25–s31. doi:10.1016/j.jadohealth.2013.04.019.

Tinker, Robert H., and Sandra A. Wilson. 1999. *Through the Eyes of a Child: EMDR with Children.* New York: W. W. Norton.

Trevarthen, Colwyn, and Jonathan Delafield-Butt. 2017. "Development of Consciousness." In *Cambridge Encyclopedia of Child Development,* 2nd ed., edited by Brian Hopkins, Elena Geangu, and Sally Linkenauger, 821–35. Cambridge: Cambridge University Press.

Tronick, Ed. 2007. *The Neurobehavioral and Social-Emotional Development of Infants and Children.* New York: W. W. Norton.

Tronick, Ed, and Marjorie Beeghly. 2011. "Infants' Meaning-Making and the Development of Mental Health Problems." *American Psychologist* 66, no. 2 (February–March): 107–19. doi:10.1037/a0021631.

Truppi, Ann Marie. 2001. "The Effects of Dance/Movement Therapy on Sexually Abused Girls in Residential Treatment." PhD diss., Walden University. ProQuest (AAT 3010680).

Tursich, M., T. Ros, P. A. Frewen, R. C. Kluetsch, Vince Daniel Calhoun, and Ruth A. Lanius. 2015. "Distinct Intrinsic Network Connectivity Patterns of Post-Traumatic Stress Disorder Symptom Clusters." *Acta Psychiatrica Scandinavica* 132, no. 1: 29–38.

van der Kolk, Bessel. 2014. *The Body Keeps the Score: Brain, Mind, and Body in the Healing of Trauma.* New York: Penguin.

van der Kolk, Bessel A., Robert S. Pynoos, Dante Cicchetti, Marylene Cloitre, Wendy D'Andrea, Julian D. Ford, Alicia F. Lieberman, et al. 2009. "Proposal to Include a Developmental Trauma Disorder Diagnosis for Children and Adolescents in DSM-V." Unpublished manuscript. February 1, 2009. https://tinyurl.com/qk6h9au.

van der Kolk, Bessel A., Joseph Spinazzola, Margaret E. Blaustein, James W. Hopper, Elizabeth K. Hopper, Deborah L. Korn, and William B. Simpson. 2007. "A Randomized Clinical Trial of Eye Movement Desensitization and Reprocessing, Fluoxetine, and Pill Placebo in the Treatment of Posttraumatic Stress Disorder: Treatment Effects and Long-Term Maintenance." *Journal of Clinical Psychiatry* 68, no. 1 (January): 37–46.

van der Kolk, Bessel A., Laura Stone, Jennifer West, Alison Rhodes, David Emerson, Michael Suvak, and Joseph Spinazzola. 2014. "Yoga as an Adjunctive Treatment for Posttraumatic Stress Disorder: A Randomized Controlled Trial." *Journal of Clinical Psychiatry* 75, no. 6 (June): e1–e7. doi:10.4088/JCP.13m08561.

Viard, Armelle, Justine Mutlu, Sandra Chanraud, Fabian Guenolé, Pierre-Jean Egler, Priscille Gérardin, Jean-Marc Baleyte, Jacques Dayan, Francis Eustache, and Bérengere Guillery-Girard. 2019. "Altered Default Mode Network Connectivity in Adolescents with Post-Traumatic Stress Disorder." *NeuroImage: Clinical* 22: 101731. doi:10.1016/j.nicl.2019.101731.

Vogt, Ralf. 2007. *Psychotrauma, State, Setting: Psychoanalytical-Action-Related Model for a Treatment of Complexly Traumatized Patients.* English edition, 2008. Giessen, Germany: Psychosozial-Verlag.

Volchan, E., V. Rocha-Rego, A. F. Bastos, J. M. Oliveira, C. Franklin, S. Gleiser, W. Berger, et al. 2017. "Immobility Reactions Under Threat: A Contribution to Human Defensive Cascade and PTSD." *Neuroscience and Biobehavioral Reviews* 76 (May): 29–38.

Warner, Elizabeth, Jane Koomar, Bryan Lary, and Alexandra Cook. 2013. "Can The Body Change the Score? Application of Sensory Modulation Principles in the Treatment of Traumatized Adolescents in Residential Settings." *Journal of Family Violence* 28 (October), no. 7: 729–38.

Warner, Elizabeth, Joseph Spinazzola, Anne Westcott, Cecile Gunn, and Hilary Hodgdon. 2014. "The Body Can Change the Score: Empirical Support for Somatic Regulation in the Treatment of Traumatized Adolescents." *Journal of Child and Adolescent Trauma* 7, no. 4 (December): 237–46. doi:10.1007/s40653-014-0030-z.

Wieland, Sandra. 2015. "Dissociation in Children and Adolescents: What It Is, How It Presents, and How We Can Understand It." In *Dissociation in Traumatized Children and Adolescents: Theory and Clinical Interventions,* 2nd ed., edited by Sandra Wieland, 1–27. New York: Routledge.

Winnicott, D. W. 1964. *The Child, the Family, and the Outside World.* London: Penguin Books.

World Health Organization. 2018. *International Classification of Diseases and Related Health Problems.* April 2019 version. https://icd.who.int/browse11/l-m/en.

Zeev-Wolf, Maor, Jonathan Levy, Abraham Goldstein, Orna Zagoory-Sharon, and Ruth Feldman. 2019. "Chronic Early Stress Impairs Default Mode Network Connectivity in Preadolescents and Their Mothers." *Biological Psychiatry* 4, no. 1 (January): 72–80. doi:10.1016/j.bpsc.2018.09.009.

Introduction to Part 2

Ogden, Pat, and Janina Fisher. 2009. "Sensorimotor Psychotherapy." In *Treating Complex Traumatic Stress Disorders: Scientific Foundations and Therapeutic Models,* edited by Christine A. Courtois and Julian D. Ford, 312–28. New York: Guilford Press.

Ogden, Pat, and Kekuni Minton. 2000. "Sensorimotor Psychotherapy: One Model for Processing Traumatic Memory." *Traumatology* 3, no. 3 (October): 149–73.

Ogden, Pat, Kekuni Minton, and Clare Pain. 2006. *Trauma and the Body: A Sensorimotor Approach to Psychotherapy.* New York: W. W. Norton.

Siegel, Daniel J. 1999. *The Developing Mind: How Relationships and the Brain Interact to Shape Who We Are.* New York: Guilford Press.

Siegel, Daniel J. 2012. *The Developing Mind: How Relationships and the Brain Interact to Shape Who We Are.* 2nd ed. New York: Guilford Press.

Chapter 3

Ayres, A. Jean. 1972. *Sensory Integration and Learning Disorders.* Los Angeles: Western Psychological Services.

Ayres, A. Jean, and Jeff Robbins. 2005. *Sensory Integration and the Child: Understanding Hidden Sensory Challenges.* Torrance, CA: Western Psychological Services. First published 1979.

Birdwhistell, Ray L. 1956. "Kinesic Analysis of Filmed Behavior of Children." Paper presented at the Group Processes: Transactions of the Second Conference, Princeton, NJ, October 1955. In *Group Processes: Transactions of the Second Conference,* edited by B. Schaffner, 141–44. New York: Josiah Macy Jr. Foundation.

Birdwhistell, Ray L. 1970. *Kinesics and Context: Essays on Body Motion and Communication.* Philadelphia: University of Pennsylvania Press.

Champagne, Tina, and Nan Stromberg. 2004. "Sensory Approaches in In-Patient Psychiatric Settings: Innovative Alternatives to Seclusion and Restraint." *Journal of Psychosocial Nursing,* 42, no. 9 (September): 34–44. doi:10.3928/02793695-20040301-01.

Feldman, Ruth. 2006. "From Biological Rhythms to Social Rhythms: Physiological Precursors of Mother-Infant Synchrony." *Developmental Psychology* 42, no. 1: 175–88. doi:/10.1037/0012-1649.42.1.175.

Feldman, Ruth. 2007. "On the Origins of Background Emotions: From Affect Synchrony to Symbolic Expression." *Emotion* 7, no. 3: 601–11. doi:10.1037/1528-3542.7.3.601.

Ionta, Silvio, Lukas Heydrich, Bigna Lenggenhager, Michael Mouthon, Eleonora Fornari, Dominique Chapuis, Roger Gassert, and Olaf Blanke. 2011. "Multisensory Mechanisms in Temporo-Parietal Cortex Support Self-Location and First-Person Perspective." *Neuron* 70 (April 28): 363–74. doi:10.1016/j.neuron.2011.03.009.

Jaffe, Joseph, Beatrice Beebe, Stanley Feldstein, Cynthia L. Crown, Michael D. Jasnow, Philippe Rochat, and Daniel N. Stern. 2001. "Rhythms of Dialogue in Infancy: Coordinated Timing in Development." *Monographs of the Society for Research in Child Development* 66, no. 2: i–viii, 1–149. www.jstor.org/stable/3181589.

Koomar, Jane A., and Anita C. Bundy. 2002. "Creating Direct Intervention from Theory." In *Sensory Integration: Theory and Practice,* 2nd ed., edited by Anita C. Bundy, Shelly J. Lane, and Elizabeth A. Murray, 266–302. Philadelphia: F. A. Davis.

Lackner, James R., and Paul DiZio. 2005. "Vestibular, Proprioceptive, and Haptic Contributions to Spatial Orientation." *Annual Review of Psychology* 56: 115–47. doi:10.1146/annurev.psych.55.090902.142023.

Lenggenhager, B., S. T. Smith, and O. Blanke. 2006. "Functional and Neural Mechanisms of Embodiment: Importance of the Vestibular System and the Temporal Parietal Junction." *Reviews in the Neurosciences* 17, no. 6: 643–57.

Malloch, Stephen N. 1999. "Mothers and Infants and Communicative Musicality." *Musicae Scientiae* 3, no. 1, special issue (September): 29–57. doi:10.1177%2F10298649000030S104.

Malloch, Stephen, and Colwyn Trevarthen. 2009. "Musicality: Communicating the Vitality and Interests of Life." In *Communicative Musicality: Exploring the Basis of Human Companionship,* edited by Stephen Malloch and Colwyn Trevarthen, 1–11. Oxford: Oxford University Press.

Margolis, Amy E., Sang Han Lee, Bradley S. Peterson, and Beatrice Beebe. 2019. "Profiles of Infant Communicative Behavior." *Developmental Psychology* 55, no. 8: 1594–1604. doi:10.1037/dev0000745.

May-Benson, Teresa A., and Jane A. Koomar. 2007. "Identifying Gravitational Insecurity in Children: A Pilot Study." *American Journal of Occupational Therapy* 61, no. 2 (March/April): 142. doi:10.5014/ajot.61.2.142.

May-Benson, Teresa A., Alison Teasdale, and Juliana Lopez De Mello Gentil. 2016. "Gravitational Insecurity in Children with Sensory Integration and Processing Problems." Poster presented at the American Occupational Therapy Association (AOTA) conference, Chicago, IL, April 7, 2016. Abstract at *American Journal of Occupational Therapy* 70, no. 4, Supplement 1 (August): 1. doi:10.5014/ajot.2016.70S1-PO2007.

Pfeiffer, Christian, Andrea Serino, and Olaf Blanke. 2014. "The Vestibular System: A Spatial Reference for Bodily Self-Consciousness." *Frontiers in Integrative Neuroscience* 8 (April): 1–13. doi:10.3389/fnint.2014.00031.

Scott, Eric, and Jaak Panksepp. 2003. "Rough-and-Tumble Play in Human Children." *Aggressive Behavior* 29, no. 6: 539–51. doi:10.1002/ab.10062.

Serino, Andrea, and Patrick Haggard. 2010. "Touch and the Body." *Neuroscience and Biobehavioral Reviews* 34, no. 2 (February): 224–36. doi:10.1016/j.neubiorev.2009.04.004.

Spinazzola, J. 2017. "Developmental Trauma Disorder: Emerging Science and Best Practices." Paper presented at the Annual International Trauma Conference, Psychological Trauma: Neuroscience, Identity and the Transformation of Self, Boston, MA, June 2017.

Stoodley, Catherine J., and Jeremy D. Schmahmann. 2009. "Functional Topography in the Human Cerebellum: A Meta-Analysis of Neuroimaging Studies." *NeuroImage* 44, no. 2 (January): 489–501. doi:10.1016/j.neuroimage.2008.08.039.

Warner, Elizabeth, Jane Koomar, and Anne Westcott. 2009. "Arousal Regulation in Traumatized Children: Sensorimotor Interventions." PowerPoint presentation, International Trauma Conference, Boston, MA, June 5, 2009.

Chapter 4

Bateson, Gregory. 1979. *Mind and Nature: A Necessary Unity.* New York: Dutton.

Bromberg, Philip. 2011. *The Shadow of the Tsunami and the Growth of the Relational Mind.* New York: Routledge.

Condon, William S., and Louis W. Sander. 1974. "Synchrony Demonstrated between Movements of the Neonate and Adult Speech." *Child Development* 45, no. 2 (June): 456–62. doi:10.2307/1127968.

Daniel, Stuart, and Colwyn Trevarthen, eds. 2017. *Rhythms of Relating in Children's Therapies: Connecting Creatively with Vulnerable Children.* London: Jessica Kingsley Publishers.

Ford, Julian D., Joseph Spinazzola, Bessel van der Kolk, and Damian J. Grasso. 2018. "Toward an Empirically Based Developmental Trauma Disorder Diagnosis for Children: Factor Structure, Item Characteristics, Reliability, and Validity of the Developmental Trauma Disorder Semi-Structured Interview." *Journal of Clinical Psychiatry* 79, no. 5 (September/October): e1–e9. doi:10.4088/JCP.17m11675.

Fosha, Diana. 2000. *The Transforming Power of Affect: A Model for Accelerated Change.* New York: Basic Books.

Herman, Judith. 1992. *Trauma and Recovery.* New York: Basic Books.

Hughes, Daniel. 2018. *Building the Bonds of Attachment: Awakening Love in Deeply Traumatized Children.* Lanham, MD: Rowman & Littlefield.

Iacoboni, Marco. 2008. *Mirroring People: The Science of Empathy and How We Connect with Others.* New York: Picador.

Kahneman, Daniel. 2015. *Thinking, Fast and Slow.* New York: Farrar, Straus, and Giroux.

Koomar, Jane, and Daniel Hughes. 2011. "SAFE PLACE: Increasing the Power of Intervention for Professionals: Improving Attachment, Regulation, and Sensory Processing." Paper presented at the Creating A SAFE PLACE for Attachment 2011 Boston Symposium: Sensory Processing, Emotion & Behavior, Waltham, MA, January 13, 2011. https://tinyurl.com/rwxapl3.

Kurtz, Ron. 2007. *Body-Centered Therapy: The Hakomi Method.* Rev. ed. Mendocino, CA: LifeRhythm.

Levine, Peter A. 2015. *Trauma and Memory: Brain and Body in a Search for the Living Past.* Berkeley, CA: North Atlantic Books.

Levy, Terry M., and Michael Orlans. 2014. *Attachment, Trauma and Healing: Understanding and Treating Attachment Disorder in Children, Families and Adults.* 2nd ed. London: Jessica Kingsley Publishers.

Ogden, Pat, Kekuni Minton, and Clare Pain. 2006. *Trauma and the Body: A Sensorimotor Approach to Psychotherapy.* New York: W. W. Norton.

Perls, Frederick S., Ralph Hefferline, and Paul Goodman. (1951) 1994. *Gestalt Therapy: Excitement and Growth in the Human Personality.* Gouldsboro, ME: Gestalt Journal Press.

Provenzi, Livio, Giunia Scotto di Minico, Lorenzo Guisti, Elena Guida, and Mitho Müller. 2018. "Disentangling the Dyadic Dance: Theoretical, Methodological and Outcomes Systematic Review of Mother-Infant Dyadic Processes." *Frontiers in Psychology* 9 (March): 348. doi:10.3389/fpsyg.2018.00348.

Rizzolatti, Giacomo, and Corrado Sinigaglia. 2008. *Mirrors in the Brain: How Our Minds Share Actions and Emotions.* Translated by Frances Anderson. Oxford: Oxford University Press.

Siegel, Daniel J. 2018. *Aware: The Science and Practice of Presence.* New York: Penguin.

Stern, Daniel N. 2008. *Diary of a Baby: What Your Child Sees, Feels, and Experiences.* New York: Basic Books.

Stern, Daniel N. 2018. *The Interpersonal World of the Infant: A View from Psychoanalysis and Developmental Psychology.* London: Routledge. First published 1985.

Streeck-Fischer, Annette, and Bessel A. van der Kolk. 2000. "Down Will Come Baby, Cradle and All: Diagnostic and Therapeutic Implications of Chronic Trauma on Child Development." *Australian and New Zealand Journal of Psychiatry* 34, no. 6: 903–18. doi:10.1080/000486700265.

Tronick, Ed. 2007. *The Neurobehavioral and Social-Emotional Development of Infants and Children.* New York: W. W. Norton.

Warner, Elizabeth, Jane Koomar, Bryan Lary, and Alexandra Cook. 2013. "Can the Body Change the Score? Application of Sensory Modulation Principles in the Treatment of Traumatized Adolescents in Residential Settings." *Journal of Family Violence* 28, no. 7 (October): 729–38. doi:10.1007/s10896-013-9535-8.

Warner, Elizabeth, Joseph Spinazzola, Anne Westcott, Cecile Gunn, and Hilary Hodgdon. 2014. "The Body Can Change the Score: Empirical Support for Somatic Regulation in the Treatment of Traumatized Adolescents." *Journal of Child and Adolescent Trauma* 7, no. 4 (December): 237–44. doi:10.1007/s40653-014-0030-z.

Winnicott, Donald W. 1967. "Mirror-Role of Mother and Family in Child Development." In *Playing and Reality* (1971), 111–18. London: Tavistock.

Chapter 5

Beebe, Beatrice. 2014. "My Journey in Infant Research and Psychoanalysis: Microanalysis, a Social Microscope." *Psychoanalytic Psychology* 31, no. 1 (January): 4–25. doi:10.1037/a0035575.

Birdwhistell, Ray L. 1970. "Kinesic Analysis of Filmed Behavior of Children." In *Kinesics and Context: Essays on Body Motion Communication*, 47–49. Philadelphia: University of Pennsylvania Press. First paperback edition 1990.

Fonagy, Peter, Michelle Sleed, and Tessa Baradon. 2016. "Randomized Controlled Trial of Parent–Infant Psychotherapy for Parents with Mental Health Problems." *Infant Mental Health Journal* 37, no. 2 (March/April): 97–114. doi:10.1002/imhj.21553.

Gottman, John, and Julie Gottman. 2017. "The Natural Principles of Love." *Journal of Family Theory and Review* 9, no. 1 (March): 7–26. doi:10.1111/jftr.12182.

Lyons-Ruth, Karlen. 2006. "Contributions of the Mother–Infant Relationship to Dissociative, Borderline, and Conduct Symptoms in Young Adulthood." *Infant Mental Health Journal* 29, no. 3 (May/June): 203–18. doi:10.1002%2Fimhj.20173.

Stern, Daniel N. 2004. *The Present Moment in Psychotherapy and Everyday Life.* New York: W. W. Norton.

Tronick, Ed. 2007. *The Neurobehavioral and Social-Emotional Development of Infants and Children.* New York: W. W. Norton.

Chapter 6

Beebe, Beatrice, and Frank M. Lachmann. 2014. *The Origins of Attachment: Infant Research and Adult Treatment.* New York: Routledge.

Emerson, David. 2015. *Trauma-Sensitive Yoga in Therapy: Bringing the Body into Treatment.* New York: W. W. Norton.

Emerson, David, and Elizabeth Hopper. 2011. *Overcoming Trauma through Yoga: Reclaiming Your Body.* Berkeley, CA: North Atlantic Books.

Fogel, Alan. 2009. *The Psychophysiology of Self-Awareness: Rediscovering the Lost Art of Body Sense.* New York: W. W. Norton.

Fogel, Alan. 2011. "Embodied Awareness: Neither Implicit Nor Explicit, and Not Necessarily Nonverbal." *Child Development Perspectives* 5, no. 3: 183–86. doi:10.1111/j.1750-8606.2011.00177.x.

Gaensbauer, Theodore J. 2016. "Moments of Meeting: The Relevance of Lou Sander's and Dan Stern's Conceptual Framework for Understanding the Development of Pathological Social Relatedness." *Infant Mental Health Journal* 37, no. 2 (March/April): 172–88. doi:10.1002/imhj.21555.

Hughes, Daniel A. 2018. *Building the Bonds of Attachment: Awakening Love in Deeply Traumatized Children.* 3rd ed. Lanham, MD: Rowman & Littlefield.

Kepner, James I. 2001. *Body Process: A Gestalt Approach to Working with the Body in Psychotherapy.* Santa Cruz, CA: Gestalt Press. First published 1987.

Levine, Peter A., and Ann Frederick. 1997. *Waking the Tiger: Healing Trauma: The Innate Capacity to Transform Overwhelming Experiences.* Berkeley, CA: North Atlantic Books.

Ogden, Pat, and Janina Fisher. 2015. *Sensorimotor Psychotherapy: Interventions for Trauma and Attachment.* New York: W. W. Norton.

Ogden, Pat, Kekuni Minton, and Clare Pain. 2006. *Trauma and the Body: A Sensorimotor Approach to Psychotherapy.* New York: W. W. Norton.

Perry, Bruce D. 2009. "Examining Child Maltreatment through a Neurodevelopmental Lens: Clinical Applications of the Neurosequential Model of Therapeutics." *Journal of Loss and Trauma* 14, no. 4: 240–55. doi:10.1080/15325020903004350.

Perry, Bruce D., and Christine L. Dobson. 2013. "The Neurosequential Model of Therapeutics." In *Treating Complex Traumatic Stress Disorders in Children and Adolescents,* edited by Julian D. Ford and Christine A. Courtois, 249–60. New York: Guilford Press.

Schore, Allan N. 2003. *Affect Dysregulation and Disorders of the Self.* New York: W. W. Norton.

Shonkoff, Jack P., and Susan Nall Bales. 2011. "Science Does Not Speak for Itself: Translating Child Development Research for the Public and Its Policymakers." *Child Development* 82, no. 1 (January/February): 17–32. doi:10.1111/j.1467-8624.2010.01538.x.

Shonkoff, Jack P., Andrew S. Garner, Benjamin S. Siegel, Mary I. Dobbins, Marian F. Earls, Laura McGuinn, John Pascoe, David L. Wood, and the Committee on Psychosocial Aspects of Child and Family Health, Committee on Early Childhood, Adoption, and Dependent Care, and Section on Developmental and Behavioral Pediatrics. 2012. "The Lifelong Effects of Early Childhood Adversity and Toxic Stress." *Pediatrics* 129, no. 1 (January): e232–e247. doi:10.1542/peds.2011-2663.

Trevarthen, Colwyn, and Jonathan Delafield-Butt. 2017. "Development of Consciousness." In *Cambridge Encyclopedia of Child Development,* 2nd ed., edited by Brian Hopkins, Elena Geangu, and Sally Linkenauger, 821–35. Cambridge: Cambridge University Press.

Tronick, Ed. 2007. *The Neurobehavioral and Social-Emotional Development of Infants and Children.* New York: W. W. Norton.

Warner, Elizabeth, Alexandra Cook, Anne Westcott, and Jane Koomar. 2014. *Sensory Motor Arousal Regulation Treatment (SMART): A Manual for Therapists Working with Children and Adolescents: A "Bottom Up" Approach to the Treatment of Complex Trauma.* 2nd ed. Brookline, MA: The Trauma Center at JRI. First published 2011.

Westcott, Anne and C. C. Alicia Hu. 2017. *How Little Coyote Found His Hidden Strength.* London: Jessica Kinsgley.

Chapter 7

Achenbach, Thomas M., and Leslie A. Rescorla. 2000. "Child Behavior Checklist for Ages 1½-5." Burlington, VT: ASEBA.

Hudak, Mark L., and Rosemarie Tan. 2012. "Neonatal Drug Withdrawal." *Pediatrics* 129, no. 2 (February): e540–e560. doi:10.1542/peds.2011-3212.

Miller, Arnold, and Eileen Eller-Miller. 1989. *From Ritual to Repertoire: A Cognitive-Developmental Systems Approach with Behavior-Disordered Children.* New York: Wiley.

Panksepp, Jaak. 2008. "Play, ADHD, and the Construction of the Social Brain: Should the First Class Each Day Be Recess?" *American Journal of Play* 1, no. 1 (Summer): 55–79.

Panksepp, Jaak, and Lucy Biven. 2012. *The Archaeology of Mind: Neuroevolutionary Origins of Human Emotions.* New York: W. W. Norton.

Parham, L. Diane, Cheryl Ecker, Heather Miller Kuhaneck, Diana A. Henry, and Tara J. Glennon. 2010. *Sensory Processing Measure.* Torrance, CA: Western Psychological Services.

Scott, Eric, and Jaak Panksepp. 2003. "Rough-and-Tumble Play in Human Children." *Aggressive Behavior* 29, no. 6 (December): 539–51. doi:10.1002/ab.10062.

Chapter 8

Finn, Heather, Elizabeth Warner, Maggi Price, and Joseph Spinazzola. 2018. "The Boy Who Was Hit in the Face: Somatic Regulation and Processing of Preverbal Complex Trauma." *Journal of Child & Adolescent Trauma* 11, no. 3: 277–88. doi:10.1007 /s40653-017-0165-9.

Chapter 9

Weller, Francis. 2017. *The Wild Edge of Sorrow: Rituals of Renewal and the Sacred Work of Grief.* Berkeley, CA: North Atlantic Books.

Westcott, Anne and C. C. Alicia Hu. 2017. *How Little Coyote Found His Hidden Strength.* London: Jessica Kinsgley.

Chapter 10

Blaustein, Margaret E., and Kristine M. Kinniburgh. 2019. *Treating Traumatic Stress in Children and Adolescents: How to Foster Resilience through Attachment, Self-Regulation, and Competency.* 2nd ed. New York: Guilford Press.

Centers for Medicare and Medicaid Services. 2014. "EPSDT—A Guide for States: Coverage in the Medicaid Benefit for Children and Adolescents." Washington, DC: Centers for Medicare and Medicaid Services. https://tinyurl.com/v939nbw.

Champagne, Tina, and Nan Stromberg. 2004. "Sensory Approaches in In-Patient Psychiatric Settings: Innovative Alternatives to Seclusion and Restraint." *Journal of Psychosocial Nursing* 42, no. 9 (September): 34–44. doi:10.3928/02793695-20040301-01.

Fleischner, Robert, Kathryn Rucker, and Susan Stefan. 2007. "Restraint and Seclusion of Children and Adolescents in Massachusetts: A Review of the Law." Northampton, MA: Center for Public Representation. https://tinyurl.com/vxdqwb5.

Keller, Heidi. 2014. "Introduction: Understanding Relationships—What We Would Need to Know to Conceptualize Attachment as the Cultural Solution of a Universal Task." In *Different Faces of Attachment: Cultural Variations on a Human Need,* edited by Hiltrud Otto and Heidi Keller, 1–25. Cambridge: Cambridge University Press.

Lieberman, Alicia, Chandra Ghosh Ippen, and Miriam Hernandez Dimmler. 2019. "Child–Parent Psychotherapy." In *Assessing and Treating Youth Exposed to Traumatic Stress,* edited by Victor D. Carrión, 223–37. Washington, DC: American Psychiatric Association.

Loomis, Alysse Melville. 2019. "Pathways from Cumulative Adversity to Self-Regulation and Early Student–Teacher Relationships: Identifying a Need for Trauma-Informed Preschools." PhD diss., University of Connecticut. Doctoral Dissertations. 2107. https://tinyurl.com/ujcv6qq.

Menakem, Resmaa. 2017. *My Grandmother's Hands: Racialized Trauma and the Pathways to Mending Our Hearts and Bodies.* Las Vegas, NV: Central Recovery Press.

National Child Traumatic Stress Network (website). 2019. www.nctsn.org.

Perry, Bruce. 2009. "Examining Child Maltreatment through a Neurodevelopmental Lens: Clinical Applications of the Neurosequential Model of Therapeutics." *Journal of Loss and Trauma* 14, no. 4: 240–55. doi:10.1080/15325020903004350.

Perry, Bruce D., and Christine L. Dobson. 2013. "The Neurosequential Model of Therapeutics." In *Treating Complex Traumatic Stress Disorders in Children and Adolescents,* edited by Julian D. Ford and Christine A. Courtois, 249–60. New York: Guilford Press.

Ullman, Sarah E. 2007. "Relationship to Perpetrator, Disclosure, Social Reactions, and PTSD Symptoms in Child Sexual Abuse Survivors." *Journal of Child Sexual Abuse* 16, no. 1: 19–36. doi:10.1300/J070v16n01_02.

US Department of Education. 2010. *Summary of Seclusion and Restraint Statutes, Regulations, Policies and Guidance, by State and Territory: Information as Reported to the Regional Comprehensive Centers and Gathered from Other Sources.* Washington, DC: US Department of Education. https://tinyurl.com/qlcsnfp.

Warner, Elizabeth, Joseph Spinazzola, Anne Westcott, Cecile Gunn, and Hilary Hodgdon. 2014. "The Body Can Change the Score: Empirical Support for Somatic Regulation in the Treatment of Traumatized Adolescents." *Journal of Child and Adolescent Trauma* 7, no. 4 (December): 237–46. doi:10.1007/s40653-014-0030-z.

Wu, Kitty K., Patrick W. L. Leung, Corine S. M. Wong, Philippa M. W. Yu, Betty T. K. Luk, Jamie P. K. Cheng, Rose M. F. Wong, et al. 2019. "The Hong Kong Survey on the Epidemiology of Trauma Exposure and Posttraumatic Stress Disorder." *Journal of Traumatic Stress* 32, no. 5: 664–76. doi:10.1002/jts.22430.

INDEX

ABOUT THE AUTHORS

Alexandra B. Cook, PhD, is a founding partner of SMART-moves, a training and development organization dedicated to educating professionals in effective treatment for traumatized children and their families. After graduating from Yale University with a bachelor's degree in psychology, Cook went on to complete her graduate work at Boston University earning a PhD in clinical psychology. She spent over twenty years at The Trauma Center beginning as a post-doctoral fellow, heading the Children's Services, and ultimately becoming the associate director. In 2018, Cook and her fellow authors left the Trauma Center to form SMART-moves Partners. She also maintains a small private practice in Brookline, Massachusetts. Her publications include *With the Phoenix Rising: Lessons from Ten Resilient Women Who Overcame the Trauma of Childhood Sexual Abuse, Complex Trauma in Children and Adolescents* (white paper for the National Child Traumatic Stress Network), and multiple journal articles focusing on psychological trauma.

Heather Finn, LICSW, is a practicing clinical social worker specializing in trauma-informed treatments for children, their caregivers, and adults. She graduated from Smith College School for Social Work in 2001 and has worked as a therapist and clinical supervisor in residential treatment, community-based, and outpatient treatment programs. Finn joined the Trauma Center at JRI in 2009 and became clinical director in 2017. During this time, she contributed to furthering the development of SMART as a member of the training and consulting team. Currently, Finn provides training and consultation services across the US and internationally as a founding partner of SMARTmoves, LLC. She also maintains an active private practice in Boston providing clinical treatment services and professional supervision. Finn is the lead coauthor of "The Boy Who Was Hit in the Face: Somatic Regulation and Processing of Preverbal Complex Trauma" published in the *Journal of Child and Adolescent Trauma* in 2017.

Photo by Darren Pellegrino

Elizabeth S. Warner, PsyD, is a clinical psychologist with forty years of practice experience in the full range of mental health settings. For ten years, she was the SMART Project Director at the Trauma Center at JRI, a center of excellence in trauma treatment, training, and research. She oversaw the development of Sensory Motor Arousal Regulation Treatment (SMART) through the use of videotape for practice, supervision, consultation, and research and published on this work. In 2018, she cofounded SMARTmoves Partners, an organization committed to training, education, and the development and study of trauma treatments for children, their caregivers, and adults in all types of settings. She has trained and taught therapists in the US and internationally.

Photo by Pierre Chiha Photographers

Anne Westcott, LICSW, is a founding partner of SMARTmoves, a training and development organization dedicated to educating professionals in effective treatment for traumatized children and their families. Westcott is a certified sensorimotor psychotherapist and a senior faculty member at the Sensorimotor Psychotherapy Institute. She trains and consults to help professionals throughout North America. Westcott has also coauthored a children's story series of resiliency in the face of difficult times (Jessica Kingsley Press, 2017). She continues to maintain a private practice in the greater Boston area.

About North Atlantic Books

North Atlantic Books (NAB) is an independent, nonprofit publisher committed to a bold exploration of the relationships between mind, body, spirit, and nature. Founded in 1974, NAB aims to nurture a holistic view of the arts, sciences, humanities, and healing. To make a donation or to learn more about our books, authors, events, and newsletter, please visit www.northatlanticbooks.com.

North Atlantic Books is the publishing arm of the Society for the Study of Native Arts and Sciences, a 501(c)(3) nonprofit educational organization that promotes cross-cultural perspectives linking scientific, social, and artistic fields. To learn how you can support us, please visit our website.